The Size of
Thoughts

ALSO BY NICHOLSON BAKER

The Mezzanine

Room Temperature

U and I

Vox

The Fermata

The Size of Thoughts

Essays and Other Lumber

———— ❧❧ ————

Nicholson
Baker

Chatto & Windus
LONDON

First published in 1996

1 3 5 7 9 10 8 6 4 2

Copyright © 1982, 1983, 1984, 1989, 1991, 1992, 1993, 1994, 1995, 1996 by
Nicholson Baker

First published in Great Britain in 1996 by
Chatto & Windus Limited
Random House, 20 Vauxhall Bridge Road,
London SW1V 2SA

Random House Australia (Pty) Limited
20 Alfred Street, Milsons Point, Sydney
New South Wales 2061, Australia

Random House New Zealand Limited
18 Poland Road, Glenfield
Auckland 10, New Zealand

Random House South Africa (Pty) Limited
PO Box 337, Bergvlei, South Africa

Random House UK Limited Reg. No. 954009

The following pieces were first published in periodicals: 'Changes of
Mind', 'The Size of Thoughts' and 'Rarity' in *The Atlantic Monthly*; 'Ice
Storm', 'Reading Aloud', 'The Projector', 'Discards', 'Clip Art', and 'Books
as Furniture' in *The New Yorker*; 'The History of Punctuation' and 'Leading
with the Grumper' in *The New York Review of Books*; 'Model Airplanes'
and 'The Northern Pedestal' in *Esquire*; and 'A Novel by Alan Hollinghurst'
in the *London Review of Books*

A CIP catalogue record for this book
is available from the British Library

ISBN 0 7011 6301 1

For my sister, Rachel

Contents

MIXED

LIBRARY SCIENCE

LUMBER

Thought

Changes of Mind

If your life is like my life, there are within it brief stretches, usually a week to ten days long, when your mind achieves a polished and freestanding coherence. The chanting tape-loops of poetry anthologies, the crumbly pieces of philosophy, the unsmelted barbarisms, the litter torn from huge collisions of abandoned theories—all this nomadic suborbital junk suddenly, like a milling street crowd in a movie-musical, re-forms itself into a proud, pinstriped, top-hatted commonwealth. Your opinions become neat and unruffleable. Every new toy design, every abuse of privilege or gesture of philanthropy, every witnessed squabble at the supermarket checkout counter, is smoothly remade into evidence for five or six sociological truths. Puffed up enough to be charitable, you stop urging your point with twisting jabs of your fork; you happily concede winnable arguments to avoid injuring the feelings of your friends; your stock of proverbs from Samuel Johnson seems elegant and apt in every context; you are firm, you think fast, you offer delicately phrased advice.

Then one Thursday, out on a minor errand, you inexplicably come to a new conclusion ("Keynesian economics is spent"), and it—like the fetching plastic egg that cruel experimenters have discovered will cause a mother bird to thrust her own warm, speckled ones from the nest—upsets your equilibrium. The community of convictions flies apart, you sense unguessed contradictions, there are disavowals, frictions, second thoughts, pleas for further study; you stare in renewed perplexity out the laundromat's plate-glass window, while your pulped library card dries in a tumbling shirt pocket behind you.

Such alert intermissions happen only infrequently: most of the time we are in some inconclusive phase of changing our minds about many, if not all, things. We have no choice. Our opinions, gently nudged by circumstance, revise themselves under cover of inattention. We tell them, in a steady voice, No, I'm not interested in a change at present. But there is no stopping opinions. They don't care about whether we want to hold them or not; they do what they have to do.

And graver still, we are sometimes only minimally aware of just which new beliefs we have adopted. If one of the wire services were able to supply each subscriber with a Personal Opinion Printout, delivered with the paper every morning, it would be a real help: then we could monitor our feelings about Pre-Raphaelite furniture, or the influences of urbanization on politeness, or the wearing of sunglasses indoors, or the effect of tort language on traditions of trust, as we adjusted our thoughts about them week by week, the way we keep an eye on lightly traded over-the-counter stocks. Instead, we stride into a discussion with our squads of unexamined opinions innocently at our heels—and, discovering that, yes, we do feel strongly about water-table rights, or unmanned space exploration, or the harvesting of undersea sponges, say, we grab the relevant opinion and, without dress rehearsals, fling it out into audibility ("*Fly,* you mother"), only to discover, seconds later, its radical inadequacy.

Let me now share with you something about which I changed my mind. Once I was riding the bus between New York City and Rochester. At the Binghamton stop, the driver noticed a shoe sitting on the ledge below the front windshield. The sight of it bothered him. He held it up to us and said, "Is this anybody's?" There was no response, so he left the bus for a moment and threw the shoe in a nearby trash can. We drove on toward Rochester. Idle, I became caught up in a little plan to furnish my future apartment: I would buy yellow forklifts and orange backhoes, *rows* of them, upholstered so that my guests might sit if they wished in the scoops or on the slings slung between the forks. I had begun to calculate how many forklifts a typical floor would sustain when a man with disorderly hair walked to the front of the bus wearing two socks and one shoe. "Did you by any chance see a shoe?" he asked the driver. The driver said: "I asked about that shoe in Binghamton. It's gone now." The man apologized for having been asleep and returned to his seat.

Since that bus trip, five years ago, I find that, without my knowledge, I have changed my mind. I no longer want to live in an apartment furnished with forklifts and backhoes. Somewhere I jettisoned that interest *as irrevocably as the bus driver tossed out the strange sad man's right shoe.* Yet I did not experience during the intervening time a single uncertainty or pensive moment in regard to a backhoe. Five years of walking around cities, flipping through seed catalogs, and saying "Oho!" to statements I disagreed with—the effect of which has been to leave me with a disinclination to apply heavy machinery to interior design.

Multiply this example by a thousand, a hundred thousand, unannounced reversals: a mad flux is splashing around the pilings of our personalities. For a while I tried to make home movies of my opinions in their native element, undisturbed, as they grazed and romped in fields of inquiry, gradually altering in emphasis and coloration, mating, burrowing, and dying, like prairie dogs, but the presence of my camera made their behavior stilted and self-conscious—which brings us to what I can't help thinking is a relevant point about the passage of time. Changes of mind should be distinguished from decisions, for decisions seem to reside pertly in the present, while changes of mind imply habits of thought, a slow settling-out of truth, a partially felt, dense past. I may decide, for instance, that when I take off my pants I should not leave them draped over the loudspeakers, as I normally do, but contrive to suspend them on some sort of hook or hanger. I may decide to ask that person sitting across from me at the table to refrain from ripping out the spongy inside of her dinner roll and working it into small balls between her palms. We are bound to make lots of such future-directed choices: they are the reason for risk-benefit analysis. But at the same time, on the outskirts of our attention, hosts of gray-eyed, bright-speared opinions have been rustling, shifting, skirmishing. "What I think about Piaget" is out there, growing wiser, moodier, more cynical, along with some sort of answer to "What constitutes a virtuous life?" Unless I am being unusually calculating, I don't *decide* to befriend someone, and it is the same way with a conviction: I slowly come to enjoy its company, to respect its counsel, to depend on it for reassurance; I find myself ignoring its weaknesses or excesses—and if the friendship later ends, it is probably owing not to a sudden rift, but to a barnacling-over of nearly insignificant complaints.

Seldom, then, will any single argument change our minds about anything really interesting or important. In fact, reasoning and argument count for surprisingly little in the alluvial triumph of a thought—no more than 12 to 15 percent. Those reasons we do cite are often only a last flourish of bright plumage, a bit of ceremony to commemorate the result of a rabblement of tendencies too cross-purposed to recapitulate. A haphazard flare of memory; an irrelevant grief; an anecdote in the newspaper; a turn of conversation that stings into motion a tiny doubt: from such incessant percussions the rational soul reorganizes itself—we change our minds as we change our character. Years go by and the movement remains unrecognized: "I wasn't aware of it, but my whole feeling about car-pool lanes (or planned communities, or slippery-slope arguments, or rhyme, or Shostakovich, or whether things are getting better or worse) was undergoing a major overhaul back then." We must not overlook sudden conversions and wrenching insights, but usually we fasten on to these only in hindsight, and exaggerate them for the sake of narrative—a tool perfected by the great nineteenth-century novelists, who sit their heroines down and have them deduce the intolerability of their situation in one unhappy night, as the fire burns itself into embers in the grate.

Consider "whether things are getting better or worse" at closer range. Impossibly vague and huge as it is, most of us nonetheless believe it to be a question that merits a periodical self-harvest of opinion. Here are some of the marginally rational things that from one season to the next may contribute to my feelings concerning progress: There is more static in long-distance calls than there was a while ago. The Wonder Bread concrete they now use for sidewalks is a real step down from the darker, pebblier substance they used to use, and that in turn was a decline from the undulant slabs of weathered blue slate, thrust into gradients and peaks by the roots of a nearby tree, that were on my street as a child. Progresso artichoke hearts frequently have sharp, thistly pieces left on them now, as they never used to. When I tip the paper boy these days, he doesn't say thank you. Cemetery statues suffer increasing vandalism. On the other hand, there is Teflon II. Reflective street signs. The wah-wah pedal. Free libraries for everyone. Central heating. Fire codes. Federal Express. Stevie Wonder. Vladimir Nabokov. Lake Ontario is cleaner. My friends like my new blue coat. Somehow the mind arrives at a moving weighted average of these apples and oranges.

Occasionally a change of mind follows alternate routes. One belief, about which initially I would admit of no doubt, gradually came to seem more porous and intricate in its structure, but instead of moderating my opinion correspondingly, and conceding the justice of several objections, I simply lost interest in it, and now I nod absently if the topic comes up over lunch. Another time a cherished opinion weakened as I became too familiar with the three examples that advocates used over and over to support it. Under the glare of this repetition, the secondary details, the richer underthrumming of the opinion, faded; I seemed to have held it once too often; I tried but failed to find the rhetorical or figurative twist that would revive it for me. I crept insensibly toward the opposing view.

How is it that whole cultures and civilizations can change their "minds" in ways that seem so susceptible to synoptic explanation? From the distance of the historian of ideas, things blur nicely: one sees a dogma and its vocabulary seeping from discipline to disciplines, from class to class; if you squint away specificity you can make out splinter groups, groundswells of opposition, rival and revival schools of thought. The smoothness and sweep is breathtaking; the metaphors are all ready-made.

But when I am at the laundromat, trying to reconstitute for myself the collaboration of influences, disgusts, mistakes, and passions that swept me toward a simple change of heart about forklifts, the variables press in, description stammers and drowns in detail, and imagination hops up and down on one shoe to little purpose. I consult more successful attempts by the major intellectual autobiographers—Saint Augustine, Gibbon, Mill, Newman, and men of similar kidney—but even their brilliant accounts fail to satisfy: I don't want the story of the feared-but-loved teacher, the book that hit like a thunderclap, the years of severe study followed by a visionary breakdown, the clench of repentance; I want each sequential change of mind in its true, knotted, clotted, viny multifariousness, with all of the colorful streamers of intelligence still taped on and flapping in the wind.

(1982)

The Size of Thoughts

Each thought has a size, and most are about three feet tall, with the level of complexity of a lawnmower engine, or a cigarette lighter, or those tubes of toothpaste that, by mingling several hidden pastes and gels, create a pleasantly striped product. Once in a while, a thought may come up that seems, in its woolly, ranked composure, roughly the size of one's hall closet. But a really *large* thought, a thought in the presence of which whole urban centers would rise to their feet, and cry out with expressions of gratefulness and kinship; a thought with grandeur, and drenching, barrel-scorning cataracts, and detonations of fist-clenched hope, and hundreds of cellos; a thought that can tear phone books in half, and rap on the iron nodes of experience until every blue girder rings; a thought that may one day pack everything noble and good into its briefcase, elbow past the curators of purposelessness, travel overnight toward Truth, and shake it by the indifferent marble shoulders until it finally whispers its cool assent—this is the size of thought worth thinking about.

I have wanted for so long to own and maintain even a few huge, interlocking thoughts that, having exhausted more legitimate methods, I have recently resorted to theoretical speculation. Would it be possible to list those features that, taken together, confer upon a thought a lofty magnificence? What *makes* them so very large? My idle corollary hope is that perhaps a systematic and rigorous codification, on the model of Hammurabi's or Napoleon's, might make large thoughts available cheap, and in bulk, to the general public, thereby salvaging the nineteenth-century dream of a liberal democracy. But mainly I am hoping that once I can coax from large thoughts the rich impulses of their power, I will be able to think them in solitude, evening after evening, walking in little circles on the carpet with my arms outspread.

In my first attempt to find an objective measure for the size of thoughts, I theorized (as most of us have at one time or another) that I had only to mount the narrow stairs to my attic, stand in the hypotenuse of sunlight that passed through the window there in midwinter, and, concentrating, punch the thought in question once firmly, as if it were a pillow. The total number of tiny golden dust-monads that puffed forth from the thought's shocked stuffing would indicate, I believed, its eternal, essential size.

I found this to be a crude technique, and rejected it. Next, influenced by Sir John Eccles, the neurophysiologist, who used the axon of the giant-squid neuron to arrive at truths about the chemistry of human nerve fibers (small truths, needless to say: all scientific truths are small), I cast about for a suitably large thought existing in a form compact enough for me to experiment on it intensively. I tried a line of Wordsworth's,

> . . . steps
> Almost as silent as the turf they trod.

But it wasn't really big enough for my purposes. I tried Keats's

> O, for a beaker full of the warm South,
> Full of the true, the blushful Hippocrene,

but I lost my composure every time I read it and got nowhere.
Finally I decided to think about Henry James's sentence:
"What is morality but high intelligence?" It came to seem so
conveniently vast, so ideally ample, that I handled it for several days, as if it were some richly figured object carved from
soapstone; and when it failed to relinquish the secret of its
size after that period, I discovered that I had indirectly arrived
at my first theorem regarding large thoughts, which was:

(1) *All large thoughts are reluctant.* I don't think this is
intentional on their part. It follows from the unhasty, liquid
pace of human thinking. As an experiment, overturn half a
glass of wine onto a newly starched tablecloth. Watch, wholly
absorbed, as the borders of the stain search their way outward, plumping up each parched capillary of cotton,
threadlet by threadlet, and then traveling on—a soundless,
happy explosion, with no moving parts. Thought moves at
the velocity of that stain. And since a large thought seems to
wish to pierce and acknowledge and even to replenish many
more shoots and plumules of one's experience, some
shrunken from long neglect (for every thought, even the
largest, tires, winds down, and hardens into a hibernating
token of chat, a placeholder for real intellection, unless it is
worried into endless, pliant movement by second thoughts,
and by the sense of its own provisionality, passing and repass-
ing through the many semipermeable membranes that insu-
late learning, suffering, ambition, civility, and puzzlement
from each other), its hum of fineness will necessarily be
delayed, baffled, and drawn out with numerous interstitial
timidities—one pauses, looks up from the page, waits; the

eyes move in meditative polygons in their orbits; and then, somehow, *more* of the thought is released into the soul, the corroborating peal of some new, distant bell—until it has filled out the entirety of its form, as a thick clay slip settles into an intricate mold, or as a ladleful of batter colonizes cell after cell of the waffle iron, or as, later, the smell of that waffle will have toured the awakening rooms of the house.

Yet I sensed that reluctance was insufficient. What else did a large thought have to have? Filled with an ambitious sort of wistfulness, I flung open the door of the island cottage where I was staying, nodded to the moon, and began to walk up the fairway of a golf course, repeating, to the pulse of my invisible feet, a large thought of Tennyson's on which I had decided to perform a few experiments:

> Witch-elms that counterchange the floor
> Of this flat lawn with dusk and bright

The sand traps, ghostly objects shaped like white blood cells, floated slowly past. At last I reached the green, the mooncolored green, where a dark flag flapped, and looked out over the warm white sea. I threw my arms wide, and waited. Right then my second theorem regarding large thoughts ought to have formed itself in silver characters on the far horizon, but, in fact, it reached me only some weeks later, in a public library:

(2) *Large thoughts are creatures of the shade.* Not deep shade, necessarily, but the mixed and leafy shade at the floor of large forests. Small thoughts are happy to run around in their colorful swimwear under the brutalest of noons, but large thoughts really must have sizable volumes of cool, still air, to allow room for the approach and docking of their components of sadness. Nobody can frown intently at a delicate task sitting on the floor of a large forest, and large thoughts,

too, evade the pointedness and single-purposiveness of a frown; instead, they assert with a general pressure, and avoid contentiousness, and limit themselves to the suggestion that not far off, not far off, there are wholly convincing marginalia of still-undiscovered feeling, stored like heaped carpets in unlit vaults: they exhibit, then, a lush shadiness, as do the purple fastnesses in one's lungs, or the wrought, jeweled, dark interiors of water-resistant watches. All large thoughts are also patched and played over by leaf-shadows of slight hesitation and uncertainty: this tentativeness gives the thought just enough humility for it to be true. (All that is untrue is small.) Indeed, dusk—the moment of planetary shade—is the most likely time to encounter large thoughts. Because of some power struggle between the retina's rods and cones brought on with the coming of darkness, there is a quarter-hour or so when colors, though less distinct, seem superbly pigmented, and the important things, faces and especially the teeth of smiles, become sources of genial light: it is then that large thoughts may best be observed, strolling on their somber porches, and reciting from their codices.

As you may imagine, by the time I had successfully formulated this second theorem regarding large thoughts, I was desperately tired of them. If I felt one looming up in a page of Tolstoy, I ran off; I hid. The party seemed over: Dave Peters and his orchestra had packed up, and the devitalized balloons scudded about the floor.

I took a chair. More than anything else, I wished just then for the minty breath of a slighter truth or two in my ear. A minor botanical discovery concerning an unusual species of fern, perhaps; a paradox or an aperçu would do; faint harpsichord music; tricks with coins or cards; witty biographies of peripheral Victorians. What was so very contemptible about small thoughts? Where, indeed, would we be without Cornish game hens such as "It is one of the chief merits of proofs that they instill a certain skepticism about the result proved," which came to rest in Bertrand Russell's lucky mind one day? Or Charles Churchill's little two-step:

> With curious art the brain, too finely wrought,
> Preys on herself, and is destroyed by thought.

Or this, from Pater: "There is a certain shade of unconcern, the perfect manner of the eighteenth century, which may be thought to mark complete culture in the handling of abstract questions"—a thought that bounds beamingly, radiantly skyward for an instant, but is then, like many fine small thoughts, snuffed out on the second bounce by a bookish delegation of counterexamples. If we exiled all that is nifty, careless, wildly exaggerated, light-footed, vulnerable, or circumspectly spiced from our spiritual landscape, we would be in terrible shape. I scolded myself for my callousness toward the small. "We must refine all epics into epigrams!" I said. "We must measure only the flares and glimmers of the world, thimbleful by peerless thimbleful; nor should we grudge even the jingle of a lightbulb filament the silence of an enraptured continent!"

But this extreme reaction missed the point, which was, as I found out not long afterward, that:

(3) *Large thoughts depend more heavily on small thoughts than you might think.* Why does velvet feel smoother than chrome? Because smoothness is a secondary inference on the part of the confused fingertip, based on its perception of many fleeting roughnesses running underneath it too quickly to be individually considered. This suggestion of resistance in all truly smooth surfaces, like the sense of ornamental insurrection in all truly graceful lines, is analogous to the profusion, the anarchy, of lovely, brief insights that we often

experience as we read or listen our way through a great work of the mind, a work that, once completed, will leave us filled with large, calm truths. The villi on the inside of the small intestine—dense groves of microscopic protuberances—constitute a total surface area dedicated to the absorption of nutrients that, if flattened out, would shade the entire island of Manhattan, I am told. Large thoughts, too, disembellished of and abstracted from the small thoughts that diversify their surface, become sheer and indigestible. Consider the infinitesimal hooks on horsehairs that draw from the cello string its lavish tone; consider the grosgrain in silk, the gargoyles on a cathedral, the acanthus sprays or egg-and-dart molding along the tasteful curve of a chair, the lumps of potato that, by exception, prove the otherwise fine uniformity of a cream soup; consider the examples that enforce a moral essay, the social satire in a novel with a tragic ending, the sixteenth notes in a peacemaking melody, the incessant roadside metaphors in a work of metaphysics; consider all the indefensible appliances, the snags, the friction, the plush, that seem to hinder the achievement of a larger purpose, but are, in fact, critical to it. Major truths, like benevolent madonnas, are sustained aloft by dozens of busy, cheerful angels of detail.

I have tested these three theorems—the theorem of reluctance, the theorem of shade, and the theorem of dependency—on as many of the artifacts of reason as I could while holding a steady job. My results may have a certain severe appeal. Few indeed are the hobbyists in human memory who have known the craft of building a spacious, previously unthought thought of their very own: how to obtain, in arranging its long hallways and high, ornate rooms, that pull of an ever-riper deferment, by returning to it again and again, after some studied distraction—now full-face, now three-quarter view, now very near, now far off; how to gather in its huge, slow force with an encircling persistence that is three parts novelty, two parts confirming, strengthening repetition. I count Henry James, Brahms, Bellini. Burke, Bach, Pontormo. A mere eighty-six others.

And now, in a mood of icy impartiality, I am going to test the size of the thought I am offering you right here, which I expect to see peter out very shortly with few surprises, wrapped up after another two or three breaths of the mind, extended perhaps by a last, gravelly spatter of instantiation, unless, O yearn! I just happen to happen upon that loose-limbed, reckless acceleration, wherein this very thought might shamble forward, plucking tart berries, purchasing newspapers, and retrieving stray refuse without once breaking stride—risking a smile, shaking the outstretched hands of young constituents, loosening its tie!—no, that's all, I believe: this thought has rounded itself out, and ratified itself, despite all of its friendly intentions, as small.

(1983)

Rarity

Has anyone yet said publicly how nice it is to write on rubber with a ballpoint pen? The slow, fat, ink-rich line, rolled over a surface at once dense and yielding, makes for a multidimensional experience no single sheet of paper can offer. Right now dozens of Americans are making repetitive scrolly designs on the soft white door-seals of their refrigerators, or they are directing their pens around the layered side-steppes and toe-bulbs of their sneakers (heads bent, as elders give them advice), or they are marking shiny initials on one of those gigantic, dumb, benevolent erasers (which always bounce in unforeseen directions when dropped, and seem so selfless, so apolitical, so completely uninterested in doing anything besides erasing large mistakes for which they were not responsible), and then using the eraser to print these same initials several times, backward, on a knee or forearm, in a fading progression. These are rare pleasures.

And then someone mentions several kinds of rubber penmanship in his opening paragraph. Has a useful service been performed? A few readers, remembering that they did once enjoy taking down a toll-free phone number on the blade of a clean Rubbermaid spatula, react with guarded agreement: "Yes, I guess I am one of those not-so-uncommon people who have had that sort of rare experience." Infrequent events in the lives of total strangers are now linked; but the pleasure itself is too fragile, too incidental, to survive such forced affiliation undamaged. Regrettably, multiplying the idea of a thing's rarity is nearly identical in effect to multiplying the thing itself: its rarity departs. Some readers may never again engage so unthinkingly in this particular strain of idleness. It is no more common than it was before I brought it up, but it is more commonplace.

Rarity, then, is an emotion as much as it is a statistical truth. Just say the word over to yourself: *Rare. O rarer than rare.* A long, piercing curve of light appears and fades in one's darkened memory. It's like that diminishing cry of cartoon characters when they are tricked into running off a cliff. *The rare book room. A rare disease. Rarefied air. A miracle of rare device.* Comprehended in the notion are all sorts of contributory pangs: brevity, chances barely missed, awe, the passing of great men and glorious eras. Frequency is a sudden movement of many wings, a riffle through a worn paperback; rarity holds the single hushing index finger raised. And yet the absolute number of "raremes" is enormous—too large, in fact, for us to give each one of them the rapt monocular attention it deserves. Not only are there priceless misstamped nickels, oddball aurora borealises hanging their ball-gowns over unpopulated areas, fraternal bananas enclosed in a single skin, holes-in-one, and authentic Georges de La Tours; there are also all the varied sorts of human talent and permutations of character: the master mimic of frog sounds, the memory prodigy, the man who can mix wit with sympathy. The universe of rares is surprisingly crowded, and yet it is somehow capable of holding its inmates in seeming isolation, each of them floating in a radiantly placental, fluid-filled sphere of amazement, miles from any neighbor.

But there is ferment, too, in this universe. The turnover rate is very high. One disk jockey, in a fit of inspiration, will substitute *colder in the shrubs* for *colder in the suburbs,* or *T-storms* for *thunderstorms;* within two weeks every keen-eared DJ in the country is in step, and these phrases, cooling quickly, are soon remaindered to lesser microphones. Forgotten commonplaces rare up their heads, and soiled rarities are tossed back into the commonplace, twenty-four hours a day, in processes as inevitable as the cycles of rain and evaporation. But in this churning lies our perplexity. Since rarity constitutes part of the pleasure we take in many of the things we value, how rare should we allow a rareme to remain when it is in our power to influence its frequency?

Maybe good ideas should supplant bad ones without the resistance of prejudice or habit; maybe inside information should become public knowledge with the shortest possible delay. We act as if it should. Automatic mechanisms are in place for the efficient display of any hidden gem—a clever household hint, a new theory, a patent, a fairly good poem. Seed money is everywhere. Venture capitalists, those sleepless invigilators, roam the laboratories for the tiniest tremor of a possibility, force-feed it ten million dollars, pump it up, bring it public, and move on. Grants committees and arts competitions chew through the applicant pools, funding anything that moves. Contrarians trample one another to buy unfashionable stocks. "New and Noteworthy" columns take any gruntling of an innovation and give it a paragraph, a title with a pun in it, and a close-cropped picture. We are chastened by past mistakes: Mendel died ignored; Brahms was hissed; Harvey's patients dropped him when he came out with *The Cir-*

culation of the Blood. This kind of embarrassment must not happen in our lifetime!

At times it's fun to be part of a society so intent on institutionalizing its response to novelty. Our toes are curled right around the leading edge of the surfboard. Nothing far out will catch *us* off guard. We will monitor left field continually, and no hint of activity from that quarter will elude our scrutiny.

But there are ill-effects, nervous tics, symptoms of exhaustion, that arise in an audience when it oversolicits the heteroclite. Newness ought to suffer a period of frost—it should even have to submit, for its own good, to entrenched and outraged resistance. Neglect gives a winsome oddity more time to perform important tests on itself; widespread narrow-mindedness shelters surprise. No one will blame a publisher who has discovered an out-of-print minor masterpiece and feels it his duty to enrich and uplift the human spirit by publishing it in paperback, with a beautiful, spare, up-to-the-minute cover design. That is his job. But sometimes we can't help wishing he would wait, and just buy one old copy for himself from an antiquarian dealer, preserving for at least a few more years the delight of private, proprietary knowledge, the ecstasy of arriving at something underappreciated at the end of a briareous ramification of footnotes, since the hope of such secrets is one of the things that keep us reading.

Rough timetables, "appreciation schedules," may be of some guidance. That pad dotted on both sides with suction cups, to which you can vertically affix a wet bar of soap while you are in the shower? It should remain unmentioned by any magazine's "New and Noteworthy" column for six months. Each of us should have a fair chance of finding it, hanging unheralded from a hook in the hardware store, on our own. A good poem, as Horace suggested, ought to have a nine-year news blackout. And a major leisure item—a new sort of inflatable raft, for example—deserves at least five summers of quiet superiority before it gets a Best Buy rating from *Consumer Reports* and leans against the wall in the sporting-goods department at the high-volume discounters. After all, this successful raft—with its revolutionary osmotic inflater-valve—displaces several other very good makes of raft, which once so proudly rode the crest; and when we look through the still-hopeful catalogs of these inferior raft-crafters, and sense their anguish, deepening monthly, as they watch their sales go into steep decline, then *they* begin to take on rarity—the rarity of the underdog, one of the most seductive kinds—and we discover ourselves feeling, too soon, that we must root for the second-rate product. (Haven't you felt a peculiar sort of worry about the chair in your living room that no one sits in? Haven't you sometimes felt sleeve-tugs of compassion and guilt over an article of clothing that you dislike and therefore scarcely wear? Haven't you at least once secretly sat down in the hardly-sat-in chair, wearing that ugly shirt, in order to rectify these inequities?) A little lengthening of the time it takes for new merit to out, for rare proficiencies to make their sudden bundle, would allow our sympathy for the underdog and our excitement in superiority to coincide; too rapid a transmittal of the knowledge of relative greatness, on the other hand, eliminates that beautiful period when these emotions overlap.

Subtotaling, then, we note that civilization ought to be superficially pigheaded, suspicious of all subversion, so that rarity can leap in with her accordion and startle the anatomy lesson. If the sadly underrated is kept sadly underrated, righteousness and a sense of urgent mission stay on the side of the deserving. But when all the goodies are pincered the moment they surface, when zoning rules demand public art in exchange for additional floor space, when writers curtail their finer efforts because the merest suggestion of expertise is enough to coast on for a decade, then one is unwillingly forced, in behalf of originality itself, to defend authority, stringency, unbend-ingness—not things one defends with real moral relish. So let the rare stay rare, at least for a while. Every piece of bad design praised does its bit to keep good designs under wraps. We need many incompetent arbiters; we need more choices to be foolish and uninformed.

Some desert fathers have gotten carried away, though. Say you are a genius, and you have just done something that has never been done before. There it lies, on your legal pad or your patio, as rare as it could possibly be. In a week or a year it might glint in thousands of other minds, like the tiny re-peating images in a beetle's eye. Paul Valéry has some stern words for you: "Every mind considered powerful begins with the fault that makes it known," he writes. And: "the strongest heads, the most sagacious inventors, the most exacting con-noisseurs of thought, must be unknown men, misers, who die without giving up their secret." Even putting an idea in words, according to Arthur Schopenhauer, is a sellout: "As soon as our thinking has found words it ceases to be sincere or at bottom serious. When it begins to exist for others it ceases to live in us." The self-canceling quality of these verbal arguments for silence is obvious. Still, if behind them is sim-ply the wish for a kind of privacy, for the insulation of inat-tention, for a few delays in the final sentencing of a thought, for a little sorrow intermixed with one's eager self-expression, then any prudent introvert would raise a concurring absinthe glass.

Things often work better, too, when the portions of each person's life that are wholly devoted to a quest for the rare are themselves somewhat infrequent. The staggering fluke and the exhilarating pathology ought to surprise their first discoverers as much as they surprise the rest of us. It is always more pleasing when the sweepstakes is won by the family who sent off their entry distractedly, in the midst of errands and trips to the vet, than when it is won by that man with the flat voice, in the hooded parka, who sent in five hundred thirty-seven separate entries—except that ultimately rarity accrues to him as well, once we contemplate him: all those unshaven mornings at the post office, those readings of the fine-print contest guidelines, those copyings of "Dove is One Quarter Cleansing Cream" on three-by-five pieces of paper.

For everyone besides that rare man in the parka, the provisional moral may be: Pursue truth, not rarity. The atypical can fend for itself: our innate, unconquerable human appetite for it will never let it lie low for long. And very often, when we are looking over several common truths, holding them next to one another in an effort to feel again what makes them true, rarities will mysteriqusly germinate in the charged spaces between them, like those lovely, ghostly zings that a guitarist's fingers make, as they clutch from chord to chord.

(1984)

Machinery

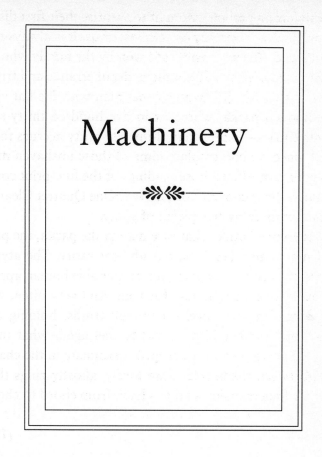

Model Airplanes

You don't need a set of Pactra enamels, or airbrush equipment, or jewelers' files; not forceps or a pin vise; you don't need to know the variations in camouflage adopted by the F-5E Tiger II 527th Aggressor Squadron at Alconbury from 1976 through 1988, or know, indeed, anything at all about war or history or military hardware; you don't need to harbor angry thoughts toward enemies abroad or at work. But a simple *tube of glue,* at the very least, might seem necessary for any appreciation of the plastic model-airplane kit. And some minimal grade-school exposure to glue, or "cement," as the technical prefer to call it, is an important early step toward the attainment of later, simpler, unpolymerized pleasures. Certainly glue, especially during those long summer afternoons in the late sixties and early seventies, before oil of mustard was added to the recipe to discourage any direct attempts at mood alteration, was lovely stuff. When you tweaked off the dried wastrel from an earlier session and applied a gentle pressure to the Testor's tube, a brand-new Steuben-grade art-blob of cooling poison would silently ensphere itself at the machined metal tip, looking, with its sharp gnomonic surface highlights and distilled, vodkal interior purity, like a self-contained world of incorruptible mental concentration, the voluptuously pantographed miniaturization of the surrounding room, and the artist's rendering on the Monogram box top, and the half-built fighter itself, along with the hands that now reached to complete it; and as the smell of this pellucid solvent, suggestive of impossible Mach numbers and upper atmospheres and limitless congressional funding, drove away any incompatible carbon-based signals of hunger or human frailty, you felt as if your head had somehow gained admission to and submerged itself within that glowing globule of formalism and fine-motor skills. When you held a pair of halved components tightly together for ten minutes, glaring at them, *willing* the tiny, glue-dolloped pins to turn to toffee and join forever their complementary sockets, you weren't worried by, you even welcomed, the bead that often reemerged along the seam as evidence of the static force of your grip, and you waved the subassembly around to speed its drying, in this way separately "flying" each wheel or pitot tube or stabilator, in order to extract its unique contribution to overall airworthiness, before you united it with the Spartan society of the fuselage. Glue was the jet fuel of 1:72 scale—inflammable, icy, dangerous. Its end wasn't speed itself, but the appreciation of speed—an idea that needed to be pieced together slowly, over hours of chair-bound, stiff-necked application, until vibration and afterburners and the sense of being almost out of control all rotated and mapped themselves onto an alternative imaginary dimension, where they were represented by an out-of-focus desert of clean newsprint, by the weightless reflection of a watch crystal across a high wall, and by a large whitish thumbprint permanently imprinted on green plastic.

Yes, glue was good and helpful in its place, but we must now put it aside. For who has the kind of time it takes to *build* plastic models? Eight years ago, during a time of professional disappointment, I bought an MPC '57 Chevy—A GREAT GASSER WITH A FLIP-UP FRONT END! read the box copy—with the idea that in putting it together I would pull myself together, since I was a '57, too. The kit cost about as much as a paperback, and would have required roughly the same number of hours to finish, but it would have bypassed the verbal lobe completely, a promise not all paperbacks can truthfully make. Yet it sits before me now, emboxed, unbuilt. For some years I justified my failure on the grounds that I had never liked building model cars as much as building model airplanes (the discount drugstore had only had model cars for sale that impulsive afternoon)—but in the past several weeks I have bought Monogram's USAF F-101B Voodoo and Soviet MiG-29 Fulcrum (both made in the USA), Revell's F-15A Eagle and Israeli F-21 Kfir (both made in Japan), Revell's Soviet Sukhoi-27 Flanker (made in Korea), Revell's B-2 Stealth Advanced Technology Bomber (made in the USA), DML's combined B-2 and F-117A Stealth kits (made in Hong Kong), Hasegawa's Kfir C2 and F-14A Atlantic Fleet Squadrons and MiG-29 Fulcrum (all three made in Japan), AMT's F-14A Tomcat (made in Italy), Lindberg's X3 Stiletto (made in USA), and Testor's Tomcat and MiG-29 (Italy and Japan, respectively), plus a few others—$211 worth of intercontinental plastic from three retail stores—and though I have very much enjoyed opening the boxes, though I have even made Canon copies that record exactly how each box's contents looked when I first lifted its top, I have built none of these aircraft. But now at least I know why.

The reason is simply that, despite the compensating attractions of glue, the activity of model construction goes to its final rest in one's memory as a long, gradual disappointment. You think deludedly that you want to own the finished thing, joined, puttied, painted, decaled, and set under glass in a diorama made of bits of hot-mounted sponge and distressed Kleenex. But what you really want is to own, say, the Monogram MiG-29 kit at the apex of its visual complexity, where it can stimulate every shock and strut of your craftsmanly ambition, before it has been harmed by the X-acto knife and pieces of things have been bonded in permanent darkness within other things; you want it to be yours when both lateral aspects of each three-dimensional component, numbered for quick reference, hang symmetrically and simultaneously available to the eye in an arrangement of rectilinear runners and fragile jointure as fully intricate and beautiful as the immense wrought-iron gates that protect the fabled treasures in the Armorer's Chamber of the Kremlin.

Straight from the store, these kits are museums: Kremlins and Smithsonians of the exploded view, wherein you may fully and rapturously attend to a single airplane, which exists planarly, neatly espaliered, arranged not by aerodynamic or military function, but by the need for an orderly flow of hot plastic through the polished cloisters of the mold in which it was formed—the largest and tiniest pieces nearest the *sprue,* or point of injection, the middle-sized pieces farther away, where they will successfully fill with a lesser fluid impulse. Nothing is hidden on these architectures; all the complex curves of wings and tailpieces are there, but everything is "straightened up," as a hotel maid rationalizes the top of a bedside table simply by reorienting the mess at right angles, throwing nothing away; one gazes and thinks less of air-to-air combat than of those alluring ads for closet organizers or for garment bags fitted with specialized pockets. A pilot, adroitly sliced in two, headless, awaits recomposition in one crowded narthex. The elegant landing gear, twice as impressive as the real thing, is on view in the south transept. Some of the pieces don't even offer up their final disposition at first glance: the truth—that they are relatively unconvincing bits of cockpit decor, or segments of a petty canard—would only cause unhappiness were you actually to engage with the kit and prove its necessary unfaithfulness to the real fighter. "It's real because it's Revell" was the manufacturer's tag in the years I was building them; but the realism, I now realize, delights most piercingly when it is taken on faith.

The box, then, is the basilica of the unbuilt. You never quite rid yourself of the illusion that you will want to get to work on it as soon as you find a suitable chunk of time. Meanwhile you are content to wander these galleries of imaginary hobbyistic space with the indefinitely postponed intention of deacquisitioning their contents and leaving their mounts as raw and wanting as stems plucked free of after-dinner grapes. The kit is informationally richer than the completed plane. Yet *richer still* is the mold from which the kit limply falls, pushed out from the hand-finished, water-cooled steel cavities by a forest of long ejector pins. From this vantage, the model kit becomes the middle term, the precious domestic intermediary between the technology of injection molding and the technology of air defense. And if the injection-molding presses, the sophisticated Van Dorns or the older Cincinnati Milacrons at the Revell/Monogram factory in Morton Grove, Illinois—machines the size of locomotives, capable of animating a few hot cupfuls of viscous gray plastic into palmate arrangements of engine cowlings and smooth leading edges and external "stores" (that is, bombs and missiles), all overgrown with a fioritura of rivet heads, every half minute or so—if these massive presses had *cockpits,* the model enthusiast would perhaps more appropriately recline here, enthroned in the pacific din of high-volume toy manufacturing, rather than in the Kfir's or Voodoo's or Tomcat's ejector seat. Fighter planes are fussy and expensive to maintain, but with oil and minimal tinkering, injection-molding machines will, in the words of Dan Burden, Revell/Monogram's plant manager, "just run forever." The aim of the Pratt & Whitney jet engine is to generate thrust with a spinning turbine; the aim of the Van Dorn is to move plastic along a rotating horizontal screw and force it to submit to prearranged detail with a minimum of flashing. The outcome of the Pratt & Whitney is turbulent exhaust and scattered applause at air shows; the outcome of the dutiful tonnage of the Cincinnati Milacron is a better preadolescent brain. (Hasegawa, the high-end Japanese manufacturer, includes, in a kit entirely devoted to U.S. guided bombs and rocket launchers, this educational word to parents: "It is reported that building plastic-model kits improves a child's capability in understanding and in patience. Moving fingers helps his brain grow faster.") The aerobatic F-15A Eagle can exceed the speed of sound in a vertical climb (at least that's what Revell's instruction sheet claims); the arobotic Cincinnati Milacron sits immovably anchored to a rubber shock-pad in a hangar full of its hulking, squirting confreres, slowly depreciating, ministered to by taciturn women who, but for their safety glasses, might have been milkmaids in another life. The plastic model you buy at the store is poised between these two rival poles of might, military-industrial and civilian-industrial. Its alliances are unsettled; the cozy homage it pays to lethal force is part of its attraction.

And now, with this mention of homage, we arrive, full of hushed deference, before the large blue box that holds the Stealth B-2 Bomber. Revell's version ($12.99 at Toys R Us) is molded, quite properly, in black plastic, and comes shrouded in a clear sack with a prominent warning in French and English about the danger of suffocation. The full-scale Stealth is beautiful from a distance, although in a worrisomely Transylvanian sort of way. It is reportedly the result of astounding advances in computer-aided design and manufacturing processes. But unfortunately its continuous curves and unmitigated blackness do not seem to make for a satisfying scale model. Perhaps this is because the real Stealth, so completely the result of composite-molding machinery, itself too closely approximates the fluent, impressionable greatness of molded styrene. It is a model, and therefore a model of it can't show off the extraordinary talent plastic has for the mimicry of other materials and textures. The kit-makers can't be held responsible for the fact that the B-2 is so maddeningly smooth, that its featurelessness soaks up the eager radar of the visual sense and sends little back. The Cold War has moved from the upper atmosphere of spy photography to the wind tunnel, and aerodynamic drag has effectively replaced the Soviet Union as the infinitely resourceful enemy. But drag, unwelcome though it is to the airplane designer, is everything to the plastic-model enthusiast, because drag means rivets, knobs, holes, wires, hinges, visible missiles, sensors, gun blisters—all those encrustations that inspire study, and make imitation (in all-time bestselling models like the Monogram Mustang P-51 fighter) difficult enough to be worthwhile. And this consideration, oddly enough, may constitute a compelling argument against the B-2 program: the Bomber may represent an act of industrial will more impressive than anything since the Second World War; it may indeed harbor genius and patents and spin-off potential in every undulant inch; but it doesn't at this moment look as if it will ever fill the demanding hobbyist with delight when he opens the box. And the fulfillment of that single recreational requirement, after all, given the inevitable shift away from vengeance and toward ornament that is history's principal sequel, is the B-2's only long-term reason for being.

But if, on the other hand, Revell/Monogram were to offer a 1:48 model of the automated tape-lamination machine that Northrop designed to manufacture the composite materials that are molded into its plane, I would sit up very quickly. There is a kit I would buy *and* build. And now a regressive vision rises up before me—a vision of a whole Revell/Monogram "Factory Floor" series, marketed along the lines of the "Yeager Super Fighters" series, with Eli Whitney giving the thumbs-up sign on the box in place of the craggy test pilot: authentic scale replicas of great production-lines from new and mature industries around the world. The masterpiece of this urgently needed set of kits, the one that would exact an unprecedented level of artistry from the talented mold-makers in Morton Grove—who follow, incidentally, a set of milestones similar to major wedding anniversaries, from paper drawings, through overscale basswood forms (carved and sanded with Ruskinian care and thrown out once their shape has been captured in epoxy), to the final jubilee of steel molds, engraved and polished by adepts in Windsor, Canada, or in Hong Kong (where the machinists, according to one mold-layout engineer I talked to, have an especially "soft touch" with airplane likenesses)—the final masterpiece of the series would have to be a superbly detailed, vintage 1979 Cincinnati Milacron injection press, complete with warning decals, rotating screw, and a fully removable mold block ready to produce two MiG-29s a minute around the clock. When production of the toy commenced, and the real twelve-ton machine began to sigh and kick onto its conveyor belt a model of itself—in this way manufacturing not another unbuilt airplane but the unbuilt tool responsible for all unbuilt airplanes—we would be witnesses to one of the greatest moments in the Age of Plastic. And by inciting later generations of avid modelers to acknowledge the intellectual satisfactions of factory engineering early enough for any potential zealotry in that direction to take permanent hold, we might also find that in passing we had done something small but helpful toward reversing the industrial collapse of the United States.

Until this great day comes, however, we must be content to collect the airplane kits themselves, shaking them tentatively, making copies of their contents in the box, tactfully inspecting their rougher undersides, browsing their multilingual directions, and then piling them somewhere safe, unglued.

(1989)

The Projector

The finest moment in *The Blob* (1958) occurs in a small-town movie theater, during a showing of something called *Daughter of Horror*. While the pre-McLuhanite projectionist reads his hardcover book, the Blob—a giant protean douche-bag—begins to urge its heat-seeking toxic viscosity through ten tiny slits in an air vent. Past the turning movie reel, we watch the doomed projectionist glance out the viewport at the screen, preparing for a "changeover"—an uninterrupted switch from the running projector, whose twenty-minute reel is almost over, to the second, idle one, which is all threaded and ready to roll. He senses something at his back; he turns; he gives the flume of coalesced protoplasm a level look—then it gets him. Now unattended, the first projector plays past the cue for the changeover and runs out of film. The disgruntled audience looks around and spots the Blob (in an image that must have inspired the development of the Play-Doh Fun Factory) extruding itself in triumph from all four of the little windows—two projector ports and two viewports—in the theater's rear wall.

Chuck Russell's remake of *The Blob* (1988) brings every detail, or almost every detail, of the first film neatly up to date. The movie-within-a-movie is now entitled *Garden Tool Massacre.* "Isn't it awfully late to be trimming the hedges?" a camp counselor mutters while making out with his girlfriend, having noticed a masked stranger at work on the shrubbery after dark. "Wait a minute," he then says, suspicions aroused. "Hockey season ended months ago." Cut to the booth, where "Hobbs," the bored projectionist (whose life will indeed prove to be "solitary, poor, nasty, brutish, and short"), his head again seen past a turning reel of film, reads a magazine and fiddles left-handedly with a yo-yo. The second-generation Blob, far peppier and more enterprising than its forebear, pukes its way briskly up the air-conditioning duct and plasters the unhappy Hobbs to the ceiling. Moments later, the manager, looking up, discovers his colleague, a Ralph Steadman grimace on his face, half consumed in an agony of Handi-Wrap and dyed cornstarch, the yo-yo still rising and falling from his twitching finger.

Why the addition of the yo-yo? the student of film technology may wonder. Is it merely a gratuitous prop, or does it tell us something? I suspect that the yo-yo is a reference to the classical principle of the movie reel, which repeatedly rewinds and relinquishes its length of film. The reason Mr. Russell had the iconography of the movie reel very much on his mind in shooting this scene, I think, is that, despite all his diligent updating of cultural references, and despite the elaborate verisimilitude of the movie's gruesomeness, he was not quite able to bring himself to reveal to us the reality of modern theatrical-movie projection. For the terrifying reality is that *film is no longer projected from reels.*

Film is projected from platters. The platter system (Fig. 1), first invented by a German projectionist, Willie Burth, and

Fig. 1. *On the top platter (1) film unfurls from the inside out, and winds up on the middle platter (2). The lowest platter (3) is a spare, used for a second feature. The canted console (4), containing the xenon lamphouse and sound equipment, aims the image from the projector (5) through the glass projector port (6), and onto the screen. In the soundhead (7), a solar cell interprets the soundtrack. The projectionist keeps an eye on image quality through the viewport (8).*

perfected by Norelco, in the Netherlands, about twenty years ago, works this way: The film arrives from the distributor on five or six reels in an octagonal steel suitcase. The projectionist splices the film from these reels together, winding it in one big spiral onto one of (typically) three horizontal circular steel disks, each roughly four feet in diameter. When the projectionist wants to set up a show, he pulls the beginning of the film from the middle of the platter, threads it through the platter's central "brain" (its lumpily massed rollers look somewhat cerebral), thence around a few guide rollers screwed into the wall or the ceiling, and loads it into the sprockets of the projector. After it passes through the "gate" (where it is actually projected), the film usually travels through the sound head (where a light reads the optical soundtrack), loops around several more guide rollers, and ends up being wound in another huge spiral on one of the other horizontal platters. Because the film leaves from the middle of the platter, instead of the outside, rewinding between shows, reel by reel, is no longer necessary. And each theater needs only one projector per screen, rather than the traditional tag-team alternating two.

There are a few revival houses in Los Angeles and New York that continue to show films on two projectors from reels, but the vast majority of the country's theaters—art houses and mall-plexes alike—currently employ the platter system, and have for the past decade. Yet of the projector-movies from this period that I have seen (movies that include a moment or two in a contemporary projection booth, I mean), not one—not Chuck Russell's *Blob* or Joe Dante's *Gremlins* (1984: gremlins invade theater and play Reel 4 of *Snow White*), or *Night of the Comet* (1984: couple spend night in steel-firewalled projection booth and escape being turned into red dust or killer maniacs by comet), not Susan Seidelman's wonderful *Desperately Seeking Susan* (1985: we'll get to this one later) or *Gas, Food, Lodging* (1992: girl falls for Chicano projectionist)—dares give us a glimpse of a turning platter. I was sure, having read a description (in Carol J. Clover's thoughtful book *Men, Women, and Chain Saws: Gender in the Modern Horror Film*) of a despicable Italian zombie movie called *Demons* (1985), that, because its action—fountains of pus and helicopter-blade disembowelings—is set within a fully automated and (of course) transcendently evil movie theater, with an unmanned projection booth, and because the second-largest manufacturer of movie projectors in the world happens to be Milan's Cinemeccanica, that at least here, in this admittedly unsavory setting, we would be shown something approaching the technical truth about movie projection. But no: although the demonic equipment blinks with a few more lights than usual, it is fitted with the familiar pairs of reels up front.

These lapses of realism probably have more to do with iconographic inertia than with any sort of conspiracy or coverup on the part of movie people. It isn't that "they" don't want us to know that the friendly century-old reel of celluloid, the reel that has fueled a million puns and that more than any other image means movies to us, has been superseded by a separate triple-tiered mechanism that, while full of visual interest, and quite beautiful in its indolent, wedding-cake-on-display sort of way, is less intuitively comprehensible than its predecessor. Hollywood producers don't care whether we are aware that the platter system reduced the participatory role of the projectionist and helped make the multiplex theater financially attractive. (The eighteen-screen Cineplex Odeon in Los Angeles, for example, requires only two projectionists at any one time, and the twenty-six-screen complex in Brussels is comfortably tended by eight.) Nor do they care whether or not we know that platter hardware is, according to some critics, rougher on a movie print than reel-to-reel projection was.

"The platter is death to film," Dr. Jan-Christopher Horak, the senior curator of films at the George Eastman House, in Rochester, told me. A print now must twist a hundred and eighty degrees on its axis as it completes the large open-air loop that leads from the feed platter through the projector to the takeup platter; this subjects it, Horak says, to a kind of helical stress that film stock has not previously had to withstand. He has been finding "strange stretch marks that aren't vertical, as you might expect, but horizontal" on platter-fed films. And the platter system, he says, allows for unattended operation: if a hardy chunk of filth gets caught in the gate of the projector, it can scratch the film for hundreds of feet unremedied. Horak also mentions the lost-frame problem: every time a projectionist "builds" a feature on a platter, he must cut the leaders off each component reel and splice the ends in place; then, when the film is "broken down" at the end of its run, those splices are cut and the leaders reattached for shipping. In the process, each reel loses at least a frame of film. The more theaters a film visits, the shorter it gets.

Dick Twichell—a wise and careful projectionist at a twelve-screen Loew's Theatre complex in greater Rochester, not far from Horak's archival collection—admits that ambient dirt can cause serious trouble now. "Static electricity becomes more of a problem, because the film is out in the open air and attracts dust," he says. The guide rollers, often made of plastic rather than metal, contribute to, rather than dissipate, static. And when a plex theater does something called "interlocking"—the simultaneous running of a single print through two or even three separate projectors, aimed at different screens—the film can travel hundreds of feet over guide rollers, paying out along the ceiling and returning low, inches from the floor, drawing dust along the way.

On the other hand, Twichell disagrees that the round trip to and from a platter physically overstresses a print. "If that were true, the splices would come apart, and they almost never do," he says. In fact, Twichell, like many in the film industry, is of the opinion that platter hardware is far gentler on prints than reels were. A takeup reel had a primitive clutch: it pulled the film forcibly off the teeth of the projector's lower sprocket, wearing out its perforations: a print would last perhaps three hundred runs, certainly no more than seven hundred, before becoming flimsy and easily torn.

Now, on platters, a print can run almost indefinitely without sustaining that sort of mechanical damage. (There is a platter disaster known as a "brain-wrap," but it is relatively rare.) Disney routinely gets ten or twenty thousand showings from a single print in its theme parks; often the dyes in the emulsion fade before the film succumbs.

Constant rewinding, which platters eliminate, was itself a major source of harm. "Fully nine-tenths of the damage to film comes from the process known as 'pulling down' in rewinding," says the 1912 *Motion Picture Handbook*. The rainmarks, as they are called, that distance us from an old Buster Keaton picture, say, were probably made while it was being rewound, not while it was being cranked through the projector. Projectionists were traditionally tinkerers, techies, taciturn isolates with dirty fingernails; of necessity they worked (and still do work, some of them) surrounded by grease pots, oilcans, dirty rags, swapped-out components, and (before xenon bulbs came in, in the sixties) by the stubs of spent carbons from the carbon-arc lamps, each of which lasted no more than half an hour. Chuck McCann, who plausibly plays the hefty, chain-smoking hero of a 1970 film called *The Projectionist* (which is a sort of remake of the 1924 Buster Keaton movie *Sherlock, Junior:* the one about a projectionist who, dozing off on a stool by one of his machines, dreams that he has entered the film that he is showing), gets angry at Rodney Dangerfield (the manager) and slams a reel of film onto the rewinder, cranking hard and maintaining tension by resting his palm on the reel. The more brute film handling— rewinding, threading, splicing—that the typical projectionist was forced to do, the more beat-up the film became.

The Projectionist is filled with fun snippets from old movies, as is *Cinema Paradiso* (1989), a horribly sentimental Italian creation that is nonetheless accurate in portraying the local projectionist, rather than any director or studio head, as the person with the final cut. *Cinema Paradiso*'s previewing priest rings a bell anytime people kiss onscreen, and the projectionist dutifully marks the moment in the reel with a strip of paper so that he can remove the kiss later. In truth, though, projectionists, at least in the United States, were more likely to be furtive editors and clip-collectors on their own (as the creators of *The Projectionist* seemingly were) than on behalf of local censors: they would simply cut out a few feet, or a frame or two, of an image or a sequence they liked. Commonly, they collected "favorite movie stars, and especially scenes or shots that had pieces of female anatomy in them," Horak told me; the Eastman House now owns some of these collections. One projectionist told me that if you cut two frames from a scene where a camera is dollied sidewise, and you then view these frames through a stereoscope, you can simulate 3-D. After years in the projection business, this man has lost all interest in watching movies, and he has canceled HBO and Cinemax, but he continues to accumulate 3-D frames. He cuts them out, he hastened to say, only if they appear in a trailer, or at the front or back of a reel, where frames are meant to be lost anyway. Other projectionists may be less ethical. It could well be that hands-off platter automation helps projectionists resist the powerful temptation to keep souvenirs from the films that pass through their theaters.

Even with automation, though, there is a fair amount of under-the-hood maintenance connected with tending a projector. Early in *The Inner Circle* (1991), Tom Hulce, who plays Stalin's projectionist, plucks something from his shirt pocket.

"What's that you're poking in the projector?" asks the alarmed K.G.B. official.

"Toothbrush," Hulce says. "Very convenient for cleaning. I always carry one with me."

The K.G.B. man studies it, sniffs it. "The old projectionist never had anything like that," he says, impressed.

Recently, after the last show of the night of *The Remains of the Day*, I watched Stephan Shelley, senior projectionist at the Grand Lake Theatre, in Oakland, California, clean the vitals of one of his eight projectors with a pale-blue Colgate toothbrush. ("A clean, used toothbrush is ideal," advises the user's manual for the current Century MSC-TA 35-mm. projector with self-turning lens turret.) Shelley greases the rods and gears of his Century projectors every morning; he uses rubbing alcohol and Q-Tips on the equipment daily as well; and he keeps a vigilant eye on the level of the oil bath in the all-important intermittent movement. (Seventy-millimeter film, he says, which has a magnetic rather than an optical soundtrack, leaves a projector especially dirty, because ferrous particles from the magnetic strip come off in the machine.) Fully cross-trained, he also fixes popcorn poppers when they break. There are occasional reports of projectionists less knowledgeable than Shelley who, having run out of projector oil, resort in desperation to pouring popcorn butter in the machines to keep them from freezing up. This practice voids the warranty, however.

Besides platters, the other notable recent development in projectorware is the aforementioned xenon bulb, a two-thousand-watt, foot-long, thousand-dollar item that illuminates a film by sending eighty amperes of direct current through a quartz envelope containing ten atmospheres of excitable xenon. It makes a B-movie sort of zap when it comes on. Through a tiny green portal in the lamphouse, you can peer in on it and watch it radiating away, cooled by indefatigable fans. It, too, caused a flutter of dissent when first introduced: charged xenon was said to produce a noticeably harsher, bluer light than the glowing carbon tips of the arc lamp did. Also, bulbs occasionally "fail violently" (i.e., explode), damaging the focusing mirror in the lamphouse. But the arc lamp gave off toxic fumes, and it was moody: movies were especially luminous on windy days, when the exhaust chimneys drew better and the carbons consequently burned brighter. Objections to xenon have pretty much died down; the only legitimate gripe the moviegoer can make now is that when a bulb fails, even nonviolently (this usually happens after about two thousand hours of service), it takes a while to alert someone in the theater and get the projector stopped, and, since platters can't be reversed, the audience will miss the stretch of the movie that ran with sound and no picture.

We now know more of the projector's earliest history, thanks to Christopher Rawlence's recent book *The Missing Reel: The Untold Story of the Lost Inventor of Moving Pictures.* It was the movie projector, not the movie camera, that gave early visionaries trouble, since the projector must hold each frame still longer, and must snap to the next frame faster, than a camera does when it exposes film. The original invention, defined as an affair of toothed sprockets that engage with a flexible perforated band carrying sequential images, probably ought to be attributed to Louis Aimé Augustin Le Prince (1841–1890?), a ceramicist and enameler who worked in Leeds. Le Prince filed the relevant patent in 1886 but disappeared several years later, days before he was to leave for the United States with a crated demo model of his epochal "deliverer." That Thomas Edison's lawyers had him killed, Rawlence suggests, is unclear.

Edison, tireless and shrewd in his appropriation of other people's work, unsurprisingly claimed sole authorship of the "Vitascope," but he and his projector-development team had done little more than slap the Wizard's name on a machine actually built by Thomas Armat, a Washington inventor, which incorporated principles conceived by Le Prince. Armat's historic hand was working the crank when, on April 23, 1896, the screen at Koster & Bial's Music Hall, on West Thirty-fourth Street, wowed journalists with the "Perfect Reproduction of Noted Feminine Figures and Their Every Movement."

Early projectionists in the wake of Armat were inventors and repairmen, but they were also performers, interpreting the emotional tone of a film by varying the film speed. "The really high-class operator, who produces high-class work on the screen, must and will vary his speed to suit the subject being projected," F. H. Richardson's 1912 textbook advised. For example:

> [A]s a rule solemn scenes will be improved if the machine turns slowly. Take, for instance . . . the Pathé Passion Play; probably the Bible patriarchs in real life actually moved as fast as anyone else. They may have, upon occasion, even run. Nevertheless rapid action does not suit our preconceived notions of such things. I have often seen the Pathé Passion Play run at such enormous speed that the characters were jumping around the screen like a lot of school boys. Such an exhibition was disgusting to the audience and offensive to those of deeply religious inclination and who revere those characters.

Even after the electric motor eased the physical labor of the projectionist, silent film studios often furnished cue sheets along with their prints, which itemized the changes in speed that, like tempo markings on a piano score, were an important part of the experience of films such as *The Birth of a Nation*. One of the reasons silent movies can seem so ridiculous now (in addition to the fact that some of them *are* ridiculous, of course) is that they are frequently presented at the fixed, twenty-four-frames-per-second rate adopted for equipment in the late 1920s, in conjunction with the optical soundtrack (the ear can't tolerate changes in speed the way the eye can), rather than at variable rates more in the vicinity of sixteen frames a second, as was conventional until then.

But despite these momentous changes—the stabilization of film speed; sound; Technicolor; the replacement of nitrate-based film with fire-retardant acetate; xenon bulbs; platterization—the really remarkable thing about the evolution of the projector over the past century is how similar in motive essentials a 1994 Simplex machine is to the original Armat/Le Prince design. Film still moves on sprockets with sixteen teeth, and the crucial "intermittent" sprocket—the one that actually stops and starts the film—is still powered, as it was at Koster & Bial's Music Hall, by a lovely piece of precision machinery called the Geneva movement, which was first developed by Swiss watchmakers to prevent springs from being overwound. The Geneva movement has two main pieces: a Maltese cross (or star, or starwheel) and a more pedestrian cam, both of which splash around half submerged in oil. The pin on the steadily turning cam slips into the slot in the Maltese cross and forces it to rotate a quarter of a turn and then stop dead, immobilized by the cam's circular edge. When the star is stopped, a single immobile image floods the theater screen for a few hundredths of a second; when it turns, the film advances under cover of shuttered darkness. The moviegoer's brain, hoodwinked by this succession of still lives, obligingly infers motion.

"You know what a Maltese cross is?" an itinerant projector-repairman with questionable toilet habits asks an incompetent projectionist near the end of Wim Wenders' mammoth film-fleuve, *Kings of the Road*. The projectionist takes a guess: Some kind of drink? The repairman shakes his head sadly and tries to explain it to him. "Without this little thing, there'd be no film industry!" he says. The projectionist is unimpressed, and (because *Kings of the Road* is a semi-comprehensible art movie) he casually inhales the flame from a cigarette lighter to close out the scene. But the workings of the true star system, though they may take a moment to grasp

(Fig. 2), repay meditation: seldom has a mechanism so simple, so unexpectedly heraldic, persisted without modification at the center of a ruthless business that has otherwise undergone continuous technical, artistic, and financial upheavals.

The Simplex projector, which many hold to be the finest, is built in Omaha by a company called Ballantyne, which also makes theatrical spotlights and high-tech chicken cookers. The Maltese cross *within* the Simplex projector, however, is manufactured in Glendale Heights, Illinois, the work of a privately held company called La Vezzi Precision Incorporated, run by fifty-one-year-old Al La Vezzi. Al La Vezzi's grandfather, Edward La Vezzi, got his start, during the First World War, by milling the worn teeth off projector sprockets and sweating new brass ones on. Now, in a sort of benevolent monopoly, La Vezzi's company makes sprockets and intermittent movements for Simplex, Century, and Ballantyne projectors (all three brands are co-owned, and based in Omaha), and also for several companies in Europe and Asia, and for Christie projectors made in Cypress, California. For Christie, La Vezzi developed a sealed, belt-driven intermittent movement, called the Ultramittent, that never needs oiling. La Vezzi Precision is also responsible for the legendary VKF sprocket—the Very Kind to Film sprocket, that is—whose teeth are smoothed in meaningful ways by computer-controlled four-axis machining centers. The manufacture of the VKF sprocket is a "no-brainer," however, according to Mr. La Vezzi, compared to making the Maltese cross, where serious flaws are measured in millionths of an inch. "The slot of a star has to be perfect," he says, pronouncing "perfect" with inspiring plosiveness.

Will there always be intermittent sprockets, and the projectors they serve, at work in the world? Will later generations of movie watchers know how similar a projector sounds to an

Fig. 2. *The cam turns (1) until the pin engages the Maltese cross (2), giving it a quarter turn and pulling the film down one frame (3). At (4), the pin releases the cross.*

idling VW Beetle? Will they, when viewing that superb early scene in Charlie Chaplin's *Modern Times,* realize that, though Chaplin is ostensibly dragged down into the bowels of a huge "Electro Steel Corp." machine, he is really miming a piece of flexible film and threading himself through the sprockets of a movie projector? I've watched quite a few projector-movies recently (including one that I haven't been able to splice in anywhere here, called *The Smallest Show on Earth,* in which Peter Sellers plays an old projectionist who disrupts a Western when he gets drunk in the booth), but I watched every one of them on videotape. I paused, rewound, fast-forwarded, played, and paused again so much in studying the last scene of *Desperately Seeking Susan,* for instance (Aidan Quinn kisses Rosanna Arquette against a Simplex projector playing a sci-fi movie about mutant attackers—Rosanna's back arrests the winged chariot of the movie reel and the film frame melts on the screen), that the black plastic housing of the rented video gave off an unusually strong and pleasing smell of miniature VCR servomotors and hot printed-circuit boards when I at last, having subjected the lovers' frame-melting embrace to a level of scrutiny it was never meant to bear, ejected it.

But that single 35-mm. rectangle of color film contains, it is estimated, the equivalent of forty megabytes of digital information: forty megabytes, the contents of an entire small hard disk, in *every frame* of a movie. Even if one assumes all sorts of clever data compression, it is difficult to imagine digital storage systems matching the Van Eyckian resolution of the chemical grains on a strip of 35- or 70-mm. movie film anytime soon. Projectors, and the durably whirling Maltese crosses inside them, may still be around when, in another thirty years, a third, magnificently reimagined *Blob* oozes into the projection area of the local eight-plex and begins stirring up trouble. And by then, perhaps, horror-film makers will be brave enough to show us a few platters.

(1994)

Clip Art

Professional men can't wear much in the way of jewelry. The gemless wedding band, the watch, the belt buckle, the key chain—possibly the quietly costly blue-enameled pen in a shirt pocket—are among the few sanctioned outlets for the male self-embellishing urge. Occasionally permissible are the shirt stud, the cufflink, and the nautical brass blazer button. Bas-relief suspender clasps, various forms of tie and collar tackle, and chunky nonmarital fingerware are allowable on men who make a living by commission. The demotion of smoke has eliminated the ornate cigarette lighter. Neck and wrist chains are inadvisable. Metalwork for the male nostril, tongue, ear, or foreskin is an option only in outlying areas.

But fingernail and toenail clippers—the unworn but elegant accessories to all men's fashion, since no man has ever looked presentable with long nails (long being anything over three-sixteenths of an inch)—continue to glitter legitimately in an otherwise unpolished age. Like fancy pens and pocket watches, these palmable curios have a function—that of severing corneous shrapnel from key areas of the human form with a bracing abruptness, a can-do metallic snap, that leaves their user with the illusion that he is progressively, clip by hardened-steel clip, gaining control of his shambling life. They offer some of the satisfactions of working out on exercise machines without the sweat and gym shorts; some of the pleasures of knuckle manipulation without the worry of arthritic deformity; some of the rewards of cracking a nut without having to eat it. You may crouch over the wastebasket while you operate, but there is happily no assurance that anything clipped will end up there; for just as certain insects will hop or fly off so fast that they seem not to displace themselves physically but simply to disappear on the spot, so the clipper chip vanishes at the very instant the jaws meet and chime, propelled toward a windowsill or on some other untraceable tangent, never to trouble anyone again unless a bare foot happens to rediscover it.

The market for clippers is apparently unsaturable. This year, millions of men will buy one, as they have for decades, despite the fact that these maintenance tools almost never wear out and are entirely unnecessary. You can cut your nails just fine with a decent pair of scissors, assuming a rudimentary ambidextrousness; in fact, from one point of view a scissor cut is less labor-intensive than clipping, since, despite the helpful curvature of the clipper jaws, it often takes three angled snips to approximate the arc of a given fingernail. (The cut facets thus formed are surprisingly sharp the first time you scratch an itch, but they wear away in a day.) Clippers sell steadily because, like clippings, they disappear (in the backs of drawers, in glove compartments) and must be replaced, and because they are beautiful and cheap. A big clear drum of ninety-nine-cent Trim brand clippers sitting near the drugstore's cash register like a bucket of freshly netted minnows is an almost irresistible sight. They are the ideal weight and smoothness; they exploit the resiliency of their material both to maintain their assembly without rattling and to hold their business edges apart. They appear to have aerodynamic virtues. And, once bought, they can alter their profile in a single puzzle-solving flip-and-pivot of the lever arm, without excessive play or roughness or torn rotator cuffs, from minnow shape to grasshopper shape and back again. They were our first toy Transformers: metallic dual-phase origamis that seem triumphantly Japanese and yet happen to be, in their perfected form, a product of the small town of Derby, in southern Connecticut, near the Sikorsky helicopter plant.

In the forties, the W. E. Bassett Company made "washers" for the rubber heel pieces on men's shoes (these stopped nails from piercing through to the foot area) and artillery components for the Army. After the war, William E. Bassett, founder, retooled his equipment in Derby, and devoted himself to the production of a superior jaw-style nail clipper, the Trim clipper. The jawed design had been around since the nineteenth century, but Bassett was its Bernini. He added, for example, two thoughtful nibs near the base of the tiny (and, in the experience of some, unused) nail file that together keep the lever arm aligned in its closed position; and he replaced the unsatisfactory pinned rivet with the brilliant notched rivet. (The Chinese still use pinned rivets in their mediocre but cute baby-nail clipper, manufactured for Evenflo.) The stylish thumb-swerve in the Trim's lever (patent pending) was Bassett's idea, too.

According to William's brother Henry (who died, as the chairman of the board, in May of 1994, at the age of eighty-four), the best fingernail clipper Bassett ever made was the Croydon model of the late forties. It was stamped with a clipper-ship emblem and was promoted in *Esquire* for the jewelry-store trade. (It flopped—a case of overqualification.) But William Bassett's sons William C. Bassett, now the president and treasurer, and Dave Bassett, now the company's manufacturing engineering manager, continue the work of innovation and cost-manicuring. Despite some exciting recent work by the Koreans, who manufacture all Revlon's more expensive but not quite so well-finished clippers, along with the Gem line, the Trim clipper by Bassett continues its reign as the best on the planet. (Clippers are chrome-plated after being assembled. The finished Revlon clippers frequently betray their undercoating in those areas where one part obscured another in the electrolyte solution; Trim clippers, designed to minimize this shadowing, almost never do.)

In fact, all Bassett's grooming aids—from emery boards to tweezers—earn high marks among power users. This past August, for example, Jerry Lewis's secretary called the company directly to order a dozen five-inch triple-cut Trim nail files (with accompanying blue vinyl protective sheaths), because Mr. Lewis couldn't obtain them locally. "The tweezer is a very fussy item," Dave Bassett said recently; each Bassett tweezer tip (its inner edge ground "to help grab that hair") is inspected manually, under a magnifier. The company makes nail clippers plated in gold as well as in chrome; its Heirloom line offers gift sets like the Saddlebag, which includes scissors, a bottle opener, and folding nail files, along with an anchor pair of clippers. This Christmas, Bassett will be selling the Holiday Family Manicure Kit, with a fingernail clipper and a toenail clipper, two wooden cuticle pokers, some emery boards, and a pair of tweezers, displayed against a background of falling snow and rising reindeer. (What better way to spend Christmas morning with one's loved ones?) For Dr. Scholl's, Bassett has created an extraordinary matte-black and gold-plated piece of toenail-cleaving insanity that would not be out of place dangling from the rearview mirror of a new forty-valve 3.5-liter Ferrari 355.

It won't do to labor the parallels between caring for a fingernail and manufacturing a fingernail clipper. Making a clipper is considerably more complex. Still, it is striking how reminiscent of human clippings are the spurned little pieces of scrap metal exiting from the side of the deafening Minster stamping press. Once cut (from rolls of Midwestern steel, at an impact force of roughly fifteen tons), the clipper "blanks" must be cleaned of oil, spot-welded, racked, hardened for two hours in a massive furnace, then oil-quenched, cleaned again, tempered in a second furnace to limber them up a little, and finally revolved in huge barrels with sixty thousand of their fellows for several days in a slurry of metal slugs, abrasives, and lime, to smooth away unhandy burrs. Vibrating bowls dither the components into sequential position, preparing them for a definitive riveting, which is accompanied by a Fred Astaire-like volley of air-cylinder taps and flourishes. Each clipper gets a sharpened cutting edge; a digital image system checks the finished edges for truth. Eyelets, shot in at the caudal end, affix the nail files; then the entire splayed clipper, racked on hooks, proceeds through the plating sequence—ten minutes in a warm nickel bath, a minute or two of chrome. A nimble piece of pneumatics straightens the akimbo file and closes the lever. At last the basic Bassett fingernail clipper is ready for action. You can determine the year your clipper was made by referring to the inside of the lever arm.

Nail care has been weighing on my thoughts recently, I confess, because the great Stephen King, in an introduction to his recent short-story collection, *Nightmares & Dreamscapes,* describes one of my books as a "meaningless little fingernail paring." Are we to infer from "paring" that the Bard of Bangor doesn't possess or know how to operate a Trim (or a Gem, or a

Revlon, or even a La Cross) clipper of his own? Does he envision himself as the heir of Joyce's artist-hero, in *A Portrait of the Artist as a Young Man,* who was "refined out of existence, indifferent, paring his fingernails"? Does he still whittle? (Bassett's sales are "really taking off" in Ireland right now, according to Barbara Shannon, the company's marketing manager; it seems that the Irish are through with Joyce's manual methods and insist on taking, with Trim's help, the shortcut to artistry.) Or is Mr. King rather implying that someone like me disdainfully pares and fiddles while he, market-wise progressivist, hacks on with the latest technology?

If so, I can assure Mr. King that I, too, clip—not as often as I should, perhaps, but with genuine enthusiasm. When I want a really authentic experience, I sometimes use a toenail clipper on my fingernails, shuddering with the thrill of fulcrumed power; and then, for my toes, I step on up to Revlon's veterinary-gauge Nipper, a parrot-beaked personal-pruning weapon that, despite its chrome plate, looks as if it should be stored in the toolshed. A dense, semiopaque shard cut by this nineteen-dollar piece of spring-loaded Brazilian craftsmanship recently rose from what was left of my ravished toenail and traveled across the room, landing in a box of tax records, where it remains.

We can say with some certainty (and sadness) that Nabokov did not use nail clippers. That is, John Shade, *Pale Fire*'s poet, did not:

> The little scissors I am holding are
> A dazzling synthesis of sun and star.
> I stand before the window and I pare
> My fingernails. . . .

The cutting of a fingernail is important in Nabokov: it may constitute for him the act of self-liberation from annotative servitude, since he is demonstrably aware of the traditional scholarly use of the nail's edge as a marginal place-inscriber. In Pushkin's *Eugene Onegin,* Tatiana learns about Onegin's mind by studying his library, and she notices (in Nabokov's translation) that

> Many pages preserved
> the trenchant mark of fingernails.

Nabokov's commentary to these lines mentions Sheridan's *The Rivals* (dismissing it in passing, with his usual harshness, as a "singularly inept comedy"), in which someone "cherishes her nails for the convenience of making marginal notes." Nabokov adds, puzzlingly, "The art is a lost one today." Hardly so: even with a closely clipped and manly thumbnail, the reader can and very often does, today, in America, score a visible double line to mark an interesting passage, if it appears in a book that he is prevented for one reason or another from defacing. In those midnight moments of the misplaced pencil, too, a nail impression is a less destructive and more spatially precise aid to memory than a turned-down corner. Moreover, the pressure of the reader's nail, deformed by its momentary trenchancy, against the tender hyponychial tissues it protects, creates a transient thumbwide pleasure that is, or can be, more than literary.

But the most troubling feature of Stephen King's assessment of my alleged "nail paring" of a novel is his apparent belief that a bookish toe- or fingernail scrap can be justifiably brushed off as meaningless. Last September, Allen Ginsberg sold a bag of his beard hair to Stanford. Surely Mr. King ought to be saving for the ages whatever gnarled relics he clips or pares? And the Master Spellbinder, of all people, should be able to detect the secret terrors, the moans of the severed but unquiet soul, that reside in these disjecta. Think of the fearful Norse ship of the apocalypse, *Naglfar,* made of dead men's nails, which will break loose from its moorings during the Monstrous Winter, when the Wolf has swallowed the Sun—"a warning," in Brian Branston's retelling, "that if a man dies with his nails unshorn he is adding greatly to the materials for Naglfar (a thing both gods and men would be slow to do)." Gertrude Jobes's mythological dictionary cites a related Finno-Ugric tradition in which the Evil One collects any Sunday nail parings and "with them builds the boat for transporting the dead." Lithuanian folklore contends (per Stith Thompson) that "from the parings of man's nails devils make little caps for themselves." I didn't have a chance to ask any of the employees at the factory in Derby, Connecticut, many of whom are first- or second-generation Polish, whether they had heard similar tales.

Lest someone unknowingly aid the devils in their hattery (would a fingernail hat resemble a miniature wicker knick-knack basket, one wonders, or would the snippets be sewn or glued on, like sequins?), the Bassett Company, in 1990, launched the Easy Hold clipper. The Easy Hold line features an unusual pair of either-handed cuticle scissors, with forefinger-rests that aid fine work (U.S. Design Patent No. 331,867); a foam emery-board holder; and an enhanced tweezer that makes the removal of other people's splinters even more of a wicked joy than it always has been. But the new nail clippers go further: in addition to a considerate plastic thumb element, they include a housing for the jaw that catches nearly every snippet the moment it is clipped.

Eric Rommerdale, the head of laboratory technology at the University of Mississippi School of Dentistry, in Jackson, is the principal figure behind the development of all the Easy Hold grooming products. Mr. Rommerdale, fifty-two, a white-mustached ex-Navy man, is no stranger to inventive self-care, having in his off-hours developed Sunbeam's triple-brush, hands-free toothbrushing system (now sold by DKI Inc.) and the mouth-stick-activated urine-bag release valve, both for the wheelchair set. His big fingernail moment came in November of 1987, in a Stop-n-Go, while he was watching a man in his seventies with "hands the size of baseball mitts" trying to clip his nails. Three times the clipper fell to the floor. Out of polymer resin (often used in dental work) Rommerdale built a pair of add-on clipper grips and tried to interest Revlon in them. Revlon said no, unequivocally. But in 1988 William Bassett the younger listened to a pitch by Rommerdale in the lobby of the Bridgeport Hilton, liked what he heard, and asked the inventor to rethink the graspability of the entire manicure line. The University of Mississippi Medical Center then evaluated and refined the prototypes (under a grant from the Bassett Company), videotaping and surveying a group of talkative elderly beta-testers.

Although Rommerdale's original rounded design gained, in its final, blister-packed form, a few unwelcome projections and some squared-off edges that call out for smoothing ("We could have done a better job on that," William Bassett admits), it is nonetheless heartening to find that the stylistic history of the clipper—one of the great bureau-top products of the century—is not over. This coming January, all plastic Easy Hold fittings, at present colored a battleship-gray, will turn teal-green, after extensive mall-site interviewing. Eric Rommerdale, using his patent royalties, recently expanded his backyard workshop, and he is currently developing safer tools for meat cutters and a jar opener for the disabled. It looks as if there will still be time for us to clip our nails closely and carefully, as if nothing else mattered, before the coming of the Monstrous Winter, when *Naglfar* will set sail.

(1994)

Reading

Reading Aloud

A few years ago I did my first reading. It was at the Edinburgh Festival in Scotland, under a tent. Several others read, too; we all sat on independent sections of a biomorphic orange modular couch, our heads bowed as we listened, or half listened, to each other. Eventually my turn came, and the words that I had written in silence (an earplug-enhanced silence, as a matter of fact, that amplified the fleeting Chiclety contact of upper and lower incisors, and made audible the inner squirt of an eyeball when I rubbed it roughly, and called to my attention the muffled roar of eyelid muscles when my eyes were squeezed shut in an effort to see, using the infrared of prose, whatever it was that I most wanted at that moment to describe)—these formerly silent words unfolded themselves like lawn chairs in my mouth and emerged one by one wearing large Siberian hats of consonants and long erminous vowels and landed softly, without visible damage, here and there in the audience, and I thought, Gosh, I'm reading aloud, from Chapter Seven!

Things went pretty well until I got to a place near the middle of the last paragraph, where I began to feel that I was going to cry. I wouldn't have minded crying, or at least pausing to swallow down a discreet silent sob, if what I'd been reading had been in any obvious way sad. When people on TV documentaries tell their stories, and they come to the part where the tragedy happens and they have to say over again what, in silent form, they adjusted to years earlier, and they choke up, that's fine, they should choke up. And I've heard writers read autobiographical accounts of painful childhood events and quaver a little here and there—that's perfectly justifiable, even desirable. But the sentence that was giving me difficulty was a description of a woman enclosing a breakfast muffin in bakery tissue, placing it in a small bag, and sprinkling it with coffee stirrers and sugar packets and pre-portioned pats of butter. Where was the pathos? And yet by the time I delivered the words "plastic stirrers" to the audience, I was in serious trouble, and I noticed a listening head or two look up with sudden curiosity: Hah, this is interesting, this American is going to weep openly and copiously for us now.

Why that sentence, though? Why did that image of a succession of small white shapes, more stirrers and sugar packets and butter pats than I needed, and in that sense ceremonial and semi-decorative rather than functional, falling, falling over my terrestrial breakfast, grab at my grief-lapels? There were a number of reasons. In college I had once competed for a prize in what was called the "Articulation of the English Language," for which the contestants had to read aloud from set passages of Milton and Joyce and others. I got to the auditorium late, having bicycled there while drinking proudly from a shot bottle of Smirnoff vodka that I'd bought on an airplane, and, as planned, I read the Milton in a booming fake English accent and read the Joyce excerpt—which was the last paragraph of "The Dead"—first in a broad bad Southern accent, then in a Puerto Rican accent, and then in the Southern accent again, and to my surprise I'd found that the Joyce suddenly seemed, in my amateur TV-actor drawl, extremely moving, so that the last phrase, about the snow "faintly falling . . . upon all the living and the dead," was tragic enough to make it unclear whether my rhetorical tremor was genuine or not—and my voice box may have remembered this boozy Joycean precipitation from college as I read aloud from my own sugar-packet snowfall.

Also, a version of the chapter I was reading in Edinburgh had appeared in *The New Yorker*, and I'd had a slight disagreement, a friendly disagreement, with a fact checker there over the phrase "tissue-protected muffin." She'd held that the word "tissue" implied something like Kleenex, and that it should be a "paper-wrapped muffin," and I'd said I didn't think so. On the way home from work the next day I'd stopped in a bakery and spotted a blue box of the little squares in question and I'd seen the words "bakery tissue" in capital letters on the side; and, exulting, I'd called the manager of the store over, a Greek man who barely spoke English, and offered to buy the entire box, which he sold me for nine dollars, and I called my editor the next day and said, "It's tissue, it is tissue," and as a compromise it became in their version a "tissue-wrapped muffin"—but now, reading it aloud in Scotland, I could turn it into a "tissue-protected muffin" all over again; right or wrong, I was able in the end to shield the original wordless memory from alien breakfast guests with this fragile shroud of my own preferred words. It had turned out all right in the end. And that might have been enough to make me cry.

But it wasn't just that. It was also that this tiny piece of a paragraph had never been one that I'd thought of proudly when I thought over my book after it was published. I'd forgotten it, after writing it down, and now that my orating tongue forced me to pay attention to it I was amazed and moved that it had hung in there for all those months, in fact years, unrewarded but unimpaired, holding its small visual charge without any further encouragement from me, and, like the deaf and dumb kid in rags who, though reviled by the other children, ends up saving his village from some catastrophe, it had become the tearjerker moment that would force me, out of pity for its very unmemorableness, to dissolve in grief right in the midst of all my intended ironies. That was a big part of it.

Contrition, too. Contrition made its contribution to the brimming bowl—for these Edinburgh audience members didn't know how much pure mean-spirited contempt I had felt back in my rejection-letter days for writers who "gave readings," how self-congratulatorily neo-primitivist I'd thought it was to repudiate the divine economy of the published page and to require people to gather to hear a reticent man or woman reiterate what had long since been set in type. Ideally, I'd felt, the republic of letters was inhabited by solitary readers in bed with their Itty Bitty Book Lights glowing over their privately owned and operated pages, like the ornate personal lamps that covertly illuminate every music stand in opera pits while the crudest sort of public melodrama rages in heavy makeup overhead. There was something a bit too Pre-Raphaelite about the regression to an audience—I thought of those reaction shots in early Spielberg movies, of family members gazing with softly awestruck faces at the pale-green glow of the beneficent UFO while John Williams flogged yet more Strauss from his string section. And there were the suspect intonation patterns, the I'm-reading-aloud patterns—especially at poetry readings, where talented and untalented alike, understandably wishing in the absence of rhyme to give an audible analogue for the ragged right and left margins in their typed or printed original, resorted to syllable-punching rhythms and studiously unresolved final cadences adapted from Dylan Thomas and Wallace Stevens, overlaid with Walter Cronkite and John Fitzgerald Kennedy. These handy tonal templates could make anything lyrical:

> This—is a Dover—edition—
> Designed—for years—of use—
>
> Sturdy stackable—beechwood—bookshelves—
> At a price you'd expect—to pay—for plastic—

And yet, despite all this sort of easy, Glenn-Gouldy contempt in my background, there I was physically in Edinburgh, under that tent, among strangers, finishing up my own first reading, and, far from feeling dismissive and contemptuous before my turn came, I'd been simply and sincerely nervous, exceedingly nervous, and now I was almost finished, and I hadn't done anything too humiliating, and the audience had innocently listened, unaware of my prior disapproval, and they had even tolerantly laughed once or twice—and all this was too much: I was like a crippled unbeliever wheeled in and made whole with a sudden palm blow to the forehead by a preaching charlatan. I'm reading aloud! I'm reading aloud! I was saying, my face streaming with tears—I was cripple and charlatan simultaneously. Evidently I was going to cry, out of pure gratitude to myself for having gotten almost to the end without crying.

And then, as the unthinkable almost happened, and the narcissus bulb in the throat very nearly blossomed, I recognized that if I did break down now, the intensity of my feeling, in this supposedly comic context, would leave the charitable listeners puzzled about my overall mental well-being. At the very least I would be thought of as someone "going through a stressful time," and it would be this diagnosis they would take home with them, rather than any particular fragment from what I'd read that they liked, and whenever I tried to write something light 'n' lively thereafter I would remember my moment of shame on the orange couch and to counteract it I'd have to invent something bleak and brooding and wholly out of character. I couldn't let it happen; I couldn't let reading aloud distort my future output. I started whispering urgent ringside counsel to myself: *Come on, you sack of shit. If you cry, people will assume you're being moved to tears by your own eloquence, and how do you think that will go over?* That was frightening enough, finally, to stabilize the nutation in my Adam's apple, and I just barely got through to the last word.

Since that afternoon in 1989, I've read aloud from my writing a number of times, and each time I've been a little more in control, less of a walking cripple, more of a charlatan. I've reacquainted myself with my larynx. When I was fourteen I used to feel it each morning at the kitchen table, before I had any cereal. It was large. How could my throat have been retrofitted with this massive service elevator? And what was I going to say with it? What sort of payloads was it fated to carry? First thing in the morning I could sing, in a fairly convincing baritone, the alto-sax solo from *Pictures at an Exhibition*—and as I went for a low note there was a unique physical pleasure, not to be had later in the day, when the two thick slack vocal cords dropped and closed on a shovelful of sonic peat moss. Sometimes as I sang low, or swung low, it felt as if I were a character actor in a coffee commercial, carelessly scooping glossy beans from deep in a burlap bag and pouring them into a battered scale—the deeper the note I tried to scoop up, the bigger and glossier the beans, until finally I was way down in fava territory. I was Charles Kuralt, I was Tony the Tiger, I was Lloyd Bridges, I was James Earl Jones—I too had a larynx the size of a picnic basket, I felt, and when you heard my voice you wouldn't even know it was sound, it would be so vibrantly low: you'd think instead that your wheels had strayed over the wake-up rumble strips on the shoulder of a freeway. Just above the mobile prow of the Adam's apple, just above where there should properly be a hood ornament, was a softer place that became more noticeable to the finger the lower you spoke or sang, and it was directly into this vulnerable opening, this chink in the armor of one's virility, that I imagined disk jockeys secretly injecting themselves with syringes full of male hormones and small-engine oil, so that they could say "traffic and weather together" with the proper sort of sawtooth bite.

And though my own voice has proved to be—despite my high secondary-sexual expectations, and even though I was pretty tall and tall people often have voice boxes to match—not quite the pebbly, three-dimensional mood machine I'd counted on, I do occasionally now like reading aloud what I've written. I get back a little of the adolescent early-morning feeling as I brachiate my way high into the upper canopy of a sentence, tightening the pitch muscles, climbing up, and then dropping on a single word, with that Doppler-effect plunge of sound, so the argument can live out its closing seconds at sea level. I feel all this going on, even if it isn't audible to anyone else. And sometimes I know that my voice, imperfect medium though it may be, is making what I've written seem for the moment better than it is, and I like playing with this dangerous intonational power, and even letting listeners know that I'm playing with it. It's not called an Adam's apple for nothing: that relic of temptation, that articulated chunk of upward mobility, that ever-ready dial tone in the throat, whether or not it successfully leads others astray, ends by thoroughly seducing oneself.

(1992)

The History of Punctuation

The nine basic marks of punctuation—comma, dash, hyphen, period, parenthesis, semi-colon, colon, space, and capital letter—seem so apt to us now, so pipe-smokingly Indo-European, so naturally suited in their disjunctive charge and mass to their given sentential offices, that we may forgivably assume that commas have been around for at least as long as electrons, and that while dialects, cursive styles, and typefaces have come and gone, the semi-colon, that supremely self-possessed valet of phraseology, is immutable.

But in fact the semi-colon is relatively modern. Something medieval called a *punctus versus,* which strongly resembled a semi-colon, though it was often encountered dangling below the written line, had roughly the force of a modern period; another sign that looked (in some scribal hands) exactly like a semi-colon was a widely used abbreviation for several Latin word endings—*atque* could appear as *atq;,* and *omnibus* as *omnib;.* But the semi-colon that we resort to daily, hourly, entered the picture with the first edition of Pietro Bembo's *De Aetna* two years after Columbus reached America, the handiwork of Aldus Manutius the Elder (or someone close to him) and his tasteful punch-cutter, Francesco Griffo. The mark, we are told by Dr. Malcolm Parkes, its historian, took much longer than the parenthesis did to earn the trust of type-setters: shockingly, its use was apparently not fully under-stood by some of those assigned to work on the first folio of Shakespeare.

And it is of course even now subject to episodes of neglect and derision. Joyce preferred the more Attic colon, at least in *Ulysses,* and Beckett, as well, gradually rid his prose of what must have seemed to him an emblem of vulgar, high-Victorian applied ornament, a cast-iron flower of mass-produced Ciceronianism: instead of semi-colons, he spliced the phrases of *Malone Dies* and *Molloy* together with one-size-fits-all commas, as commonplace as stones on a beach, to achieve that dejected sort of murmured ecphonesis so characteristic of his narrative voice—all part of the general urge, perhaps, that led him to ditch English in favor of French, "pour m'appau-vrir": to impoverish himself.

Donald Barthelme, too, who said that the example of Beck-ett was what first "allowed [him] to write," thought that the semi-colon was "ugly, ugly as a tick on a dog's belly"—but he allowed that others might feel differently. And still the semi-colon survives, far too subtle and useful, as it turns out, to be a casualty of modernism. It even participates in those newer forms of emotional punctuation called "smileys" or "emoti-cons"—vaguely irritating attempts to supply a sideways facial expression at the close of an E-mail paragraph—e.g., :-) and >%-(. The semi-colon collaborates in the "wink" or "smirk," thus—;-).

So our familiar and highly serviceable repertoire of punctles was a long time coming; it emerged from swarms of com-peting and overlapping systems and theories, many of them misapplied or half-forgotten. Petrarch, for example, used a slash with a dot in the middle of it to signal the onset of a parenthetical phrase. A *percontativus,* or backward question mark, occasionally marked the close of a rhetorical question even into the seventeenth century—Robert Herrick wrote with it. A *punctus elevatus,* resembling an upside-down semi-colon or, later, a fancy, black-letter *s,* performed the function of a colon in many medieval texts; when used at the end of a line of poetry, however, it could signal the presence of an enjambment. A nameless figure shaped like a tilted candy-cane served to terminate paragraphs of Augustus's autobiography (A.D. 14), inscribed on his tomb. Around A.D. 600, Isidore of Seville recommended ending a paragraph with a 7, which he called the *positura.* He also advocated the placing of a horizontal dash next to a corrupted or questionable text ("so that a kind of arrow may slit the throat of what is superfluous and penetrate to the vitals of what is false"), and he relied on the ancient *cryphia,* a C turned on its side with a dot in the middle— ☉ —to be used next to those places in a text where "a hard and obscure question cannot be opened up or solved."

The upright letter C, for *capitulum,* developed into the popular medieval paragraph symbol, ¶, called at times a *pilcrow* or a *paraph.* Seventh-century Irish scribes were in the habit of using more points when they wanted a longer pause; thus a sentence might end with a colon and a comma (:,), or two periods and a comma (..,), or three commas together (,,,). At the close of the twelfth century, one of the *dictaminists,* a man named Buoncompagno, troubled by so much irreconcilable complexity, proposed a pared-down slash-and-dash method: a dash would mark all final pauses, and a slash would mark all lesser pauses. It didn't take, although the "double virgula" (//) was used to separate sentences in the fifteenth century, and Edmund Spenser and Walter Ralegh sometimes hand-wrote with single slashes, rather than commas. A plus sign (+) stood for a period in a few early printed books; in others, it could set off a quotation.

Printing eventually slowed the pace of makeshift invention, forcing out many quaint superfluities, but novel marks, and surprising adaptations of old marks, may appear at any time. Besides smileys, online services have lately given rise to the ecstatic bracket hug of greeting: {{{{{{{{{Shana!!!}}}}}}}}}. Legal punctuation continues to thrive—the ™, the ®, and the © are everywhere. (The title of *Jurassic Park* is not *Jurassic Park*, but *Jurassic Park*™; likewise David Feldman's *Why Do Clocks Run Clockwise and Other Imponderables*™.)

Especially fashionable now is the ^SM, as in "Forget Something?^SM"—observed not long ago on a plastic notice beside the bathroom sink in a room at a Holiday Inn: a mark that modifies the phrase it follows to mean, "This is not merely a polite question regarding whether you have successfully packed everything you require during your stay, this utterance is part of our current chain-wide marketing campaign, and we are so serious about asking it of you that we hereby offer fair warning that if you or anyone else attempts to extend such a courtesy to another guest anywhere in the hotel industry in printed or published form, either on flyers, placards, signs, pins, or pieces of folded plastic positioned at or beside a sink, vanity, or other bathroom fixture, we, the owner of this service mark, will torment and tease you with legal remedies." Even the good old comma continues to evolve: it was flipped upside down and turned into the quotation mark circa 1714, and a woman I knew in college punctuated her letters to her high school friends with homemade comma-shapes made out of photographs of side-flopping male genitals that she had cut out of *Playgirl*.

Until now, readers have had to fulfill their need for the historical particulars of this engrossingly prosaic subject with narrow-gauge works of erudition such as E. Otha Wingo's sober *Latin Punctuation in the Classical Age,* or John Lennard's extraordinary recent monograph on the history of the parenthesis, *But I Digress* (1991)—a jewel of Oxford University Press scholarship, by the way, gracefully written and full of intelligence, decked out with a complete scholarly apparatus of multiple indices, bibliographies, and notes, whose author, to judge by the startling jacket photo (shaved head with up-sticking central proto-Mohawk tuft, earring on left ear, wilted corduroy jacket, and over-laundered T-shirt bearing some enigmatic insignia underneath), put himself through graduate school by working as a ticket scalper at Elvis Costello concerts. (A discussion of Elvis Costello's use of the parenthesis in "Let Him Dangle" figures in a late chapter.)

At last, however, we have *Pause and Effect,* Dr. Malcolm Parkes's brave overview: "an introduction," so he unassumingly subtitles it, though it is much more than introductory, "to the history of punctuation in the West." Not in the East, mind, or elsewhere—Arabic, Greek, and Sanskrit customs await a final fuse-blowing collation. (And according to the MLA index, there is Nanette Twine's 1984 article on "The Adoption of Punctuation in Japanese Script," in *Visible Language,* a journal that has recently done exciting things for the study of the punctuational past, to be absorbed; and, for canon-stretchers, John Duitsman's "Punctuation in Thirteen West African Languages" and Carol F. Justus's "Visible Sentences in Cuneiform Hittite.") Though his punning title promises sprightliness, Dr. Parkes—fellow of Keble College and lecturer in paleography at the University of Oxford—has produced a rich, complex, and decidedly unsprightly book of coffee-table dimensions, with seventy-four illustrative plates, a glossary, and, regrettably, no *index rerum.*

It is not an easy book to read in bed. Because of the oversized folio format, each line on the page extends an inch or so longer than usual, resulting in eye-sweeps that must take in fourteen words at a time, rather than the more comfortable ten or eleven. As his shoulder muscles tire of supporting the full weight of the open book, the reader, lying on his left side, finally allows it to slump to the mattress and assume an L-position, and he then attempts to process the text with one open eye, which, instead of scanning left to right, reads by focusing outward along a radically foreshortened line of type that is almost parallel with his line of sight, skipping or supplying by guesswork those words that disappear beyond the gentle rise of the page. The gaps between each word narrow, hindering comprehension, although they never achieve that incomprehensible Greek ideal of page-layout called *scriptio continua,* in which the text is recorded unspaced as solid lines of letters.

And why, in fact, did the Greeks relinquish so sensible a practice as word-spacing, which even the cuneiformists of Minoan Crete apparently used? Lejeune, for one, finds this development "remarquable"; but even more remarquable is the fact that the pragmatic Romans had word-spacing available to *them* (via the Etruscans), in the form of "interpuncts," or hovering dots between each word (a practice successfully revived by Wang word-processing software in the 1980s), which they too abandoned in early Christian times. "For this amazing and deplorable regression one can conjecture no reason other than an inept desire to imitate even the worst characteristic of Greek books," scolds Revilo P. Oliver. Dr. Parkes, on the other hand, theorizes that class differences between readers and scribes may have had something to do with the perseverance of *scriptio continua*—a scribal slave must not presume to word-space, or otherwise punctuate, because he would thereby be imposing his personal reading of the constitutive letters on his employer. There were also, in monkish contexts, quasi-mystical arguments to be made for unspaced impenetrability: a resistant text, slow to offer up its literal meaning, encouraged meditation and memorization, suggested Cassian (a prominent fifth-century recluse); and the moment when, after much futile staring, the daunting word-search-puzzle of the sacred page finally spaced itself out, coalescing into comprehensible units of the Psalter, might serve to remind the swooning lector of the miracle of the act of reading, which is impossible without God's loving condescension into human language and human form.

Amid all this phylogeny, Parkes does not mention, nor should he necessarily mention, the more mundane developmental fact that *scriptio continua* comes naturally to children:

DEARANDREWH

APPYBIRTHDA

YILOVEYOULO

VEALICEXXOX

Children aren't *taught* to forgo spacing; all their written models are properly spaced. Occasionally, as a concession to the recipient (or adult onlooker), they will go back and insert a virgule here and there between words for clarity. There is something so exciting about writing, perhaps, that, like barely literate five-year-olds, civilizations in the midst of discovering or rediscovering its pleasures and traditions take a while before they begin to care about casual readability—and consequently their scholars are said to study *litterae,* "letters," not words.

In part as a result of the unspaced line, pointing was viewed from the beginning as a form of ornament, as well as a means of what Parkes calls "disambiguation." Cassiodorus, the first great biblical pointillist, advised sixth-century monks to add punctuation "in order that you may be seen to be adding embellishment." Alcuin wrote Charlemagne that "*Distinctiones* or *subdistinctiones* by points can make embellishment in sentences most beautiful." Early medieval readers like Dulcitius of Aquino would decorate a work with dots and diples and paragraph marks as they read it and then proudly sign their name on the page: "I, Dulcitius, read this." Punctuation, like marginal and interlinear commentary, seems at times to have been a ritual of reciprocation, a way of returning something to the text in grateful tribute after it had released its meaning in the reader's mind.

Somewhat surprisingly, scholastic philosophy of the thirteenth and fourteenth centuries, which is, as Francis Bacon uncharitably observed, a vast and intricate cobweb spun from Aristotle, "admirable for the fineness of thread and work, but of no substance and profit," and thus ideally decorative and mannerist rather than functional, pushed by logical and disputational energy rather than pulled by truth—the sort of era, then, in which you might expect punctuation to *thrive*—turns out in fact to be a dark, sad time for *subdistinctiones*. Parkes explains that the paradigmatic nature of the scholastic manuscript, with its repetitive *queriturs* and *quaestios* signaling to the reader precisely where he was in the formal structure of the argument, made a sophisticated punctuational tool-set unnecessary.

On the other hand, it may just be that the schoolmen, spending their days reading awful Latin translations from the Arabic of translations from the Greek, had no ear. Cicero himself disdained punctuation, insisting that the well-cadenced sentence would audibly manifest its own terminus, without the need of any mere "stroke interposed by a copyist"; but those who afterward took punctuation, and took Cicero, seriously—Cassiodorus, Isidore, Bembo, Petrarch—proved their allegiance by their virgulae: like archaizing composers who want to ensure a certain once-standard performance practice and therefore spell out every trill and every *ritenuto,* though their historical models offer only unadorned notes, these admirers could hear the implied punctuation of Ciceronian rhythm, and could in some cases duplicate his rollaway effects in their own writing, but they didn't trust their contemporaries to detect a classicizing *clausula* without the help of visual aids.

Dr. Parkes's own prose is serviceable and unprecious, if non-passerine. For those of us whose Latin never quite took flight, he has provided translations of every passage he quotes. He takes care from time to time to mention political developments as they impinge on the punctuational sphere: if some depredation or upheaval happens to have brought on "a situation hostile to grammatical culture," he says so. The puzzling thing, though, is how casual Parkes is—this eagle-eyed paleographer, who has worked so hard to "raise a reader's consciousness of what punctuation is and does"!—about his commas. Where *are* they? "Pausing therefore was part of the process of reading not copying." "Before the advent of printing a text left its author and fell among scribes." "The printing process not only stabilized the shapes and functions of the symbols it also sustained existing conventions that governed the ways in which they were employed." And: "This increase in the range of distinctive symbols also promoted new developments in usage since the symbols not only enabled readers to identify more easily the functions of grammatical constituents within a sentence but also made possible more subtle refinements in the communication of the message of a text."

Were it not for Dr. Parkes's surefooted employment of the comma elsewhere, one might almost suspect that his was a case reminiscent of those psychotherapists who enter their profession because they sense something deeply amiss within themselves, or of those humorless people who buy joke books and go to comedy clubs to correct internal deficiencies. In a commentary accompanying a fascinating page of Richard Hooker, Parkes, or someone with whom he has shared (as he nicely says in his preface) "the burden of proofs," flouts even the sacred law of the serial comma: "The notation series for indicating glosses notes and citations in the margins, based on letters of the alphabet in sequence, was also used in the Geneva Bible of 1560."

Once, however, Parkes surprises us by unconsciously using the old-fashioned, eighteenth-century *that*-comma. It is the comma of Gibbon—

> It has been calculated by the ablest politicians, that no state, without being soon exhausted, can maintain above the hundredth part of its members in arms and idleness.

And of Gibbon's model Montesquieu, in Nugent's 1750 translation (twice)—

> Plato thanked the Gods, that he was born in the same age with Socrates: and for my part, I give thanks to the Almighty, that I was born a subject of that government under which I live; and that it is his pleasure I should obey those, whom he has made me love.

And of Burke (twice)—

> Mr. Hume told me, that he had from Rousseau himself the secret of his principles of composition. That acute, though eccentric, observer had perceived, that to strike and interest the public, the marvellous must be produced . . .

And of Burke's brilliant adversary, Thomas Paine—

> Admitting that Government is a contrivance of human *wisdom*, it must necessarily follow, that hereditary succession, and hereditary rights (as they are called), can make no part of it, because it is impossible to make wisdom hereditary.

Parkes writes, "The punctuation of the manuscript has been so freely corrected and adapted by later scribes, that it is not easy to determine whether any of the other ecphonetic signs are also by the original scribe or whether they have been added." The only other person I can think of who uses old-style *that*-commas with any consistency is Peter Brown, who, like Parkes, spends his time with Latin *quod*-clauses that have been punctuated by old German commentators. (A comma is still regularly used before a *daß*-clause in German.)

Another rarity in Parkes's book, perhaps the very first of its kind, is the occurrence of the two halves of *semi-colon* linked, not by a hyphen, but by a full-scale em-dash: *semi—colon*. This elongation could be Parkes's secret way of protesting American trends in copy-editing, which would have the noun-unit spelled without any divisive internal rule at all: *semicolon*. Truly, American copy-editing has fallen into a state of demoralized confusion over hyphenated and unhyphenated compounds—or at least, *I* am demoralized and confused, having just gone through the manuscript of a novel in which a very smart and careful and good-natured copy-editor has deleted about two hundred of my innocent tinkertoy hyphens. I wrote "stet hyphen" in the margin so many times that I finally abbreviated it to "SH"—but there was no wicked glee in my intransigence: I didn't want to be the typical prose prima donna who made her life difficult.

On the other hand, I remembered an earlier manuscript of mine in which an event took place in the back seat of a car: in the bound galleys, the same event occurred in the "backseat." *The backseat.* Grateful for hundreds of other fixes, unwilling to seem stubborn, I had agreed without protest to the closing-up, but I stewed about it afterward and finally reinserted a space before publication. ("Backseat" wants to be read as a trochee, BACKseat, like "baseball," when in reality we habitually give both halves of the compound equal spoken weight.) Therefore, mindful of my near miss with "back seat," I stetted myself sick over the new manuscript. I stetted *re-enter* (rather than *reenter*), *post-doc* (rather than *postdoc*), *foot-pedal* (rather than *foot pedal*), *second-hand* (rather than *secondhand*), *twist-tie* (rather than *twist tie*), and *pleasure-nubbins* (rather than *pleasure nubbins*).

The copy-editor, because her talents permit her to be undoctrinaire, and because it is, after all, *my* book, indulged me, for better or worse. In passing, we had a stimulating discussion of the word *pantyhose,* which she had emended to read *panty hose.* My feeling was that the word *hose* is unused now in reference to footwear, and that *panty,* too, in its singular form, is imaginable only as part of *pantywaist* or in some hypothetical L. L. Bean catalog: "Bean's finest chamois-paneled trail panty." *Pantyhose* thus constitutes a single, interfused unit of sense, greater than the sum of its parts, which ought to be the criterion for jointure. And yet, though the suggested space seemed to me mistaken, I could just as easily have gone for *panty-hose* as *pantyhose*—in fact, normally I would have campaigned for a hyphen in this sort of setting, since the power-crazed policy-makers at Merriam-Webster and *Words into Type* have been reading too much Joyce in recent years and making condominiums out of terms (especially *-like* compounds, which can look like transliterated Japanese when closed up) that deserve semi-detachment. (Joyce, one feels, wanted his prose to look different, Irish, strange, not tricked out with fastidious Oxford hyphens that handled uncouth noun-clumps with gloved fingertips: he would have been embarrassed to see his idiosyncratic *cuffedge* and *watchchain* and famous *scrotumtightening* acting to sway US style-shepherds.) A tasteful spandex hyphen would have been, so my confusion whispers to me now, perfectly all right in *panty-hose,* pulling the phrase together scrotumtighteningly at its crotch.

I offer this personal note merely to illustrate how small the moments are that cumulatively result in punctuational thigmotaxis. Evolution proceeds hyphen by hyphen, and manuscript by manuscript—impelled by the tension between working writers and their copy-editors, and between working copy-editors and their works of reference ("I'll just go check the big *Web*," a magazine editor once said to me cheerfully); by the admiration of ancestors, and by the ever-imminent possibility of paralysis through boredom. Are the marks that we have right now really enough? Don't you sometimes feel a sudden abdominal cramp of revulsion when you scan down a column of type and see several nice little clauses (only one per sentence, of course: *Chic. Man. St.* § 5.91) set off by cute little pairs of unadorned dashes?

The nineteenth century didn't think the dash on its own was nearly enough. Dr. Parkes ends his brief discussion of "The Mimetic Ambitions of the Novelist and the Exploitation of the Pragmatics of the Written Medium" with Virginia Woolf, so he (pardonably) avoids treating the single most momentous change in twentieth-century punctuation, namely the disappearance of the great dash-hybrids. All three of them—the *commash* ,—, the *semi-colash* ;—, and the *colash* :— (so I name them, because naming makes analysis possible)—are of profound importance to Victorian prose, and all three are now (except for certain revivalist zoo specimens to be mentioned later) extinct.

Everyone used dash-hybrids. They are in Dickens, Wilkie Collins, Charlotte Brontë, and George Meredith. They are on practically every page of Trollope—

He was nominally, not only the heir to, but actually the possessor of, a large property;—but he could not touch the principal, and of the income only so much as certain legal curmudgeons would allow him. As Greystock had said, everybody was at law with him,—so successful had been his father, in mismanaging, and mis-controlling, and misappropriating the property.

Rapid writing will no doubt give rise to inaccuracy,—chiefly because the ear, quick and true as may be its operation, will occasionally break down under pressure, and, before a sentence be closed, will forget the nature of the composition with which it commenced.

The novels of a man possessed of so singular a mind must themselves be very strange,—and they are strange.

They are in Thackeray—

[. . .] the Captain was not only accustomed to tell the truth,—he was unable even to think it—and fact and fiction reeled together in his muzzy, whiskified brain.

And in George Eliot—

The general expectation now was that the "much" would fall to Fred Vincy, but the Vincys themselves were surprised when ten thousand pounds in specified investments were declared to be bequeathed to him:—was the land coming too?

The toniest nonfictional Prosicrucians—De Quincey, Carlyle, Ruskin, Newman, Doughty—also make constant use of dashtards, often at rhetorical peaks:

It is well to be a gentleman, it is well to have a cultivated intellect, a delicate taste, a candid, equitable, dispassionate mind, a noble and courteous bearing in the conduct of life;—these are the con-natural qualities of a large knowledge; they are the objects of a University: I am advocating, I shall illustrate and insist upon them; but still, I repeat, they are no guarantee for sanctity or even for conscientiousness, they may attach to the man of the world, to the profligate, to the heartless,—pleasant, alas, and attractive as he shows when decked out in them.

Pater, though he has been charged with over-sonorous purism, and is unquestionably at times a little light in his Capezios (to steal a phrase from Arsenio Hall), depends on punctuational pair-bonding to help him wrap up his terrific essay on style and his "Conclusion" to *The Renaissance*. Sydney Smith wrote that if Francis Jeffrey were given the solar system to review—Francis Jeffrey being the sour critic who said "This will never do" of Wordsworth's *Excursion*—he would pan it: "Bad light—planets too distant—pestered with comets—feeble contrivance;—could make a better with great ease." Emerson was a huge user of the semi-colash; in fact, of the fifty-two dashes in "The American Scholar," only four, by my count, appear unaccompanied by either a semi-colon or a comma.

Hybrids become somewhat less common, though they are still easily found, after the turn of the century. Henry James employed a few in his early writing, but revised them out in the *édition de luxe* that began appearing in 1907. The 1911 *Encyclopaedia Britannica*, a good test bed of Edwardian norms, resorts to them fairly frequently:

> A large screw can, however, be roughly examined in the following manner:—(1) See whether the surface of the threads has a perfect polish . . . (2) mount it between the centres of a lathe . . . (4) Observe whether the short nut runs from end to end of the screw without a wabbling motion when the screw is turned and the nut kept from revolving. If it wabbles the screw is said to be drunk.

And Edmund Gosse's 1907 *Father and Son* has a lovely comma-softened dash that can be read as a wistful farewell to a form of punctuation in its twilight:

> These rock-basins, fringed by corallines, filled with still water almost as pellucid as the upper air itself, thronged with beautiful sensitive forms of life,—they exist no longer, they are all profaned, and emptied, and vulgarised.

They pop up here and there in Norman Douglas, early J. B. Priestley, and Cyril Connolly. J. M. Keynes used a scattering of all three forms in his 1920 *Economic Consequences of the Peace*. For instance:

> The policy of reducing Germany to servitude for a generation, of degrading the lives of millions of human beings, and of depriving a whole nation of happiness should be abhorrent and detestable,—abhorrent and detestable, even if it were possible, even if it enriched ourselves, even if it did not sow the decay of the whole civilized life of Europe.

But hybrid punctuation was doomed by then. Proust used two pre-war semi-colashes in the enormous "bedrooms I have known" sentence in the opening of *A la rehash;* Scott Moncrieff removed them in his post-war 1922 translation. (Terence Kilmartin, good man, restored the original punctuation in 1981.) The dandiest dandy of them all, Vladimir Nabokov (who, I think, read *Father and Son* just as closely as he read Proust, drawn to its engaging combination of literature and amateur naturalism), used over sixty excellent comma-dash pairings in his first and quite Edwardian English-language novel, *The Real Life of Sebastian Knight* (1941). (For example, " 'A title,' said Clare, 'must convey the colour of the book,—not its subject.' ") He used none at all in *Speak, Memory: The New Yorker* had sweated it out of him. In all of his later work I have noticed only one precious semi-colash: Humbert writes, "I remember the operation was over, all over, and she was weeping in my arms;—a salutary storm of sobs after one of the fits of moodiness that had become so frequent with her in the course of that otherwise admirable year!"

More precious still, to the punctuational historian, are the two instances of *reversed* commashes in Updike's early novels—one in the Fawcett edition of *The Centaur,* and one on page 22 of the Fawcett *Of the Farm:*

> As Joan comforted him, my mother, still holding the yardstick—an orange one stamped with the name of an Alton hardware store—, explained that the boy had been "giving her the eye" all morning, and for some time had been planning to "put her to the test."

This extremely rare variant form hearkens back to forties Mencken—

> My father put in a steam-heating plant toward the end of the eighties—the first ever seen in Hollins Street—, but such things were rare until well into the new century.

And again to Proust: "Que nous l'aimons—comme en ce moment j'aimais Françoise—, l'intermédiaire bien intentionné qui" etc.

But Updike, our standard-bearer, never stands up for dashtards now. Even John Barth's eighteenth-century pastiche, *The Sot-Weed Factor,* where they would have been right at home, doesn't use them. (They were everywhere in the eighteenth century, too.) What comet or glacier made them die out? This may be the great literary question of our time. I timidly tried to use a semi-colash in an essay for *The Atlantic Monthly* in 1983: the associate editor made a strange whirring sound in her throat, denoting inconceivability, and I immediately backed down. Why, why are they gone? Was it— and one always gropes for the McLuhanesque explanation first—the increasing use of the typewriter for final drafts, whose arrangement of comma, colon, and semi-colon keys made a quick reach up to the hyphen key immediately after another punctuation mark physically awkward? Or was it— for one always gropes for the pseudo-scientific explanation just after McLuhan—the triumphant success of quantum mechanics? A comma is indisputably more of a quantum than a commash. Did the point-play of the Dadaists and E. E. Cummings, and the unpunctled last chapter of *Ulysses,* force a scramble for a simple hegemony against which revolt could be measured?

The style manuals had been somewhat uncomfortable with hybrid punctuation all along—understandably so, since it interferes with systematization. The most influential Victorian antibarbarus, John Wilson's *A Treatise on English Punctuation,* which went through something like thirty editions in England and America, tolerated mixed points; indeed, later editions offered pages of exercises, written and oral, intended to help the student refine his dexterity with the commash. But "the unnecessary profusion of straight lines," Wilson warned, as others had warned before him, "particularly on a printed page, is offensive to good taste, is an index of the *dasher's* profound ignorance of the art of punctuation . . ." In *"Stops" or, How to Punctuate,* Paul Allardyce, the Edwardian successor to Wilson, was more severe: "There is seldom any reason for the use of double points." G. V. Carey, in *Mind the Stop* (1939), was unequivocal: "The combination of other stops with dashes is even less admissible than with brackets." There was a glimmer of hope in Eric Partridge's *You Have a Point There* (1953)—he advised that, yes, compound points should be used with "caution and moderation," but he had the courage to admit that "occasionally [they] are, in fact, unavoidable."

But that was 1953, in fault-tolerant England. According to the *Chicago Manual of Style* (§ 5.5), dash-hybrids are currently illegal in the U.S. In the name of biodiversity, however, I stuck a few of them in out-of-the-way places in my first novel, over the objections of the copy-editor, in 1988. I thought I was making history. But Salman Rushdie had beaten me to it, as it turned out: *The Satanic Verses,* which appeared a few months before my book, uses dozens and dozens of dashtards, and uses them aggressively, flauntingly, more in the tradition of Laurence Sterne than of Trollope. Brad Leithauser's arch, *Sebastian Knight*-like frame-narrator, in *Hence* (1989), uses many commashes; and Leithauser discussed Rushdie's "Emily Dickinsonian onslaught of dashes" in a *New Yorker* review that same year—although somehow

Emily Dickinson doesn't seem quite right. But we're just playing at it now, the three of us—we aren't sincere in our dashtardy;—we can't be.

It would be nice to see Dr. Parkes or Dr. Lennard (of parenthetical fame) attempt a carefully researched socio-historical explanation of the passing of mixed punctuation. Unfortunately, a full explanation would have to include everything—Gustav Stickley, Henry Ford, Herbert Read, Gertrude Stein, Norbert Weiner, Harold Geneen, James Watson, Saint Strunk, and especially *The New Yorker*'s Miss Eleanor Gould, whose faint, gray, normative pencil-point still floats above us all. And even then the real microstructure of the shift would elude us. We should give daily thanks, in any case, to Malcolm Parkes, for offering us some sense of the flourishing coralline tidepools of punctuational pluralism that preceded our own purer, more consistent, more teachably codified, and perhaps more arid century.

(1993)

A Novel by
Alan Hollinghurst

Alan Hollinghurst is better at bees than Oscar Wilde. On the opening page of *The Picture of Dorian Gray*, Wilde has them "shouldering their way through the long unmown grass." A bee must never be allowed to shoulder. Later that afternoon, Dorian Gray, alarmed by Lord Henry Wotton's graphic talk of youth's inevitable degeneration, drops a lilac blossom that he has been "feverishly" sniffing. Bee *numero due* appears, taking most of a paragraph to "scramble all over the stellated globe of the tiny blossoms" and further interrogate the "stained trumpet of a Tyrian convolvulus." Here again, when you're talking about bee-legs and their prehensile dealings with plant tissue, "scramble" doesn't quite do the trick.

In *The Folding Star*, on the other hand, Alan Hollinghurst's narrator (who has several traits in common with Wilde's disillusioned, youth-seducing Lord Henry) describes lying on a bench in the sun, "breathing the seedy vanilla smell of a bush on which half a dozen late bees still dropped and toppled." "Dropped and toppled," with its slumping music, is brief and extremely good: avoiding the mention of blossoms altogether, it nicely captures the heavy, dangled, abdominal clumsiness of those end-of-shift pollen-packers.

There are things like this, and better than this, to be grateful for on almost every page of Hollinghurst's new book—in almost every paragraph, in fact. And yet it isn't glutting to read because its excellences are so varied and multiplanar. Hollinghurst, it seems, has an entirely sane and unmanic wish to supply seriatim all the pleasures that the novel is capable of supplying. The conversation, especially, is brilliant, but everything—depraved or refined or both—is tuned and compensated for, held forth and plucked away, allusively waved at when there's no time for a thorough workover, and neatly parsed when there is. The narrator is a sad man, past-besotted, unachieving and "drinky" if not drunken, with moments of misanthropic Larkinism ("Books are a load of crap," he unconvincingly quotes near the beginning), but his lost-youth mood is the opposite of depressing because he describes whatever suits him with an intelligence that cheers itself up as it goes.

He—Edward Manners—has come to a mythical, silt-choked, fallen Flemish city (Ghentwerp? Brugeselles? some hybrid, anyway) to start fresh by tutoring two boys in English. One is the son of an art historian who has been plugging away at a *catalogue raisonné* of a minor (and fictional) Burne-Jonesite Symbolist and syphilitic with the wonderful name of Orst—Edgard Orst, that is, depicter of fabric-draped interiors, spare seascapes, and allegorical women with orange hair and racy chokers made of Roman medals. But this first boy has asthma and is plump, so forget him. The other "lad," Luc Altidore, seventeen, he of the wide shoulders and wondrously puffy upper lip, is the descendant of an eccentric luminary named Anthonis Altidore, a sixteenth-century printer (Christophe Plantin?) who, so we learn, successfully traced his ancestry straight back to the Virgin Mary. ("One imagines some pretty murky areas around, say, the third century," somebody comments.) Despite the presence of a bewildering array of men and their variously sized and angled organalia in Edward Manners's gay bar-coded sensibility, young Luc, though he may possibly be a heterosexual (mixed blessing!), and though the thought that he is related to Jesus Christ is "slightly unnerving," utterly appropriates our likable if occasionally glum hero's romantic imagination. Luc is no rocket scientist. "I could have impressed him, even gently squashed him with my knowledge," Manners thinks, but allowances must be made for the language problem, and anyway, as Lord Henry Wotton explains, "Beauty is a form of Genius—is higher, indeed, than Genius as it needs no explanation." Manners, in a fever of early-thirties infatuation, can't stop thinking about that cursed "molten trumpeter's lip" which blows all the available competition away; like some "creepy old hetero," he finds himself sniffing used lad-undies and crusty lad-hankies, tasting dry toothbrushes and stealing negatives in order to get closer to this unattainable Altidorian Gray, who though he is at his best in white jeans can "ironise" even a pair of khakis, leggy piece of work that he is.

Like Hollinghurst's great first book, *The Swimming-Pool Library*, *The Folding Star* has many characters but few women. The author takes pains to greet them and make them feel welcome in a chapter or two, and he clearly bears them no ill-will, but he can't focus on them for longer than half an hour. It's too bad that we don't have a little more time with the charming (and page-boyish) Edie, for example, who is willing to listen to any lurid sketch of gay fetishism with "the open-minded expression of someone on holiday good-

naturedly learning the rules of a foreign national game." But
Edward is fundamentally suspicious of, or at least uninterested in, the "never fully plausible world of heterosexual feeling." An awed or intrigued reference to the male "genital
ensemble" occurs every fifteen pages or so, as well it should.
(For instance: "sometimes modest and strong, sometimes lol-
loping and heavy-headed, its only constants an easy foreskin,
a certain presence, and a heather-honey beauty"; or, he
"pissed fiercely in the bushes; then stood for a while slapping
his dick in his palm as a doctor smacks a vein he wants to
rise.") An analogous visual insatiability within the straight
world, however, Edward views with fastidious distaste. Presented with some antique dirty pictures of a laundrywoman,
he says: "I made my interest scientific, dimly thinking what a
prig I was when it came to women and the indignities men
demanded of them."

All this seems both true and funny—there is a deep chasm,
no doubt essentially vulval, of reciprocal incomprehensibility
that normally separates the gay cosmology from the prevailing straightgeist; we might as well recognize the obvious
cleavage and wrest some entertainment out of (for example)
our mutually baffling pornography. Manners, with refreshing
intolerance, goes so far as to say that "there was always
something lacking in those men who had never had a queer
phase as boys, it showed in a certain dryness of imagination,
a bland tolerance uncoloured by any suppression of their
own, a blindness to the spectrum's violet end."

Blind and violet-deprived though we few remaining creepy
heteros are (and sleep-deprived, as well—Hollinghurst includes a glimpse of a new father, who "yawned like a dog,
with a whine too"), we nonetheless do our best to learn as
much as we can about our cross-pollinating betters, and we
welcome, or ought to welcome, with foot-stamping and cheers

and the earnest rattling of our model-airplane kits, the inspired historical verisimilitude that Hollinghurst brings to bear in both his books on the making of an alternative creation-myth of artistic evolution. The retroactive homosexualization of poetic history, and especially of the tradition of pastoral elegy and rustic reflection as it works its way down through Milton, William Collins, Wordsworth, and Shelley all the way to the fictional Georgian poet "Sir Perry Dawlish," is accomplished with astonishing ease and plausibility in *The Folding Star.*

In one scene, the adolescent Edward waits outdoors for the evening star to come out and thinks over his phrase-hoard of nature poetry and "becomes a connoisseur of the last lonely gradings of blue into black"; and in doing so somehow leads us to the conviction that all the grunting, groping, and "stubbly frenching" that apparently goes on at dusk between men and boys in decrepit parks and overgrown commons, in ruined abbeys and hermitages and other handy arcadias, has always gone on and is good and worthwhile—is, indeed, the secret triumphant undertheme of all pastoral verse. Edward looks over the trees at that trope of tropes, Hesperus, star of the muse and of poetic attainment, the "folding-star" of Collins's "Ode to Evening" or (as in Milton's "Comus") the "Star that bids the shepherd fold," and it seems to become for him the winking lure and symbol of all things perseveringly evanescent, immortally short-lived, bravely tearful and impeccably campy. Edward never goes so far as to say that his private muse, his beloved vespertine twinkler, is actually *puckered,* forthrightly anal, but he is too visually on the ball not to want to allow us to infer that cinctured sense of "folding star," as well—he refers to Luc (the name is a broken spangle from "Lucinda," perhaps) as a "star" and as "starlit" and we concede the point. And it's a star of mourning, too; the AIDSy sadness of so much recent loss, the disappearance of brilliant youths and the disappearance of one's own youth's brilliance, and the more general sadness of the unknowable generations of self-stifled and closeted poets that preceded our outspoken time, and then, too, the simple asexual unattainability of much of what we really want and the unretrievability of what we best remember, are some of the emotions toward which Hollinghurst shepherds us.

The Folding Star turns out to be one of the few satisfying books around that treat the relationship between art and life and the secrets they keep from each other. The thirteenth-century English exported wool to Bruges, where Flemish guild-members wove it into cloth and tapestry. Edward Manners here exports himself, his native language, his wool-gathered raw material of educated reading, his sexual appetite, to a Brugesed and battered city that goes to work on him and knots him as we read into a figure in its ancient hieratic carpet. The allegory in the book is thick and ambiguous and un-Jamesian: like a well-hung (shall we say) Flemish tapestry—like the Flemish tapestry, perhaps, that hangs in the childhood room where Dorian Gray secretly stores his horrifying portrait, or like the tapestries Edgard Orst paints behind his mysterious orange-haired models—it's decorative and plush and fine, exuberantly pictorial but uninsistently in the background.

Given the man-boy theme, we may be forgiven for keeping half an eye out for gender-flipped Lolitanisms. There are at least two: a pointed passage about the pronunciation of "Lucasta" ("the darting buss with which it began, the upward and downward flicker of the tongue against the teeth"); and the Frenchified "dream palindrome" of "Luc" and "cul." One could conceivably call these defects, but they aren't—as a matter of fact, the play on "Luc" and "cul" helps dissolve another minuscule potential reproof, which is that there are a few too many uses of the vogue word "clueless." For "clueless" is only a dream anagram of "Luc-less"—and the pain of Luc-lessness is what this clue-laden book, lucky for us, is all about.

(1994)

Leading with the
Grumper

This[1] may be the funniest and best-smelling work of profound lexicographical slang-scholarship ever published.
Some may respect the hint of Elmer's glue in recent printings
of Partridge's *Dictionary of Slang and Unconventional English
(8th ed.),* or the faint traces of burlap and cocoa-bean that
linger deep in *The Oxford Dictionary of Modern Slang,* or
even the fume of indoor swimming-pool that clings to the
paper-bound decolletage of *Slang!: The Topic-By-Topic Dictionary of Contemporary American Lingoes.* But a single deep
draught of J. E. Lighter's magnificent *Historical Dictionary of
American Slang (Volume I, A–G)* is a higher order of experience: it smells like a high-ceilinged bare room freshly painted
white—clean and sunlit, full of reverberative promise and
proud of its mitered corners, although with a mildly intoxicat-
ing or hyperventilational "finish." Since these one thousand
and six pages embrace more concentrated filth, vilification,

[1] *Historical Dictionary of American Slang (Volume 1, A–G),* edited by
J. E. Lighter.

and depravity than any contiguously printed sequence is likely to contain until Lighter's Volume II (H–R) appears in the spring of 1996, we may momentarily question the appropriateness of so guileless a fragrance. Yet reading onward (and Lighter really must be read, or at least deeply browsed, rather than consulted—the book belongs on every patriotic coffee table) we begin to acknowledge its aptness, for this work makes us see American slang—a dingy, stuffy, cramped apartment that we've lived in for so long now that it bores and irritates us—with sudden latex-based clarity and awe. What a spacious, cheery gallery we now have in which to tour our swear-words! How delightfully chronological and typographically tasteful it all is! How firmly principled, how unchaotic, how waltzable-in!

And mainly, how unexpectedly funny. To judge by his helpful introduction, Mr. Lighter, who has been laboring on this project for twenty-five years, is not himself a wildly comic person, but he is an exact and deliberate and historically minded person, and he has a rare ability for positioning formerly funny words and phrases in settings that allow them to become funny once more. He is slang's great straight man. I never suspected that I would again laugh aloud at the phrase "broken-dick motherfucker," having found it inert for some time—but no, reading (on the plane) one of the several citations under "**broke-dick** *adj.* worthless.—usu. considered vulgar," I was suddenly, mystifyingly, pounding the tray-table. So too with the entry for *airhole*:

> **airhole** *n.* [partly euphem.] ASSHOLE, 1 & 2.
> *a*1925 in Fauset *Folklore from N.S.* 134: Mary had a little lamb,/Its face was black as charcoal,/Every time it shook its tail,/He showed his little airhole.
> 1985 *Webster* (ABC-TV): I wear socks with black shoes. A lot of people think I'm an airhole.

And *fern:*

> **fern** *n. Stu.* the buttocks. *Joc.*
> **1965** N.Y.C. high-school student: How's your fern [after a fall]?
> **1965** Adler *Vietnam Letters* 99: You know, the hardest part of all this is the feeling of sitting around on our ferns, doing nothing.

And even:

> **asshole** *n.* [ME *arce-hoole*] Also (*Rare* in U.S.) **arsehole.**—usu. considered vulgar. [See note at ASS, *n.,* which is usually considered to be less offensive. Additional phrases in which these words appear interchangeably may be found at ASS.]
> **1.** the anus or rectum [. . . .]
> **1987** D. Sherman *Main Force* 183: when I tell you to do something, I expect to hear your asshole pop, do you understand me?

You enter, while studying this book, the west wing of verbal consciousness—the realm of *slangfarbenmelodie,* of alliterative near-similarity and drunken lateralism and chiming hostility purged of its face-to-face context and abstracted into music: you are in the presence, at times, of the only good things that a million anonymous bullies and sadistic drill-sergeants and cruel-minded, mean-spirited frat boys or sorority girls have bequeathed to the world:

> **chicken-fucker** *n.* a depraved or disgusting fellow.—usu. constr. with *baldheaded.*—usu. considered vulgar.
> **1953** in Legman *Rationale* 20: Suddenly two bald-headed men enter, and the parrot says, "You two chicken-fuckers come out in the henhouse with me." **1976–79** Duncan & Moore *Green Side Out* 276 [ref. to *ca*1960]: All right ya baldheaded chicken-fuckers, I want this area policed the fuck up. **1967–80** McAleer & Dickson *Unit Pride* 287 [ref. to Korean War]: Heave in the first shovelful . . . and run like a baldheaded chicken-fucker.

Of course, nice, gentle people invent slang, too, once in a while. And nice, gentle people can take private satisfaction in slang that they would never more than mutter. In the trance of linguistic close scrutiny that this book induces, terms which would simply be tiresome or embarrassing if actually employed in speech—if used by a winking wall-to-wall-carpeting salesman or an obnoxious dinner guest, say—may without warning deviate your septum here. That we manage to see them as harmless and even possibly charming is entirely to Lighter's credit; the trick seems to hinge, curiously enough, on the repeated use of a single abbreviated versicle: "usu. considered vulgar."

A *donkey dick,* for example, meaning "a frankfurter, salami, or bologna," is "usu. considered vulgar." Few observers would disagree. A *fartsack,* defined as "a sleeping bag, bedroll, bunk, cot, or bed; SACK" is, again justifiably, "usu. considered vulgar." The morning request to "Drop your cocks and grab your socks!" is "usu. considered vulgar." To *have a bug up (one's) ass [and vars.]* (meaning to "have an unreasonable, esp. obsessive or persistent, idea") is "usu. considered vulgar." A *come-pad* ("mattress") is "usu. considered vulgar." *Cunt-breath* and *dicknose* are "usu. considered vulgar." This phrase is probably the one most frequently used in the dictionary, with "usu. considered offensive" a distant second; the introductory material explains that *usu.* actually means "almost always, though not inevitably," since " 'mainstream standards' are flexible and are primarily based on situation and speaker-to-speaker relationships." But the exoticizing Urdic or Swahilian symmetry of "usu." gives it comic authority, as well: it serves up each livid slangwad neatly displayed on a decorative philological doily.

What is not "usu. considered vulgar" is of some interest, too. The word *grumper* (buttocks) is not considered vulgar, perhaps because it is relatively rare. (The citation, from 1972, reads: "Some chicks lead with the boobs. . . . This chick leads with the grumper.") A *Knight of the golden grummet,* listed under *grommet* and meaning, according to a 1935 definition quoted by Lighter, "a male sexual pervert whose complex is boys," does not rate the "usu." phrase. To *deep-throat* is not vulgar. A *dingleberry* (cross-referenced with the earlier *dill-berry* and *fartleberry*), painstakingly defined in a 1938 cita-tion as "Tiny globular pieces of solidified excreta which cling to the hirsute region about the anal passage"—or, if you pre-fer a pithier 1966 definition, as a "piece of crap hanging on a hair"—is not flagged as vulgar, although *eagle shit* ("the gold ornamentation on the visor of a senior officer's cap") is, and *dingleberry cluster,* meaning a military decoration, does receive a "used derisively." The English, who sometimes become confused about such things, used *dingle-berries* to mean "Female breasts: low and raffish," according to Par-tridge, a sense that doesn't, on Lighter's evidence, seem to have reached these shores—although other unvulgar Ameri-can meanings Lighter does record (and which illustrate slang's resourceful opportunism, its indifference to anatomi-cal inconsistency) are "a doltish or contemptible person," "the testicles," "the clitoris or vagina," and "splattered mol-ten particles around a metallic weld on a pipe or vessel."

Not only is Lighter choosy (a *chooser,* incidentally, is a neglected vaudevillism meaning "plagiarist") about what words are truly vulgar, he is also interestingly selective about what words he includes in the book at all. *Butt plug* only appears by virtue of its derisive sense, meaning a "stupid or contemptible person.—usu. considered vulgar," where it is followed by a corroborative quotation from *Beavis and Butt-head.* ("Nice try, . . . butt plug.") The primary, artifactual usage of *butt plug* does not appear, apparently because it is (to quote the press release that accompanied review copies of the dictionary) "a descriptive term that cannot be said [i.e., expressed] with any other word." In Lighter's system, a word, however informal, that has no convenient synonyms proba-bly isn't slang—*butt plug* is jargon, perhaps, a "term of art" in some advanced circles. Slang is by definition gratuitous; slang words most commonly travel in loose packs of unnecessary cognates or rhymes. (Viz., *breadhooks, cornstealers, daddles, flappers, flippers, grabbers,* and *grabhooks* for "hands"; or, for "sanatorium," *booby hatch, brain college, bughouse, cackle factory, cracker factory, fool farm, foolish factory, funny factory, funny farm, giggle academy,* and so on, all chronicled by Lighter; the bucolic "farm" variants are generally predated by the "factory" variants—idiomatic insanity in America seems to begin as an industrial symptom.) Even stand-alone units like *cookie-duster* (mustache), *crotch rocket* (motorcycle), *dusty butt* (short person), *drum snuffer* (safe-cracker), *blow blood* (have a nosebleed), *flannel-buzzards* (lice), or *boom bucket* (an aircraft's ejection seat) are slang by virtue of their appreciable emotional distance from, and yet complete referential synonymy with, a unit of Standard English. Only when our culture evolves at least one other word for a butt plug will the term—if I understand Lighter—merit his definitional attention.

The truth is, though, that I probably don't understand Lighter and I'm probably not doing justice to the complex algorithms that allow him to discriminate between slang and other kinds of verbal festivity. Why is *butt plug* out and *French tickler* in? If a lack of standard English synonyms is one of the tests for exclusion, why is an admittedly fine term like *gig-line* (meaning "a straight alignment of the buttons of a shirt and jacket, the belt buckle, and the fly of the trousers") included? Is there really a standard English equivalent for such a disposition of one's wardrobe? And why is *bong,* in the sense of a water-filtered pot-smoking mechanism, not to be found, while the related but more recent *bong* meaning a "device consisting of a funnel attached to a tube for drinking beer quickly" is? Lighter includes *fluff* ("the usu. passive partner in a lesbian relationship") and sister words *femme* and *fuckee,* and even *bender* ("a male homosexual who habitually assumes the passive role in anal copulation"—also known as an *ankle grabber*), but not the related S/M sense of *bottom. Fender-bender,* in the automotive sense, is in, as is *cluster-fuck, fuckhead,* and even *fenderhead,* but *gender-bender* and *genderfuck* are out—hardly surprising or scandalous omissions, although both are interesting meldings, part of the steady slanging down of the High Church word *gender,* which only a few years ago was esteemed by language reformers for its lack of connotative raciness, and which is now quietly de-euphemizing, thanks to the work of gender-fuck pioneers like Kate (*née* Albert) Bornstein, lesbian transsexual author of a play called *Hidden: A Gender.* In the area of lit-crit and genre studies, *fuck-book* is here (along with *dick-book* and *cunt book*), but *friction-fiction* is possibly too recent or too technical.

Lighter is at his most severely exclusive regarding authorial or journalistic neologisms. For instance, his entries for *bush, crank,* and *fudge-packer* quote lines from a book of my own, being pre-existent words, whereas none of the A-through-G novelties in that same book (*bobolinks, candy-corn, clit-cloister, cream horns, frans,* etc.)—novelties, may I say, on which I expensed some spirit and wasted some shame—were allowed in. Coinages, Lighter explains, "owe their birth partly to high spirits but chiefly to the coiner's forgivable desire to impress the public with his or her wit." He censures earlier works of reference such as Berrey and Van den Bark's *The American Thesaurus of Slang* (1942) for including such "ephemera," contending that

> slang differs . . . from idiosyncratic wordplay and other nonce figuration in that it maintains a currency independent of its creator, the individual writer or speaker.

Lighter's experience tells him that

> Most words and phrases claimed as "slang" are nonce terms or
> "oncers," never to be seen or heard of again. Some become true
> "ghost words," recorded in slang dictionaries for many years but
> never encountered in actual usage. We have attempted to exclude
> such expressions from this dictionary.

("Ghost words" must never be confused with *ghost turds*—
"accumulations of lint found under furniture.—usu. considered vulgar.") Occasionally a fetching journalistic invention
will prosper—notably the creative work of writers at *Variety*
in the twenties and thirties, who brought us such necessities as
turkey, lay an egg, and *flop.* But Lighter plays down the importance of print in slang's genesis and dissemination: "although
journalism has often encouraged the spread of slang, the chief
method of popularization has always been the shifting associational networks among individuals"—particularly, he con-
vincingly asserts, the associational networks within the U.S.
armed services. (Lighter's command of the history of military
slang is stunning: the entry for *gook* has over fifty citations; it
is three times longer than the entry for *chick.*) Real slang just
happens: "lexical innovations are traceable only rarely to specific persons; the proportion of slang actually created by identifiable individuals is minute."

Despite slang's usually anonymous and often paramilitary
origins, hundreds of identifiable individuals have a place in the
Dictionary, doing their bit to substantiate the existence of a
given piece of loose language. Perhaps the most cheering thing
about this awesome project is how seriously it takes the trade
paperback. As one would expect, there are crumbs collected
from movies, newspapers, TV series, linguistic research interviews, and celebrity profiles—as when Steve McQueen is
quoted as saying, "I chickenshitted on the second turn"—but
there are also innumerable illustrative quotations drawn from

the work of novelists and litterateurs and even poets. Lighter and his colleagues really read books. It is a delight to encounter so many writers through their passing use of some regionalism, obscenity, or malediction. In this snickerer's *OED*, William Faulkner appears not for some high-flown word like *endure*, but for *ass-scratcher*. Sandburg is immortalized as a user of *arky malarky*. I also ran into (in alphabetical order by term) Thomas Berger (*ass-wipe, dinkum*), Cheever (*asshole* used adjectivally), Sorrentino (*banana nose*), Eudora Welty (*bohunkus*), John Sayles (*boot* in the sense of vomit, *dead presidents*), Woody Allen (*bowels in an uproar*), Camille Paglia (*breeders*), Joseph Mitchell (*bums*), A. J. Liebling (*pain in the butt*), Philip Roth (*circle-jerker*), Harlan Ellison (*clock* and *grease-burger*), Northrop Frye (*clueless*), Barry Hannah (*cockhead, dicking off*), Henry Miller (*crap*), Kerouac (*crock-ashit*), and Erica Jong (*crotch rot*).

And there is Joseph Wambaugh (*cumbucket, don't know my dick from a dumplin*), Saul Bellow (*candy kid, cunt-struck*), Bernard Malamud (*dead-to-the-neck*), Maya Angelou (*dick-teaser*), William Burroughs (*doodle, glory hole*), Danielle Steele (*dumb cunt*), Stephen King (*el birdo, cock-knocker*), Bellow (*fart-blossom*), Hunter Thompson (*big spit*), Coover (*flagpole* meaning penis), Grace Metalious (*frig you*), John O'Hara (*frig*), S. J. Perelman (*frigged*), Edmund Wilson (*friggin'*), H. L. Mencken (*frigging, crap*), Dos Passos (*frigging, gash*), Larry Heinemann (*fuck the duck, crapola*), Mailer (*fuck yourself, cream*), Tom Wolfe (*go-to-hell* as an adj.), Donald Barthelme (*grog*), and Robert Heinlein (*grok,* of course, but also *go cart* for "car").

Parnassian sources such as *The New York Review of Books* are not neglected either—*corn-holed* and *do* (in the sexual sense) appeared there, per Lighter. The *Atlantic Monthly* supplies the first citation for *doghouse,* musician's slang for "double-bass" (1920). *Esquire* pops up as a locus for a rare 1976 use of *dog water,* which, Lighter informs us, means "clear drops of seminal fluid." *The New Yorker* makes many appearances, some for nice old words like *brads* ("cash"), *cluckhead,* and *cheesy.* (Lighter's crew has, by the way, come up with a sentence employing *cheesy* that predates by over thirty years the first *cheesy* citation in the Supplement to the OED. In 1863 someone named Massett wrote: "The orchestra consisting of the fiddle—a very cheezy flageolet, played by a gentleman with one eye—a big drum, and a triangle.") *The New Yorker* also substantiates the word *fucking* used adverbially, thanks to its recent explosion of profanity, and it furnishes two separate nuances of *asshole* dating from 1993.

For obvious reasons, though, the magazine that is most often quoted in *The Historical Dictionary of American Slang* is *The National Lampoon.* Lighter and his crew have combed its back issues carefully in quest of elusive flannel-buzzards, and they have not gone unrewarded. Yet here the editors must have had difficulty at times deciding which words were merely "nonce figuration," to be excluded from the dictionary, and which words had obtained a "currency independent of the speaker." The fact that *The National Lampoon* uses *cock-locker* or *flog the dolphin* or *get your bananas peeled* (all with sexual meanings) is taken to be an indication that this recherché vocabulary enjoyed a currency independent of the humorist during the period in question. It may have; *Lampoon* writers were expert listeners and diligent field-workers. But they were, as well, habitués of the reference room; in some cases at least, one suspects that they simply pulled down a few slang tomes, found a "ghost word" they thought was funny, and resurrected it for the greater good. P. J. O'Rourke recently told a lunch-table that he owns a whole shelf of unconventional lexicography; he and Michael O'Donohue, another *Lampoon* contributor and professional slangfarber, were particularly fond of one major thesaurus dating from (he thought) the thirties—by which he surely meant Berrey and Van den Bark's huge "ephemera"-filled collection from the forties. In this way, out of the dried mud-flats of old reference books, to one-time creative placement in a humor magazine, to further climate-controlled stasis in Lighter's *Dictionary,* are some words blessed with "currency" after a single recycling. And the language is happier for it.

Using *The Historical Dictionary of American Slang* will probably have long-term side effects. A three-week self-immersion in Lighter's initial volume significantly altered this suggestible reader's curse-patterns. I swore more often and more incomprehensibly while reading it than ever before; the "Captain Haddock syndrome" was especially noticeable while driving. (Captain Haddock is the character in the Tintin series who, when drunk, showers puzzling nonce-abuse on people: Poltroons! Iconoclasts! Bashi-bazouks!) To a slow motorist (with windows closed, of course, so he couldn't hear), I would call out, "*Go,* you little scum-jockey!"—or "corn-pad" or "dirt-bonnet." None of these formulae is to be found in Lighter (at least, there is no reason to expect *scum-jockey* to appear in Volume III), but reading Volume I made me say them. Furthermore, under Lighter's fluid spell I spent several hours working on a matrix of related insults:

You	bag!	ball!	bomb!	wad!	wipe!	loaf!
cheese-		x		?	?	?
corn-		x		?	?	
dirt-	x	x	x			
grease-		x				
hose-	x			x	?	
jiz-	x			x	x	?
scum-	x	x		x		
scuzz-	x	x			x	?
sleaze-	x	x	x	x		
slime-		x		x		

(An *x* indicates an existing piece of slang; a question mark indicates a plausible compound, which may or may not appear in the future. Whether there is any linguistic point to building such a predictive matrix is an open question.)

Some of these behavioral aberrations will pass in time, but it is at least possible that by the spring of 1997, when the final installment of this mighty triptych assumes its place in the library, those of us who have been diligently reading and waiting will discover ourselves to be marginally better people, or at least more cheerful and enlightened and tolerant swearers, as a result of what Jonathan Lighter and his cohorts have done for the massive and heretofore unmanageable dirtball of American slang.

(1994)

Mixed

The Northern
Pedestal

Esquire sent out hundred-dollar bills to writers and artists and asked for contributions in return. I found some old pages I had produced in an altered state, cut them down, and added commentary. Except for several corrected typos, the quoted text is reproduced exactly as it was first written.

In the spring of 1982, having received a piece of unwelcome news, the Subject, a male, aged twenty-five, not a habitual drug-user, smoked nearly a hundred dollars' worth of marijuana at his portable typewriter. Subject produced a document that is three single-spaced pages long. It begins:

> There is that feeble urgency behind all forced mannerisms of finery—haste and pomp cannot coincide.

Six lines later, there are preliminary indications of a disabled rationality:

> A logic of the ears, certainty of outer crust. Changing pleasures in misstatements. Maintenance of patternability. Hold on to the camel marts. Feebler lessons in disenchantment, supererogation of the lymphatic spatial asymmetries. Power lessons in discontinuity,

retinue of the unfamiliar, flip the reversal tiny efforts of bettering the grimp instinct retractions, flipping up of y behavior patterns, total housal shift unmanageability . . .

A little further on, Subject accidentally burns his finger:

Odd, dual penetration of pain: veers upward to mind chambers, and through the physical breezes of manual realms. A white veil of pain, but centered, dotlike. Change through further, more rhomboid patterns. Get it round before it fails, or spatial locations nets the prize. It failed. Pods defer to red-shift memory blossoms.

Subject then attempts to analyze his interior state:

I am not so much speechless, as placing further the northern pedestal. Chasten the memory switching houses. Decorum focuses the hiss momentarily, but the roar prevails. A smooth, bouldered impact, torsal conjunction, indwelling machinations; though choice motorizes the wilderness. Corn ligaments of taste-cramp. Changed veldt diagrams of powerhungry tortoise blossoms, of cold trustworthies; noun or verb? Nevermore the chancy apostles of hope. Oh Joyce, you sad intimate. I see your blind bane now. Adam woke. Cluster globe tendencies; meld proliferation. Debug the profanities!

The Subject goes on to spell out exactly what is at stake:

The courts of gyrations exact the reciprocal chinook tapestries. Vestpocket parks of error. Or, perhaps, conversely, victories of fresher tin villages. Vibratations of the seat cushion.

Subject's girlfriend has fallen asleep on the couch, and a worry about disturbing her with the sound of his typing momentarily intrudes on his reflections:

But doth movement occur, and if so, how can she sleep with same sound: re noise.

Immediately, however, Subject reproaches himself for the use of an archaic construction like "doth":

Take care to avoid those Simonized orations. Which? doubt begs. But I vanquish and banish him. And so avoid the avoidable. A mush of relapses. Flatness a primer and more sinister virtue. Tender our resignation at coherent sources of Hermetic entrancement. Detest the relief of stupefaction, because only of the mogul's gurgle.

Presently Subject begins to enjoy himself:

Enticed offshoots of rationality spice the general curve. Drunken soliloquies of spree. Melded enticements. Seasoned intermingling. Dense near-visions. A tongue eruptions, oxygen feist, holdup, metered youth distillation. Change dereliction of patterned play-things. Pull those cotton shadow-pockets into the light. Find the newer presences. Frocked with light, the cave-dweller chimes out the night. Held with motile polliwogs, reason coys at plaything we. Try again, Oh witless raisin!

Soon, though, Subject has some doubts about the medical advisability of what he is doing:

Certain it harms, and virtues not later kiln utterances can't breach. Regain high gain drift basis. Allow permeables to photoreact to bisections into health arrangements.

And yet, by the bottom of page two, Subject has regained his characteristic cheer:

All goes well. Fortune smiles. Torrid mannequins field northern rotund light blue pained warmness, and misapplied filth. Blending the apple-blossoms of the event. Noticed her unguent catalepsis. Ching the item of motiveless blandishment. A store of future irre-mediables. Critic spanglers. Or no.

Several minutes later, Subject again becomes aware that he is not quite himself. He wonders if he is perhaps "crashing":

Notice of infringement. Telltale signals of final-phase ache. Mem-ory shrivels, grows glittered and void. Blackness sheds its para-doxical deposit. One more casualty to finer concentrations. Too powerful to contain such mortal ironies. Veneered hotel migrant vortices. Total mystery midget cone devour fence brigand devour-ers. Signature of betrayal. Tone-spun disservice, rampant dis-avowel. Changed prophets of upward disdainments. No higher enervations possible; the myths of disorder cannot moult. Firm dog blossoms oystered rout.

In hopes of reversing his mood, Subject smokes the last of the marijuana. He is moved to reflect further on the possible discomfort of his girlfriend:

> Pale sprung-wound home treatment seminars. Found awesome subscription from loneliness. Avoid incurring the doubts of competitors. Love belays a pull at cherished cult vacuum. Swarm of bedevilled blueness, or anise afternoon helter mortal filches. Ah, Stanislawski. Poor Margaret who lieth in the blue of the poned couch, space fails her leg and she must toss till woken. Trees quench their interior field finery.

Then Subject is distracted by some physical symptoms:

> But tremors persist, and worsen, and failure begins to inflict larger worries. How do failings quiet themselves to approximate competence? No-one cohered to these rods.

Increasingly enfeebled, his face hanging an inch above the keys of his typewriter, Subject exhorts himself to carry on with his literary efforts:

> Toast dread insufficiency or cramp its claws! Find the later shadroed strewings time defrayed. Demonstrate the dream terror vagueness.

But the spell has irrevocably passed:

> Clenchings in midtorso. Vision restores. Slowed all conjectured field going functions or rather hope nods.

Tired, depleted, Subject nonetheless ends on a note of muted optimism:

> Keep willing the cool intervention.

(1982, 1993)

Wedding

My sister, Rachel Baker August, got married on July 11, 1987. This is a slightly shortened version of what I read that day.

In a few minutes, Rachel and Bob are going to be pronounced husband and wife. These are excellent words, husband and wife—they lean toward each other, they exist in reference to each other, they link arms. "Wife" especially seems druidic and traditional: like "life" but with the addition of the womanly W. "Husband," despite its traces of Saxon farming methods, makes me think most of "hatband"—and this seems right, if you imagine a conventional movie image of a man in a 1955 hat, with a nice gray hatband. Not a mobster hat, just the hat of a good man—a husband. Boyfriends don't wear hats.

After my own honeymoon a year and a half ago, I got a phone message at work. It was the conventional pink WHILE YOU WERE OUT message, with the little box next to "Please call back" checked, and at the bottom was written: "Your wife called." The secretary who had taken the call was not particularly interested in the fact that I had just gotten married; and yet she was kind enough to apply that word and phrase to me. If it had read, "Your girlfriend called," it would have seemed frivolous and unprofessional; but no, it was my wife, and so it was big-league, it had to do with my home and even my hearth (assuming I had a hearth)—it was about my whole life. And I, her husband, would call her back. I saved that message, because the secretary was pronouncing us husband and wife. The world, whether it cared about our marriage or not, had a slot for us; and in a few minutes the world will have a similar place for Bob and Rachel, and I predict that for them, too, the early moments, when the language that people use to talk about them falls suddenly into place, and the old message pads sing in new ways, are going to be some surprisingly fine moments.

And at the same time, while we get to exercise our categories and conventions in shameless fashion, the two of them now have the freedom, as they didn't quite have before, to go wild with their own private language, and invent many strange, embarrassing names for each other, with the knowledge that these, too, though kept secret from us, will last—they will last their whole lives, and evolve just as public speech does.

So I'm very happy that Bob and Rachel are getting married. Bob will be a good husband, and Rachel a good wife. They are proud of each other, and this mutual pride is one of the nicest things you can sense about a couple. I love them both, and I love the fact that in this evening of silk sleeves and white chairs, of taut tenting and rustling relatives, their lives are being changed forever, and they are being wed.

(1987)

Mlack

Keyboard work creates a class of unwanted things—one-letter typos, failures of phrasing, bad punctuation. If you don't want to delete these entirely, you can use the Return key to push them to the bottom of the screen. What gathers, a few lines ahead of the growth bud of your final intention, is a concentrated, enantiomorphic residue; a backward parody of each session's prose-in-progress. When Larry Dark asked writers for work that hadn't seen print, for his anthology called *Outtakes,* I sent him the accumulation at the bottom of the last screen-page of *Room Temperature,* written on Father's Day, 1989.

three days a week oruhizzing bubbling llbbing   e
to finish the article.
turned above her, ent
Bugdolatry
mere six months oldbshe had fallen aseep sucking from a
l;home
hs etcu the Bug, inconceivably grown, Everything wen
s'
owl and nrtz t, which a plastic bagn

mpinrotn
own mouth: eventually, after ten minutes of
   :
in the grass in
direct sun in a stream
unpleasant tickling of the sharp stream of water against the
roof
   of your mouth,   a stream fin
sensation of the Bug must have felt as she drew in the warm
milk from her plastic bottlehthour r, against the roof
of your
had it as: the   and saliva combined, a taste similar to et
o prove that   ere
fall overand tacar
]   ,   some change and rubber bands at th bottom; and the
very
      eom
hourfr:chewed on for several weeks while writing ;
el s and several ix
hterd
from i   once to
,   ginn

But I had the bug!

for larice or sehalf r
k crichad changedexpectedhl
but I had the
Bugtact
my energies, colliding with my uncertainty about mlack of

(1989)

Recipe

The Monroe County Library System, of Monroe, Michigan, asked for a recipe to include in a collection of "Favorite Recipes by Favorite Authors," entitled *Read 'em and Eat*.

Take one ingot of unsweetened Baker's chocolate, remove the paper, and drop it in a tiny saucepan settled over an adjustable heat-source. Then unfold one end of a brand-new silver bar of unsalted Land O Lakes butter and cut a chunk off roughly comparable to the piece of Baker's chocolate, which has by this time begun to smear slightly. (An old stick of butter has too much refrigerator flavor in its exposed end.) The butter will melt faster than the chocolate. Entertain your-self by breaking the ingot of chocolate into its two halves and pushing the halves and the subsiding chunk of butter around with the tip of the butter knife. Then abandon the butter knife and switch to a spoon. When the unmelted chocolate is no more than a small soft shape difficult to locate in the larger velouté, shake some drifts of confectioners' sugar into the liquid. You're aiming for a bittersweet taste, a taste quite a bit less sweet than ice cream—so sprinkle accordingly. But you'll find that a surprising amount of sugar is necessary. Stir idly. If the mixture becomes thick and paste-like, add another three-eighth-inch sliver of butter; to your relief, all will effortlessly reliquefy. Avoid bubbling or burning the mixture, which can now be called sauce. Turn off the heat, or turn it down so low that you don't have to worry about it. Spoon out some premium plain vanilla ice cream. Lately this has become hard to find—crowded out by low-fat premiums and Fragonard flavors. But you want the very best vanilla ice cream available in your area; you have to have that high butterfat content for it to be compatible with the chocolate sauce. Spoon the sauce over the ice cream. It will harden. This is what you have been working for. Once cooled, it will make a nice sound when you tap it with a spoon. If you want more tappable chocolate sauce and you have already covered your scoop or scoops of ice cream with a complete trelliswork, simply turn over one of the scoops and dribble more over the exposed underside. Eat with haste, because premium vanilla ice cream melts fast. Refrigerate the unused sauce right in the original saucepan, covered with tinfoil, with the spoon resting in it; that way, when you put it back on the heat-source, you'll be able to brandish the whole solidified disk of chocolate merely by lifting the spoon. It looks like a metal detector.

(1991)

Ice Storm

I grew up in Rochester, so I should probably know what an ice storm is, but what has just happened here is brand-new in my experience. On the night of March 3, a Sunday, some sort of strange, gentle, superchilled rain came down over a large part of western New York. It coated every power line with a perfect cylinder of ice nearly an inch thick, from which ideally spaced icicles, like the tines on a soil rake, descended, all exactly the same length. The freeze held through early Tuesday. On Monday, if you looked out any window for a few minutes, you were certain to see, against a background of glittering Ace combs, the bough of a tree come crashing down. There was no wind, nor had there been any the first night. It seemed more a demonstration of the patient principles of candlemaking than a storm. At a distance, the ice effects were white, but when you drew close enough to a tree to be surrounded by the continual worry-bead crackling of its fretwork, and stood there, ready to duck at any moment, you saw that it had become incorporated into a clear and disturbingly clinical arrangement of pristine pipettes and test tubes, each holding a once-natural element of the organism—a bud, a twig, one of those perky citizens you had been counting on to function as usual in a few months—in an elaborate cryopharmaceutical experiment.

I drove down the streets today (Tuesday) feeling at times that it was all very familiar, that Ansel Adams calendars had prepared me for this, but then, jumping out again and again from the arty, grainy black-and-white photography that slowly moved past was a sudden apricot-colored splash of discomfort where a bough had torn itself free or a trunk had split in half. On the streets I've seen, half of the good big trees are ravaged. The younger ones, planted about twenty years ago to replace all the elms, are especially painful broken sights. Conifers did somewhat better than deciduous trees. The tall weeping spruce next to our house weeps more than usual but has lost no limbs. Stuck high up in it before the storm was a plastic dragon kite, which we had repeatedly tried and failed to extricate; the morning after the storm, it lay in two pieces on the grass. My wife said, "Well, at least something good has come out of this." I said yes, it was like bombing all of Iraq to get rid of Saddam Hussein. She reminded me of Frost's poem about whether the world will end in fire or in ice. And if we hadn't just flown more than a hundred thousand sorties over a distant place, I would give in more to grief about all these trees, but in the face of that devastation this sort of rare and unmalicious natural catastrophe, in which nobody dies, and some leftovers spoil in some refrigerators, and people go out on tentative camera expeditions to pass the time until the cable TV comes on again, makes me think that we over here have gotten off very easily. We deserve at least this much ice after that much fire. Many of the trees will grow back, after all, as from a bad pruning. As they thaw now, the water is hearteningly visible, hurrying along the bark underneath the ice layer, like blood.

(1991)

Library
Science

Discards

One sunny afternoon in October of 1985, a crowd of librarians and library administrators gathered near the venerable card catalog of the Health Sciences Library of the University of Maryland at Baltimore. It was time for a little celebration. Hundreds of red and blue balloons gently exerted themselves against the acoustical-tiled ceiling. From each balloon hung a piece of string; at the end of each string, tied by its guide hole, dangled a card that had been plucked at random from the library's catalog. On the back of every card was a stamped message: GENUINE ARTIFACT FROM THE CARD CATALOG OF THE HEALTH SCIENCES LIBRARY, UNIVERSITY OF MARYLAND AT BALTIMORE. A TV crew was there, along with a few local dignitaries and a reporter from the *Baltimore Sun*. The group stood among the hovering cards and listened to some speeches about what a landmark day it was for the library, and about the many decisive advantages of online library catalogs—remote access, a more efficient flow of information, reduced costs, lives saved (for this was a medical institution)—and then Chancellor Edward N. Brandt, Jr., wearing a red T-shirt that said "The

Great Discard," chose a drawer of the catalog and pulled it from the cabinet. With the help of a beaming Cyril Feng, who was then the director of the library, he drew the retaining rod from the chosen drawer and let its several hundred cards ceremonially spill into a trash can decorated with colored paper.

When the applause died down, the onlookers (there were about a hundred of them, including, in addition to librarians, a number of nursing students invited to swell the crowd) gathered as many of the balloons as they could and made their way out to a grassy plaza across the street. Reassembled, at the count of three, they released their balloons. The sunlit bibliographic payloads twirled picturesquely as they rose. Soon the wind caught them, and they disappeared off to the northeast. Some days later, one of the cards was returned to the library from a place across the Chesapeake Bay by some resident who thought, foolishly, that it was of value. Another card floated all the way to Connecticut.

Since then, as universities and public libraries have completed the "retrospective conversions" of their catalogs to computer databases (frequently with the help of federal Title II-C money, as part of the "Strengthening Research Library Resources" program), hundreds of card catalogs, tens of millions of individual cards—cards typed on manual typewriters and early electric models; cards printed by the Library of Congress, Baker & Taylor, and OCLC; cards whose subject headings were erased with special power erasers, resembling soldering irons, and overtyped in red; cards that have been multiply revised, copied on early models of the Xerox copier, corrected in pencil, color-coded, sleeved in plastic; cards that were handwritten at the turn of the century; cards that were interfiled by generations of staffers, their edges softened by innumerable inquiring patrons—have been partially or completely destroyed, many in the past year.

The main subject card catalog of the University of California at Berkeley was thrown out in the summer of 1993 to make way for eight study tables. Bryn Mawr's main catalog is gone. The University of Hawaii's main catalog is just about gone. A recycling firm called Earthworm, Inc., carted off the bulk of MIT's cards in 1989—these now mingle unintelligibly as shoe or cereal boxes, or constitute a kind of electrical insulation known as "creping tissue." The cards for the Math, Africana, Engineering, and Physical Sciences collections at Cornell's John M. Olin Library are gone, with others to follow. The subject catalogs at Dartmouth, Kent State, and Boston University are gone. Harvard's cards are going. Cards representing classical literature and philosophy have been pulled from the University of Chicago's main catalog; some of the American-literature cards are being tossed out now.

The New York Public Library, ahead of the game, renovated the entire ten-million-card catalog of its Research Libraries between 1977 and 1980, microfilmed it, and threw it out. Stanford is discussing when and how to recycle its catalogs. The cards dating from 1911 to 1975 at the New York State Library in Albany (where Melvil Dewey was librarian from 1889 to 1906) were thrown away last month as a consequence of a historical-preservation project involving the building in which they were stored. The catalog for the Hawthorne-Longfellow Library at Bowdoin College is 95 percent gone. The cards from UCLA's main library are nearly gone. My own college, Haverford, stored its card catalog in an attic for two years after finishing its retrospective conversion, in 1991. But when I talked to the director of the library in August 1993, the catalog (including many thousands of handwritten cards) was being thrown out, and the cabinets were down at the physical plant being dismantled and scrapped.

One of the odder features of this national paroxysm of shortsightedness and anti-intellectualism ("In a class with the burning of the library at Alexandria," Helen Rand Parish, a historian specializing in the sixteenth century, said to me) is that it isn't the result of wicked forces outside the library walls. We can't blame Saracen sackers, B-52s, anarchists, or thieves; nor can we blame propagandistic politicians intent on revising the past, moralistic book banners, or over-acidic formulations of paper. The villains, instead, are smart, well-meaning library administrators, quite certain that they are only doing what is right for their institutions.

And, incredibly, nobody is making an audible fuss about what they are up to. Nobody is grieving. On the contrary, there are balloons and nursing students; there are festive pictures in trade magazines and industry newsletters of smiling department heads wearing aprons as they dump trays of cards into rolling trash carts. At Cosumnes River College, in California, the card catalog was ceremonially put out of its misery by an official who pointed a gun at it and "shot" it. Dickinson College held a mock wake: veils were worn, hymns were sung, and the doomed catalog was decked with wax flowers and black garbage-bag bunting. "We are only too happy to throw the cards away when we're finished," Judith Brugger, Cornell's catalog management and authorities librarian, told me. As an added publicity flourish during the Great Discard celebration, the Maryland Health Sciences Library published a commemorative chapbook called *101 Uses for a Dead Catalog Card*. Some of the suggested uses: tablecloth-crumb scrapers, space-shuttle tiles, garden compost, fish scalers, cat litter, jousting targets, and serial way-markers for spelunkers. Use No. 100 was "Make a bonfire out of them to celebrate the end of the card catalog."

Is this glee really justified? Is it seemly? I called up Dale Flecker, associate director for planning and systems for the

Harvard University Library, and asked him if he felt any regret at the throwing out of card catalogs. "In general not," he said. "They were a wonderful idea for their time. Their time was about a century, and it's now coming to a close." Mr. Flecker is currently overseeing what is perhaps the largest single retrospective-conversion project ever attempted: the transfer of the information on five million pre-1980 cards, taken from approximately a hundred libraries in the university—including millions from Widener, the main library—to Harvard's online catalog, HOLLIS. The conversion of the Widener catalog is in a fairly early stage, and it is in many ways a model of planning and forethought. Each of Widener's cards was microfilmed before the catalog was "disassembled," using a custom-made card-feeding machine. (Microfilming is, of course, a luxury few libraries can afford. Half the cost of Harvard's campus-wide conversion project is being funded with federal grants and large private gifts.) An image of the front of every card for Widener thus now exists on microfiche, available to users in a room off the lobby. (Any information on the backs of the cards—and many notes do carry over—was not photographed.) Every Tuesday, Harvard sends batches of cards, twenty thousand or so at a time, via UPS, to a nonprofit corporation in Dublin, Ohio (a suburb of Columbus), called OCLC.

These initials once stood for Ohio College Library Center, but now—since the company has grown over the past twenty-three years into an international eminence in the information industry, with yearly tax-free revenues of close to a hundred million dollars—they stand for Online Computer Library Center. OCLC owns the largest database of bibliographic information in the world, and it offers a service called RETROCON, contracting with libraries to transfer old catalog cards to "machine-readable form," at anywhere from fifty cents to six dollars per card.

The RETROCON business is good right now. When I visited OCLC in September 1993, there were three shifts of sixty operators each, plowing through RETROCONs for about forty different libraries, including, besides Harvard, the Los Angeles Public Library, a consortium of French libraries, Hughes Aircraft, Brown, Queen's University of Belfast, Northwestern, the library at Kew Gardens, the Cincinnati Public Library, the San Francisco Public Library, and Waseda University in Japan. Each operator, though initially hired as a temp, and, in some cases, no more than high-school-educated, is the survivor of a rigorous two-week training program. (Most hires do not make it through training.) At first their work is reviewed every day by a supervisor, and subsequently it is spot-checked for accuracy at unexpected times. "Our standards are very, very high," OCLC's Maureen Finn told me as we stood next to shelves holding hundreds of long gray cardboard boxes that said "Widener." "Libraries are entrusting us with the history of their library collection. We have to make sure that we've got good people who are going to do the work correctly, and that we can trust them."

Maureen Finn runs RETROCON and, from what I saw, she runs it exceedingly well. Some of her people have been converting catalog cards, with apparent contentment, for ten years or more. It is true that they seldom have formal training in the intricacies of the cataloger's art: they are not necessarily up on the elaborate Anglo-American cataloging rules, nor are they current concerning the periodic RI's, or Rule Interpretations, issued by the Library of Congress, which—like hermeneutical dispatches from the IRS or the Financial Accounting Standards Board—adjudicate perplexing cases as they emerge. Most operators have had no library-school courses in the Dewey decimal system (still thriving, by the way, and very big in Europe), or the Sears List of Subject Headings, or Cutter numbers, or the

abbreviational niceties of the International Standard Bibliographic Description (ISBD) format—but they do apparently
pick up a great deal as they go. "I would put any of these people up against an MLS cataloger any day," Ms. Finn said to
me—"MLS" meaning Master of Library Science. "I think that
their breadth of knowledge is quite extensive."

Well, it better be. The next card that a second-shift operator props onto the top of the keyboard, at ten-fifteen at night,
could be in any of three hundred roman-type or transliterated
languages, about anything at all, covering any period of
human or interstellar history. His or her job is to find a
match, or "hit," for that card in OCLC's huge database. A hit
brings up a specially formatted computer record called a
MARC record (MARC stands for MAchine Readable Cataloging)—a daunting set of numbered fields and odd symbols
developed by the Library of Congress in the sixties, redolent
of unfriendly first-generation database interfaces—describing
the particular edition of a book (or map, or videotape) which
corresponds to the one that the physical card stands for. The
hit rate varies from project to project, but it is running at
around 70 percent for Harvard.

If the operator does find a matching record, she (there are
slightly more women than men) then must make modifications to it onscreen to suit the source library's idiosyncrasies
of call numbering, entering as much or as little of the card's
supplemental information as is required by the contract
between OCLC and that particular library. (The more modification a library demands of each MARC record, the more it
costs.) In Harvard's case she typically accepts the record as is,
even when the original card bears additional subject headings
or enriching notes of various kinds.

If her search through the database does not turn up a match
for the card, she must enter the information on it from scratch.

This is, or should be, a complex undertaking, demanding judgment as well as accuracy, since not only does the card's content need to be transferred perfectly, without reference to the book itself, in a way that will accord with records for other books by that writer in that library, but the necessary "access points" have to be tagged correctly with numeric codes—access points being those fields in the record that a library user will be able to search for, such as title, author, corporate author, and subject. If someone has a bad night and creates a flawed access point for the title of a book, library patrons will simply not find the book in the library's online catalog when they search for it by title.

We shouldn't leap to the conclusion that just because the RETROCON staff is composed of temps and ex-temps, many without BAs, it will be doing awful things to Harvard's cards. I can vouch for the devotedness and hard work of (some) temps, having temped for several years myself. And airline pilots, some of whom never went to college either, land jumbo jets a thousand times a day with an exceedingly low error rate. Still, we have to wonder whether the Harvard community is expecting something of Maureen Finn's staff at RETROCON that the staff can't possibly deliver—something, in fact, that no outside group of clerical workers, sitting hundreds of miles away from the books in question, no matter how well trained and closely monitored they may be, can deliver. Even OCLC, one of the very best retrospective-conversion contractors in the business, is bound to make thousands of typos in the course of a huge project like the Harvard "recon." There is of necessity going to be a layer of error introduced into Harvard's online catalog. (The official error rate is "less than one per cent"—which, for five million cards, is less than fifty thousand records.) And some of the mistakes, though tiny in relation to the extraordinary size of the database, will—in the same way that errors in TRW's database can do vexing things to one's credit rating—be very significant for individual scholars in quest of a particular book. Nor will there be a wave of compensating corrections as a result of the conversion, since the books themselves aren't there for a zealous operator to check against.

The Widener Library cards, once they are processed by OCLC, are packed up on Wednesdays and sent back to Harvard. There are no lost cards. ("In seventeen years, we've never lost a card," Maureen Finn said, with justifiable pride.) At Harvard, Dale Flecker's staff takes random samples from the boxes of returnees, to see whether OCLC is staying within its contractual quality-control tolerances. If the spot-checkers find unacceptable inconsistencies between a card and its computer version, they retain the card for reference and correct the record online.

And what of the rest? What of the cards that resided in their drawers for fifty or a hundred years, some of which perhaps caught the eye of Charles Cutter or Fred Kilgour or one of the other great names in librarianship who trained or worked at Harvard? What of the handwritten ones? ("Library hand" was a special kind of backward-slanting penmanship meant specifically for card catalogs, and taught in library school through the 1920s.) Where are they all going?

There have been a few requests for particular sets of cards as souvenirs. Someone, for example, wants all the cards for the Gutenberg Bible. And some undetermined but large fraction of the totality is being sent to an artist named Thomas Johnston, at Western Washington University. The rest are being "discarded." "At the end of this project," Dale Flecker told me, "there won't be card catalogs left in the university." I asked him if there were any card catalogs, anywhere in the world, that he thought worthy of preservation. "In general, they're being discarded," he said. "I'm not sure I know of anybody who's decided to preserve them as physical objects." Maureen Finn said much the same thing to me: "The institutions still want the cards back, and then I think they're storing them. But most library managers that I talk to will say, 'We are storing them because it makes the staff feel good, and we will be getting rid of them.' "

Online catalogs are wonderful things in principle—things of efficacy, and even, occasionally (as in the case of OCLC's Online Union Catalog), of grandeur. As a result of the publicly financed expansion of higher education in the sixties, and the boom in academic publishing that followed it, the holdings of the typical university library have doubled over the last twenty years. Without online catalogs, and the circulation and acquisition modules of software with which online catalogs are linked, libraries would simply not have been able to process all the books and journals that were arriving on their loading docks. By the early seventies, there was an ominous arrearage of uncataloged material waiting on herds of rolling carts near the overtaxed cataloging departments of most large libraries. Cataloging had reached a state of crisis similar to the one that forced the financial markets to close early during some of the high-volume weeks of 1969, when Wall Street's paper-based methods of order processing couldn't keep up with each day's orders to buy and sell stock. Computerized stock-execution saved Wall Street (and made program trading and Black Monday possible, too), and computerized cataloging procedures saved libraries.

So card catalogs had to be closed and "frozen." Nobody can expect a library to maintain sequences of alphabetized cardboard for a collection that is growing, as some currently are, at a rate of five hundred items a day. Even at the beginning of this century, a writer for the *Boston Evening Transcript* could playfully fret about the unwieldiness of card catalogs:

> As these cabinets of drawers increase in number until it seems as if the old joke about the catalogs of the Boston Public Library and Harvard University meeting on Harvard Bridge might become literally true, the mental distress and physical exhaustion suffered by those consulting one of them becomes too important to be disregarded.

And online catalogs, despite their neolithic screen displays and excruciatingly slow retrieval rates, offer many amenities. They do not grow mold, as the card catalog of the Engineering Library of the University of Toronto once did, following water damage. And they are harder to vandalize. Radical students destroyed roughly a hundred thousand cards from the catalog at the University of Illinois in the sixties. Berkeley's library staff was told to keep watch over the university's card catalogs during the antiwar turmoil there. Someone reportedly poured ink on the Henry Cabot Lodge cards at Stanford. The huge frozen card catalog of the Library of Congress currently suffers from alarming levels of public trauma: like the movie trope in which the private eye tears a page from a phone book at a public phone rather than bothering to copy down an address and a phone number, library visitors—the heedless, the crazy—have, especially since the late eighties, been increasingly capable of tearing out the card referring to a book they want. Indeed, one of the reasons that the New York Public Library had to close its public catalog was that the public was destroying it. The Hetty Green cards disappeared. Someone calling himself Cosmos was periodically making off with all the cards for *Mein Kampf*. Cards for two Dante manuscripts were stolen: not the manuscripts, the cards for the manuscripts. Card catalogs attract vandals because they are expressive of needful social trust and communal achievement, as are other common targets, such as subway cars, railroad bridges, mailboxes, and traffic signs. To the extent that a cluster of computer terminals linked to an online catalog protects a room full of older card cabinets by marginalizing them, they are performing a great service.

And of course an online catalog is, when viewed in just the right flattering light, extremely convenient. "It's wonderful," said Julie Miran, of Swarthmore's circulation desk, enamored of keyword searching: "It's like watching the war on CNN." I began the research for this article by dialing up an online university catalog from my computer and printing out a sixty-eight-page list of volumes relating to LIBRARIES—AUTOMATION—CASE STUDIES, LIBRARIES—AUTOMATION—CONGRESSES, and so on. Though it took ten times as long to view and reject a given irrelevant book or subject heading onscreen as it would have if I had a drawer of cards in front of me, and was able to riffle through it at medium thumb-and-finger speed, I didn't have to drive to campus and find a place to park and walk to that particular drawer in order to arrive at a useful preliminary idea of the domain of locally available knowledge concerning the demise of card catalogs. Online catalogs are wheelchair-accessible in the best possible way, and now—through Gopher software on the Internet—I can poke around in the catalogs from hundreds of libraries all over the world, despite the fact that I am not affiliated with a single one of them.

Why would I want to take a look at the online catalogs of libraries I may never actually visit? To find out what clever-clever names their administrators have given them, for one thing—possibly out of their belief that people get exasperated at CRT terminals in libraries, and curse at them, simply because people suffer from a subcortical fear of technology, and that an evocative human or animal or mythopoeic name, hallowed by the vernacular, will make everything better. Thus, the New York Public Library has CATNYP. There is BEARCAT (Kutztown University) and ALLECAT (Allegheny) and BOBCAT (NYU's Bobst Library) and CATS (Cambridge). There is VIRGO (the University of Virginia), FRANCIS (Williams College), LUCY (Skidmore), CLIO (Columbia), CHESTER (the University of Rochester), SHERLOCK (Buffalo State College), ARLO (the University of Colorado at Colorado Springs), FRANKLIN (the University of Pennsylvania), and Harvard's appropriately Eustace Tilleyish HOLLIS. There is BISON (SUNY Buffalo), OASIS (the University of Iowa), ORION (UCLA), SOCRATES (Stanford), ILIAD (Butler), EuclidPlus (Case Western), LUMINA (the University of Minnesota), and THE CONNELLY EXPLORER (La Salle). MELVYL (the University of California system) is named after Melvil Dewey; the misspelling was reportedly intentional, meant to emphasize the difference between Dewey's cataloging universe and our own. SUNY Brockport's Drake Memorial Library greets its users with a typographically generated image of a card catalog:

```
!                           !
!  [=]  [=]  [=]  [=]  [=]  !
!                           !
!  [=]  [=]  [=]  [=]  [=]  !
!                           !
!_____!
    !!                  !!
    !!                  !!
    !!                  !!
```

Your automated catalog, by DYNIX.
Copyright (c) 1992 by DYNIX, Incorporated.

Meanwhile, the cards from Drake's actual card catalogs are, according to a reference librarian I talked to in October of 1993, being used as scrap paper. The reference man gave a small, embarrassed laugh when he passed this piece of news on to me. And he is quite right to be embarrassed. Drake's physical catalog has been replaced by an eager-beaver screenful of exclamation points and bracketed equal signs, as if to insist on equivalency, when in fact *there is no equivalency*. The unfortunate truth is that, in practice, existing frozen card catalogs, which just sit there, doing no harm to anyone, are typically being replaced by local databases that are full of new errors (an early OCLC study found 1.4 errors per record input), are much harder to browse efficiently, are less rich in cross-references and subject headings, lack local character, do not group related titles and authors together particularly well, and are in many cases stripped of whole classes of specific historical information (e.g., the original price of the book, its acquisition date, its original cataloging date, its accession number, the original cataloger's own initials, the record of any copies that have been withdrawn, and whether it was a gift or a purchase) that existed free, using up no disk space or computer-room electricity, requiring no pricey software updates or daily backups or hardware service calls, right in the original Remington or Brodart wooden cabinets.

Think of yourself as a successful literary agent, with a big Ferris wheel of a Rolodex on your desk. You and your Rolodex go back fifteen years. It holds hundreds of names and numbers, many of which you have updated by hand when a writer or an editor has moved or got married or had a child or hired a new underling. Fond though you are of your Rolodex, it is hardly portable, and you are doing a lot of business on the other coast now. So you decide to get one of those electronic calendar-spreadsheet-address books—something along the lines of a Psion Series 3a, say. After careful planning, you freeze the Rolodex, and then you assign one of your interns the exacting task of keying into the Psion all the up-to-date information that your Rolodex contains. It takes the intern a solid week—there are four hundred and sixteen names. You spot-check the project as it progresses. The intern has made a few screwups here and there, reversed some numbers, made some typos in foreign addresses, but in general it's surprisingly clean work.

When this retrospective conversion is complete, however, a question arises. What do you do with the big frozen Rolodex? Burn it, pulp it, shoot it? It does take up a lot of desk space. Do you have a big party, and invite all the people in your Rolodex to join you on the roof of your building to drink champagne and tie their address cards to helium balloons and release them over West Fifty-seventh? No, because you are a literary agent, after all, not a publicist. And you quickly see that it would be an error to throw away your Rolodex cards right now, since you are going to want to refer to them from time to time in the months ahead, when there is a question of an electronic address's correctness. At one point, looking up someone's name in your Psion, you find that it isn't there: an undetected typo made by your assistant has displaced the record somewhere, hiding it from you. You find the address easily on the Rolodex. Not only that: the démodé Rolodex, you discover, groups things in a way that is at times more useful to you than Psion's rote technique. Rather than alphabetized solely by name, for instance, the old paper-based system offers you all your friends at Simon & Schuster together in one clump, a form of what librarians call "collocation."

Also, in a more reflective moment it occurs to you that there is considerable information on the Rolodex cards that didn't make its way into your new toy: old, crossed-out addresses, old phone numbers, old spouses, old editorial assistants who are now publishing titans in their own right. The very degree of wornness of certain cards that you once flipped to daily but now perhaps do not—since that author is drunk and forgotten or that magazine editor has been fired and now makes high-end apple chutneys in Binghamton—constitutes significant information about what parts of the Rolodex were of importance to you over the years. Your new Psion can't begin to tell you that: its addresses are ageless, as fresh and yellowy-gray as the current in a diode. Your Rolodex is a piece of literary history, in a way. It is also the record of some of the most cherished connections you have formed with the world. Would it be stretching things too much, you suddenly wonder, to call your Rolodex a form of autobiography—a manuscript that you have been writing these fifteen years, tinkering with, revising? Perhaps it is the only manuscript you will ever write. Throw it out? No, you will donate your Rolodex to your alma mater's library, valuing it at several thousand dollars in order to get a tax write-off, and the librarians there will recognize its importance to future scholars of late-twentieth-century publishing practices and will lovingly catalog it online, assigning it a Library of Congress call number and an appropriate list of subject headings.

Now imagine something just a little larger than your Rolodex. Think of an unbound manuscript, the only one like it, composed of a great many leaves of three-by-five-inch cardboard—a million of them, in fact—each leaf covered recto and sometimes verso with detailed descriptions of certain objects that the world has deemed worthy of organized preservation. The authors of this manuscript have worked on it every day for a hundred and twenty years. It is, then, the accreted autobiography of an institution whose job it is to store and retrieve books and book-like materials. Many of its authors were smart and careful people—perfectionists, wide readers, though by predilection keeping themselves as anonymous in their authorship as medieval cathedral builders. Some of them had specialized knowledge and idiosyncratic enthusiasms, which they worked into the pages of their creation by employing thousands upon thousands of "See" and "See also" pointers to other pages. Together, over the years, they achieved what one of their early masters, Charles Ammi Cutter, called a "syndetic" structure—that is, a system of referential links—of remarkable coherency and resolution.

The authors made one serious mistake, however. Although they had taken great pains to be sure that within their massive work every book and manuscript stored in their building was represented by a three-by-five page, and often by several pages, describing it, they had forgotten to devote any page, anywhere, to the very book that they had themselves been writing all those years. Their card catalog was nowhere mentioned in their card catalog. Dutifully, they had assigned call numbers to large-type Tom Clancy novels, to magnetic tapes of statistical data, to diskettes full of archaic software, to old Montgomery Ward catalogs, to spools of professional-wrestling magazines on microfilm, to blueprints, wills, contracts, and the archives of electronic bulletin boards, to pop-up books and annual reports and diaries and forgeries and treaties and realia of every description, but they left their own beloved manuscript unclassified and undescribed, and thus it never attained the status of a holding, which it so obviously deserved, and was instead tacitly understood to be merely a "finding aid," a piece of furniture, wholly vulnerable to passing predators, subject to janitorial, rather than curatorial, jurisdiction—even though this catalog was, in truth, the one holding that people who entered the building would be likely to have in common, to know how to use from childhood, even to love. A new administrator came by one morning and noticed that there was some old furniture taking up space that could be devoted to bound volumes of *Technicalities, The Electronic Library,* and the *Journal of Library Automation.* The card catalog, for want of having been cataloged itself, was thrown into a dumpster.

Now some history. In 1791, in Paris, the Revolutionary government, having confiscated a number of private and monastic libraries throughout France, became curious to know what interesting books it suddenly possessed. The Imprimerie Nationale issued an *Instruction pour procéder à la confection du catalogue* to those charged with watching over new state property in outlying departments. Inventorists were told to number every book in a library, and then to write down, on ordinary playing cards, each book's number, its author, its title, a brief physical description, and the name of the library where it could be found. (Aces and deuces, it was suggested, might be pulled from the deck and set aside for books with wordy titles.) These cards were to be alphabetized by author, strung together, and sent on to Paris.

In 1848, Anthony Panizzi, Keeper of Printed Books for the British Museum, had a similar notion:

> By an alphabetical catalogue it is understood that the titles be entered in it under some "headings" alphabetically arranged. Now, inasmuch as in a large library no one can know beforehand the juxtaposition of these headings, and it would be impossible to arrange them in the requisite order, if they cannot be easily shifted, each title is therefore written on separate "slips" of paper ... which are frequently changed from one place to another as required. It is self-evident that if these "slips" ... be not uniform, both in size or substance, their arrangement will cause mechanical difficulties which take time and trouble to overcome.

Slips of paper and decks of playing cards eventually gave way to drawers of annotated cardboard; these were employed, through the 1860s, not as ends in themselves, to be browsed by patrons interested in finding books, but as a convenient means for the staff to keep track of what it had, or to prepare for the publication of a formal catalog. For the ornate, expensively produced catalog in book form was the traditional way a library presented itself to the public—the way it entered, as it were, the library of libraries. And, as it happens, a more than perfunctory catalog of a library's holdings is an exceedingly difficult book to edit and publish. Charles Coffin Jewett, the librarian of the Smithsonian Institution, in his *Smithsonian Report on the Construction of Catalogues of Libraries* (1853), wrote:

> The preparation of a catalogue may seem a light task, to the inexperienced, and to those who are unacquainted with the requirements of the learned world, respecting such works. In truth, however, there is no species of literary labor so arduous and perplexing. The peculiarities of titles are, like the idiosyncrasies of authors, innumerable.

In 1850, the librarian of the American Antiquarian Society was asked to produce a new catalog for the society. "Men have become insane," the agitated librarian responded,

> in their efforts to reduce these labors to a system; and several instances are recorded where life has been sacrificed in consequence of the mental and physical exertion required for the completion of a catalogue in accordance with the author's view of the proper method of executing such a task.

One Sunday, feeling only semi-sane myself, I called up Jim Ranz, retired dean of the Libraries of the University of Kansas, from whose immortal monograph *The Printed Book Catalogue in American Libraries: 1723–1900* (1964) this last quotation is taken, and I asked him to comment on the passing of card catalogs. Mr. Ranz was not terribly concerned about their fate. "Retention of a card catalog would have to be a pretty low priority in most libraries," he said. What he really wanted to talk about was Charles Ammi Cutter (1837–1903), the author of what is in Mr. Ranz's opinion the finest library catalog ever made. Cutter's masterpiece is the five-volume catalog of the Boston Athenaeum, published between 1874 and 1882. "I'm not sure he wasn't the greatest cataloger that lived," Mr. Ranz told me. The work is 3,402 pages long, and is elaborately and commonsensically cross-referenced; it cost the Athenaeum almost a hundred thousand dollars to produce. It is still of interest and utility to historians—as is the card catalog for the Athenaeum, which Cutter also developed. So far, the library has held on to its original cards.

Surely, I insisted to Harvard's Dale Flecker, the Boston Athenaeum's card catalog, at the very least, ought to be preserved. "Oh, I don't know," Mr. Flecker replied. His indifference makes sense, in a way, since he couldn't very well advocate the preservation of the Athenaeum's catalog and at the same time defensibly jettison the older and equally rich public catalog at Harvard. The young Charles Cutter had given his energy to Harvard's cards, too; while working for Ezra Abbot, who was Harvard's assistant librarian from 1856 to 1872, he had refined his theories about how people actually perform subject searches and what they require from a library's finding list. In 1861, Ezra Abbot instituted one of the first card catalogs that were "freely and conveniently accessible," in his words, "to all who use the Library." By the turn of the century, the traditional bound catalog had become a technical impossibility for large libraries, and card catalogs, predominantly handwritten (despite the existence by then of early typewriters), were everywhere.

In January 1901 the Library of Congress began printing its catalog cards in quantity and selling them in sets to any library that wanted them. These cards—elegant in their own way, accurate, highly readable, and cheap—took off. Even Cutter himself (with good grace, since his advocacy implied the eventual death of his own artful system of subject classification) recommended the purchase of Library of Congress cards, writing in 1904 that "any new library would be very foolish not to make its catalogue mainly of them." And libraries obeyed. A 1969 study of 1,926 randomly selected cards, all plucked from drawers of the shelf list at Rice University's Fondren Library, found the following kinds:

    15 handwritten
 1,275 unmodified Library of Congress
    68 modified Library of Congress
   472 typewritten
    96 miscellaneous, describing maps, musical scores, serials, etc.

(This same pre-computer-age study, published by MIT, determined that the average number of cards in a drawer was 826, that the typical book represented by a card was 276.6 pages long, and that the growth rate of Rice's library holdings closely tracked that of the United States gross national product.)

The Library of Congress's handiwork dominated card catalogdom through the early seventies. In 1968, it was distributing about a thousand cards a minute, for around five cents a card. Meanwhile, Fred Kilgour, a chemist turned librarian, sensing that the Library of Congress was failing to exploit the full possibilities of its newly developed machine-readable cataloging techniques, formed OCLC and became, among many other things, the catalog-card printer for the world. (OCLC sprang up in Ohio, according to Kilgour, because "in Ohio, and in the eastern Midwest, people in general are more willing to accept calculated risk with reference to innovation.") Since 1970, OCLC has printed 1.8 billion catalog cards on its high-volume line printers: they're the ones with the distinctive, slightly jaunty typewriteresque typeface. Though they cost slightly more than Library of Congress cards, OCLC would automatically sort your duplicates any way you wanted—all together in one alphabet, say, or separately alphabetized for the subject catalog, the author-title catalog, and the shelf list. (A shelf list is a card catalog arranged in call-number order; catalogers use it to help them shelve like books with like.) Since the labor involved in filing cards is an enormous part of the cost of maintaining a card catalog, OCLC's adaptable presorting was a real advantage, and for years OCLC was esteemed as a card-printing service even by universities that (like Princeton) sniffed at the quality of its growing database.

But it was the massive database itself that became OCLC's real triumph. For a fee, a library became an OCLC member and got one or more dedicated Beehive terminals (advanced for their time, able to handle the diacritics that catalogers needed, when other computer interfaces generally offered only capital letters), each linked to Ohio. For two dollars per title, a member cataloger could look through OCLC's records to see whether the book before her had already been cataloged by somebody else—either by the Library of Congress (whose MARC records OCLC bought and loaded into its database) or by another member library. (Each library was identified by a three-letter tag.) If she found a record, and the record looked good, she would request that OCLC print up a set of cards for it and send them to her. In this way, a library could eventually relegate a good deal of the cataloging work that had once been performed by degreed professionals to lower-paid clerks and student assistants.

And the brilliance of Kilgour's enterprise was that if the cataloger did not find a record, she could undertake to describe the book herself, and contribute her work to the system as a "master record" for that book, for the good of all members. She wrote a sort of poem, following a set of rules more rigorous than a villanelle's; she sent it off to people in Ohio who published it for her; and then she got paid a few dollars—in the form of a cataloging credit against future OCLC charges. The more fresh "copy" a cataloging department offered OCLC, the cheaper its use of OCLC was, and thus there was plenty of incentive for all libraries, engaged in the creation of a kind of virtual community long before there were such things as Usenet and listservs, to pump up the burgeoning database. What began mainly as a handy, unilateral way of delivering the Library of Congress MARC files to member libraries turned into a highly democratic, omnidirectional collaboration among hundreds of thousands of once-isolated documentalists: currently, there are close to thirty million records in the database, only a quarter of which originally came from the Library of Congress, the majority being the work of nearly seven thousand member libraries.

But amid this public-spirited hubbub there were some signs of trouble. "Distributed computing," in the recent words of Paul Lindner, one of the architects of Gopherspace on the Internet, "is like driving a wagon pulled by a thousand chickens"—and distributed cataloging, although its principal database is anchored in central Ohio, exhibits a similar noisy, gabbling, drifting quality. Quality was, indeed, a serious problem from the start: predictably, some libraries were much more careful and skillful at describing books than others. Wright State University, out of misguided zeal or a lust for cataloging credits, reportedly pushed thousands of unwholesome records into the OCLC database—at least,

Wright State is often dumped on now, perhaps undeservedly, by the folklorists of OCLC history. Libraries began to "blacklist" institutions whose three-letter tags were sure signs of bibliographic corruption. "The scuttlebutt got around fast as to who did sloppy cataloging," one librarian told me. In truth, though, everyone made mistakes. The interactive, cooperative group authorship of a resource of this complexity was something utterly new, and since OCLC exercised no editorial control over the contributions pouring in from its members, the cumulative perils of Fred Kilgour's forward-thinking system took perhaps longer than they should have to emerge.

One source of entropy was OCLC's laissez-faire concept of the "master record." The very first attempt to catalog a book on the database, no matter how unmasterly, how inadequate it might be to the needs of other libraries, became by default the "master record" for that book. For years—until, in 1984, OCLC granted a small group of libraries enhanced-member status, allowing them to improve upon faulty or skimpy records they encountered on their own—any sort of change to the master record was a laborious manual process. If a cataloger noticed the typo herself a week after she had conclusively pressed the send key at her terminal, she could not (if another library had tagged the record with its initials by then) correct her mistake onscreen; she had to fill out an error report and mail it (not electronically but with a stamp) to OCLC. I have heard librarians and professors of library science mention errors enshrined in the OCLC database that they haven't bothered to take the time to try to fix—in some cases, serious errors affecting the retrievability of books to which they themselves have contributed.

The other serious weakness of the OCLC database was its lack of "authority control"—librarianship's grand term for the act of naming entities (people, churches, government departments, periodicals, subject headings, and so on) consistently. Assume, to take a simple example using a university database, that you are assigned the task of cataloging an eminently hummable document by a person named Pjotr Iljics Csajkovszkij. Who is he? Is he perhaps the same individual as P. I. Cajkovskij? And does P. I. Cajkovskij bear some intimate relation to P. Caikovskis? Could it be that Peter Iljitch Tschaikowsky, Peter Iljitch Tchaikowsky, Pjotr Iljc Ciaikovsky, P. I. Cajkovskij, Peter Iljitsj Tsjaikovsky, Piotr Czajkowski, P. I. Chaikovsky, Pjotr Iljics Csajkovszkij, Pjotr Iljietsj Tsjaikovskiej, Pjotr Ilitj Tjajkovskij, P. Caikovskis, Petr Il'ich Chaikovskii, 1840–1893, Peter Illich Tchaikovsky, 1840–1893, Peter Ilych Tchaikovsky, 1840–1893, and Peter Ilyich Tchaikovsky, 1840–1893, are actually all the same man? If so (and this degree of title-page variation is by no means unusual for voluminous authors, many of them less well known than Tchaikovsky), the computer has to be informed of that fact outright; otherwise, symphonies and string serenades will be sprinkled haphazardly over the alphabet and a searcher won't have any idea what he is missing.

Authority control has always bedeviled the makers of catalogs, and the bigger the catalog, the more eras of publishing history it covers, the hairier things become. For Sirine and Sirin and Nabokoff-Sirin, see Nabokov. For House & Garden, see HG. For Alexander Drawcansir, Petrus Gualterus, Conny Keyber, Scriblerus Secundus, John Trottplaid, and Hercules Vinegar, see Fielding, Henry (1707–1754). For Ogdred Weary and St. John Gorey, see Gorey, Edward (1925–   ). In the late seventies, the second version of the Anglo-American cataloging rules caused a convulsion of despair in libraries when it demanded that Samuel Clemens be officially called Mark Twain, just because more of his books appeared under his primary pseudonym than under his real name. The whine of power erasers was heard through the land. (In librarianship, "eraser lung" was the seventies equivalent of carpal tunnel syndrome.) It is safe to say, however, that the apostles of St. MARC completely failed to foresee how abysmally poor the computer would be at grasping the concept of human identity. A person—even a fairly inattentive person—paid to file cards in a card catalog all day can tell that "Alexander the Great, 356–323 B.c." is the same man as "Alexander, the Great, 356–323 b.c." and "Alexandria the Great, 356–323 B.C."; we would also expect him to sense the unitary presence behind cards for "Montagu, Lady Mary (Pierrepont) Wortley, 1689–1762" and "Montagu, Mary (Pierrepont) Wortley, Lady" and "Montagu, Mary Pierrepont Wortley, Lady, 1689–1762"—to use examples from one online catalog. "The card catalog," as Tom Delsey, of the National Library of Canada, wrote in 1989, "exhibited a relatively high tolerance for deviation from literal and logical norms. . . . Typographical errors or inconsistencies in headings could be silently corrected in the process of filing the card; added entries that did not match exactly the corresponding main entry on the card to which they were related could nevertheless be placed in their proper sequence in the file."

The OCLC database, on the other hand, was, until quite recently, intolerant of deviation. Authors get married, they receive honorific titles, they die and have a year put to the right of the hyphen. Or suddenly *The New York Times* starts spelling Mao Tse-tung "Mao Zedong." In the face of all this bewildering variability, the object of a catalog, as Charles Cutter himself suggested in his *Rules for a Printed Dictionary Catalogue,* is to group together, or collocate, all the works by a given writer, and all the editions of a given work by a given writer, and all the works about a given writer's work, and all the biographies of a given writer, in the proper groups and subgroups, rationally.

For instance, we would prefer (this example is from a search of Harvard's HOLLIS, which I did in October 1993), when attempting to view the books written by Alfred Tennyson, that they weren't arbitrarily distributed under three separately alphabetized, unpunctuated headings: TENNYSON ALFRED TENNYSON BARON 1809 1892 and TENNYSON ALFRED TENNYSON 1ST BARON 1809 1892 and TENNYSON ALFRED TENNYSON 1809 1892. Moreover, it would be nice if the first work listed as by TENNYSON ALFRED TENNYSON BARON 1809 1892 (in response to the command "Find Au Tennyson") were in fact a work by Alfred Tennyson, and not a work by Tuningius, Gerardus (1566–1610), called *Apophthegmata graeca, latina, italica, gallica, hispanica* ("Imperfect: title-page slightly mutilated"), that happens to be autographed on the front endpaper by Tennyson. And we would prefer that the second work listed as by Alfred Tennyson were not *The Kraken: for solo trombone,* by Deborah Barnekow, 7 pp. (1978). (Ms. Barnekow is right, though: if Tennyson's sea monster played an instrument, it probably would be the trombone.) It would be nice, too, if *Neuronal Information Transfer,* co-edited by Virginia Tennyson, didn't intrude between several books published by the Tennyson Society and a tempting entry for a work called "Tennysoniana"—an entry that, when I accepted it, plucked me from the Tennyson list and dropped me into a list of twenty-three books by SHEPHERD RICHARD HERNE 1842–1895, none of which was "Tennysoniana." (Many of these oddities mysteriously disappeared shortly before this article went to press, but there are thousands more. A quick check of HOLLIS on March 21, 1994, revealed that Bolingbroke, Villiers de L'Isle-Adam, Edward Bulwer-Lytton, and Bernard Berenson all have works wrongly segregated under at least three different forms of their names. Charles George Lamb's *Alternating Currents* and Charles W. Lamb, Jr.'s *The Market for Guayule Rubber* come between editions of Charles Lamb's *Essays of Elia*. And 462 records for works by Thomas Macaulay are separately alphabetized under *eight* versions of his name.) I have no doubt that Dale Flecker believed what he was saying when he told me that "the machine catalog is in almost no cases worse and in most cases better than the card catalog was." But in my experience, five minutes with any online catalog is sufficient time to uncover states of disorder that simply would not have arisen in what library administrators call a "paper environment."

When I visited OCLC, some of the staff freely admitted to me that card catalogs currently do a better job of collocation than online catalogs do. "We're only partway there," Barbara Strauss, then a senior product support specialist at OCLC, told me. (Ms. Strauss "knows cataloging like your tongue knows the inside of your mouth," one of her colleagues said.) Her boss, Martin Dillon, the director of OCLC's Library Resources Management Division, recently told an interviewer that browsing the OCLC database using "keyword indexes, author indexes, and subject-term indexes sheds a harsh light on misspellings and errors of all types." A random sample in one 1989 OCLC study found a hundred and ten separate records for Tobias Smollett's *The Expedition of Humphry Clinker* in the database, nearly half of which were potential duplicates, kept separate by minuscule variations and typos. You have to feel sorry for the sophomore accounting major who is hired as a part-time "copy-cataloger" by his university's library, given a week's training, and handed an old edition of *Clinker* left to his university's library by an alumnus; you have to forgive him when, having drifted for a time through some of the seemingly endless, code-disfigured series of records, looking for a hit, he swears, gives up, and decides that it's faster just to make up another record on the fly, further cluttering the system with the hundred and eleventh "edition" of *The Expedition of Humphry Clinker.*

In the past few years, fortunately, OCLC has done a lot of automated cleanup. (The cleanup has to be automated, for, laments Martin Dillon, "when databases get as large as ours the contribution of individual humans is severely limited. The task is so large that no practical number of humans could handle it.") OCLC's "DDR" software—"Duplicate Detection and Resolution"—which was first installed in 1991, compares two records at as many as fourteen points and decides whether they stand for the same book, and thus should be fused, or not: if they differ only by an ellipsis (. . .) at the end of a truncated subtitle, say, or if one calls the publisher "Wiley" and the other calls it "John Wiley & Sons," the two become one. Common but hard-to-see typos like "Great Britian" and "Untied States" no longer force fictional duplicates. Over six hundred thousand redundant records are gone as a result of this work. And OCLC is now refining authority-control software that becomes more experienced—crisscrossed by more specific links among separate forms of the same person's name, for example—the more it works through new data. Millions of orphaned records have been united since 1990. (There have been a few embarrassments along the way, naturally: "Madonna" was globally altered by OCLC to "Mary, Blessed Virgin, Saint" as part of an authority-control routine—a change that, before it was corrected, caused problems for libraries interested in cataloging the recent work of Ms. Ciccone.)

But no matter how clever and successful OCLC's new quality-control efforts are, they mainly benefit those libraries that have not yet converted their catalogs. Countless old errors and inconsistencies are out there still, doing indolent mischief to scholarship in the local online catalogs of the libraries that "reconned" early on. Having paid millions in fees to OCLC for the use of its database, university libraries must now scrape up the cash to pay for authority-control software just so that their online catalog will perform the minimal tasks that Charles Cutter expected of the card catalog as a matter of course. The University of Chicago, even as it pays OCLC's RETROCON department to convert cards relating to the classics, philosophy, and American literature (at a cost of around two dollars a card), is contemplating paying Blackwell North America, Inc., a database processor, at least a hundred and fifty thousand dollars for a onetime authority-control grooming. (Errors and inconsistencies that appear after Blackwell is finished will persevere, of course.) The CARL Corporation, in Denver, Colorado, charges in the six figures to license its authority-control application to a major university library. This can all suddenly seem very unfuturistic and sad—sad because the cost of technology now consumes nearly 30 percent of the typical American library's budget, according to one 1992 estimate, forcing it to cut book purchases, reference staff, and skilled catalogers, and sad because the technology that libraries are actually buying turns out to be remedial software meant to correct the hash that earlier technologies have made of information once safely stored on paper.

What we have already begun seeing, in fact, especially at state universities with dwindling budgets, is a kind of self-inflicted online hell, in which the libraries are forced to continue to pay paraprofessionals to convert their huge card catalogs, since they've already pillaged the paper database to the point where its integrity is unrestorable, and yet they aren't able to afford the continuous hardware and software upgrades necessary to make the growing mass of online records function together adequately. They can't go back, and they don't have the money to go forward.

I'm thinking, for instance, of U.C. Berkeley. Berkeley has one of the best research collections in the world, and the quality of its cataloging over the past hundred and twenty-five years has been unusually high. Thus its card catalog and its shelf list were filled with richly detailed, accurate, intelligent cards, many of which were sent to Maureen Finn's RETRO-CON staff for conversion, sent back, and scrapped. But higher education is in serious trouble in California, and, as a result, Berkeley has chosen not to pay Maureen Finn for a premium RETROCON job. For about two dollars a card, Berkeley is getting a middling RETROCON—better than Harvard's but still very plain. Typically, an OCLC operator takes a Berkeley card, finds a match in the database as fast as he or she can, and accepts what the database offers, without being able to spend additional time entering the supplemental (or superior) information—the notes, the subject tracings, the holdings records—that the original card may contain. "The standards of conversion were, of necessity, because of lack of funds and lack of staff, not exquisitely high," one Berkeley employee told me. Because it can't afford better, Berkeley (like Harvard, like hundreds of other libraries) is paying OCLC not to improve but to denature and often to mediocritize its records of old and out-of-print material. "No matter how good it is," the employee said, "you throw away that card and, in some cases, accept something that's inferior."

Berkeley's subject catalog is already gone. Though it was more or less frozen in the 1980s, it was nonetheless very efficient for some kinds of searches: if the primary sources in your field were published in the eighteenth and nineteenth centuries, you don't want your retrievals spread among the thousands of irrelevant records that a mechanical database subject haul brings up. Any drawer of an out-of-date paper catalog represents the equivalent of a filtered computer search, a Boolean date-limited search, of a very sophisticated sort—in fact, one drawer represents the outcome of a kind of search that most online catalogs can't and won't ever be able to perform, since it offers clues to what books were in the library during different eras. If in seventy years a historian of science (say) wants to know whether some Nobel-laureate physics professor could possibly have seen and been influenced by a certain out-of-the-way Dutch mathematical monograph from the thirties that bears important similarities to the professor's work—whether, that is, it was part of the library's collection during the period when the professor was developing his ideas, or was acquired only after the professor's papers were published (perhaps acquired by the library as a gift from the professor's estate, because the professor was sent the monograph by the Dutchman himself, anxious to establish primacy)—the historian of science will have little chance of finding an answer to his question now, because the computer record will bear the (to him) meaningless date of the retrospective conversion of the card, i.e., sometime in the late eighties or early nineties, which has no relation to the time that the card was originally produced (and the book placed on the shelf), whereas the original card, even if it bore no direct date of creation, would have exhibited distinct features (typewriter style, format, cataloging conventions) that might have enabled a catalog-card paleographer to place it within a five-year period.

Why, then, did library administrators order the Berkeley subject catalog destroyed? Was it really just to have the space for eight study tables? Admittedly, eight study tables, incised with the inevitable obscene drawings, declarations of love, and reciprocal ethnic slurs, and populated with thirty or forty pre-midterm Psych 101 students making soft sighing noises with their pungent highlighters and burping like moss-gorged moose from time to time for comic effect, is a noble sight to have in a library. But is it a reasonable trade-off? Library administrators always use the magical phrase "out of space" when they want to get rid of something, but this in no way constitutes an argument. Libraries have been running out of space since the Sumerians first impassioned clay, because tablets and scrolls and manuscripts and books and microforms and computer disks tend to take *up* space, and their numbers inevitably grow. There are countless duplicates of old textbooks from the sixties and seventies on the shelves of most university libraries; scholarly and scientific journals probably pump more non-unique paper into Berkeley's library system every few months than was contained in its unique subject catalog. A library continues to buy books, and it selects what it throws out, on the basis of what it judges is of value to present and future users of the library: the need for space is merely a constant, S_{NEED}, in every decision to acquire or discard.

Administrators are singling out card catalogs, I think, not as a last resort but as a first resort, because *they hate them.* They feel cleaner, lighter, healthier, more polyunsaturated, when all that thick, butter-colored paper is gone. (One Berkeley administrator was heard saying, "Oh, we're just going to get rid of those junky old cards. Nobody uses the subject catalog anyway.") "Resist the impulse to burn those old cards," gaily cautions one article on retrospective conversion, since "the staff will experience withdrawal symptoms." The impulse to burn is there, it seems to me, because library administrators (more often male than female) want so keenly to distance themselves from the quasi-clerical associations that surround traditional librarianship—the filing, the typing, the shelving, the pasting, the labeling. Librarianship, they think (rightly), hasn't received the respect it deserves. The card catalog is to them a monument, not to intergenerational intellect, but to the idea of the lowly, meek-and-mild public librarian as she exists in the popular mind. The archetype, though they know it to be cheap and false, shames them; they believe that if they are disburdened of all that soiled cardboard, they will be able to define themselves as Brokers of Information and Off-Site Digital Retrievalists instead of as shy, bookish people with due-date stamps and wooden drawers to hold the nickel-and-dime overdue fines, with "Read to Your Child" posters over their heads and "February Is Black History Month" bookmarks at their fingertips. The proponents of computerization are such upbeat boosters of the library's potential role in the paperless society (Fred Kilgour once wrote that "not having to go to a library is a very important improvement in providing library service," and when asked in an end-of-career interview whether he felt there was any possible downside to library automation, he thought for a moment and replied, "I can't think of any negative effect") that library managers are encouraged to forget—are eventually frightened even to admit—that their principal job is to keep millions of used books dry and lend them out to people. When we redefine libraries as means rather than as places— as conduits of knowledge rather than as physical buildings filled with physical books—we may think that the new, more "visionary," more megatrendy definition embraces the old, but in fact it doesn't: the removal of the concrete word "books" from the library's statement of purpose is exactly the act that allows misguided administrators to work out their hostility toward printed history while the rest of us sleep.

Again, lest we become confused and forgetful, the function of a great library is to sort and store obscure books. This is above all the task we want libraries to perform: to hold on to books that we don't want enough to own, books of very limited appeal, unshielded by racks of Cliffs Notes or ubiquitous citations or simple notoriety. A book whose presence you crave at your bedside or whose referential or snob value you think you will need throughout life, you buy. Libraries are repositories for the out of print and the less desired, and we value them inestimably for that. The fact that most library books seldom circulate is part of the mystery and power of libraries. The books are there, waiting from age to age until their moment comes. And in the case of any given book, its moment may never come—but we have no way of predicting that, since we are unable to know now what a future time will find of interest.

So the incremental value of any one library book, even a rare and costly book, is tiny. The value of a huge collection isn't immeasurably increased by the acquisition of some out-of-date 1943 monograph on, say, granary design. And, conversely, the loss of any one book does no obvious harm to the whole. If an operator reverses two numbers in transferring the call number for a book from a card, causing you to look for the book on a shelf where it isn't, how terrible is that? The numerical typos and coding errors in online catalogs that (particularly in our era of closed, unbrowsable stacks) result in the complete disappearance of a title for the seeker—in its effective, though not physical, loss, its total unfindability, its sinking from view—can't compel outrage, or make headlines in academia, because most titles are in the minds of no more than five or ten people at a time. Sometimes the only person who has devoted fifteen minutes of mental receptivity and appreciation to a book, aside from its author and (with luck) its publisher, is the cataloger at the library who described it for the OCLC database. If a hundred thousand volumes disappeared at random from the shelves of a major university library in a single night, it might take weeks or months before graduate students compared their puzzling shelf experiences and slowly realized that something big, something on the order of *Fahrenheit 451,* had taken place. And yet, despite the insignificance of any individual wheat stalk of a book in relation to the total Nebraska of print, we demand that libraries exercise extraordinary care to preserve the ephemera they have on their shelves; we want them to get right to work microfilming or digitizing whatever starts crumbling; we want to trust that when we pass through a university library's entrance turnstile we aren't going to be missing too much of the inspiringly miscellaneous assembly of all that has been done and thought.

We certainly don't think that because a book may wait a decade or three between checkouts the library should necessarily cull it. And even if we do consent to the culling, and forgive the library for laying it out on the twenty-five-cent table, we are unlikely to agree that all copies of that book, in all libraries, private and public, ought to be rooted out and destroyed. We want the book to continue to exist somewhere, not to go extinct, because in some later ecosystem of knowledge it may be put to some surprising use—a cautionary use, a comic use, a cultural-historical use. And unforeseen secondary uses await the book that every library is certain to have self-published, as well. By studying Haverford's card catalog, Michael Stuart Freeman, librarian of Haverford College, was able to determine when his predecessors deployed their first typewriter (it was during the summer of 1916)—a tiny fact, perhaps, but one of sufficient interest to Freeman that he published a brief, thoughtful paper that discussed the history of typewriters in libraries. Freeman kept several handwritten cards as samples ("I save a few, because I'm a sentimentalist," he confided to me); but once his own passing curiosity was satisfied, he dumped the rest of his catalog.

Put in mind of mass extinctions and systems analysis, I got in touch with Jim Bradley, a programmer-analyst at the Computer Services department of Berkeley's College of Natural Resources and the author of an unfinished entomological dissertation entitled "Computer Tools for Pest Management: A Case Study of the Codling Moth." I asked him about retrospective conversion. "At universities, people get financial support if they're doing something sexy, and an awful lot of people that are running the over-all library operation today are not so much reference librarians as promoters of sexy modern technique," he promptly said. "The people who pay the bills want to get out of the stuff business. They don't want libraries to have anything in them." I fulminated ineffectually about the new typo layer in online catalogs, and he replied by making a point that seems to me undeniable: "I guess what we're really doing is we're having a short Dark Ages of scribalism as we transcribe from the original records into the electronic form. There's going to be that same blot on the historical record in our age as there was in the Middle Ages."

We should know better than to do this to ourselves. Or, if we do do this to ourselves—make a gigantic software upgrade of sorts from a paper database to an electronic one, because it's inevitable—we should, good systems managers that we are, have the sense to keep the old "software" around as a backup, in case Rev. 2.0 has strange bugs and doesn't perform as claimed. Charles Hildreth, a big name in library automation, said in a 1985 interview that "comparing the . . . card catalog to the online catalog is like comparing a bicycle to a space vehicle; they're both modes of transportation but that's where the similarities end." And the question is: Don't both modes have characteristic and complementary virtues? Which mode do you really want to ride to school? Which is going to have the brittle O-rings? Which is costlier? Which is likelier to drift aimlessly off into outer darkness? Which would you prefer to have your fourth grader ride? In a study of some fourth, sixth, and eighth graders carried out at the Downers Grove Public Library, in Illinois, Leslie Edmonds found that 65 percent of the kids' card-catalog searches were successful, versus only 18 percent of their online searches. No fourth graders used the online catalog successfully. (They were asked to look up things like "Fire Stations," "Insects—Poetry," "Octopus Pie," and "The Curse of the Blue Figurine.")

And grown-ups have problems, too. There are many more ways to go astray if you must type your way to the call number for a book than if you can flip mutely through cards to one. In 1984, Jean Dickson, in *An Analysis of User Errors in Searching on Online Catalog,* found that users of Northwestern's LUIS failed 39.5 percent of the time to type in a title at a terminal in a way that would bring up the record for something that actually existed in the database. She mentions, as one class of keyboard entries, "expressions of frustration" such as "Bleahh!" and "I hate this computer!" and various obscenities.

Under the "Bleahh!" subject heading may be adduced the Problem of Accelerating Typos. First, you type in a name and get no record. You think, Is it me, or is it that the library doesn't have anything by this person? You look at what you've typed. No obvious mistakes. You try again, several ways. Could this library possibly not have anything by this person? You have to decide whether it's a question of your having given a bad command, or a matter of a harder-to-spot typo, or a variant form of the writer's name. Some online catalogs require "A" as the author-search command, some

"A=," some "FI PA" (for "Personal Author"), some "FI PN" (for "Personal Name"), some "FI AU," some "AUT" or a number from a menu. Some screens respond as soon as you've typed the magical letter, some want you to press Return to deliver the command. It's as if you walked up to a card catalog you hadn't used in a while and weren't sure whether, in order to open a drawer, you were supposed to pull on the drawer handle, push on the drawer handle, twirl the brass end of the holding rod, or fart twice and sing "God Bless America" in a hoarse falsetto. Anger builds. You've forgotten whether you've already tried some variant, because your previous tries have disappeared off the screen. With anger comes poor typing. You can't know it, but you have finally found the proper command and the right form of the name—it's just that now you're so steamed that you're making basic typos every time. Finally everything gels, and you get 123 RECORDS RETRIEVED BY YOUR SEARCH, and then you learn, to your further dismay, how extremely long it takes to page through that seemingly small number of records ("at the simple touch of a button"), hitting Enter, Enter, Enter, or M, M, M, or F, F, F.

And if you persist in wanting to perform an online subject search, prepare for real uncertainties and dashed hopes and deep screen-scrolling tedium. The big technical push in the early development of online catalogs was for "known item" searching, in part because some card-catalog studies seemed to show that library visitors don't do all that much in the way of subject queries. Most of us come to the library, it was thought, with a specific writer or title in mind. In a monumental yearlong survey published in 1970, Ben-Ami Lipetz and his research assistants approached 2,134 pedestrians in the area of the card catalog at the Sterling Memorial Library at Yale, clipboard in hand, and politely said, "Please tell me precisely what you were about to do at the catalog the moment I interrupted you." Eighty-four percent had a title or an author or a specific bibliographic goal in mind, and only 16 percent were interested in browsing a set of subject cards. At least, that is what the respondents *said*. Subject searches are somewhat embarrassing, especially if you're a graduate student, and a graduate student at Yale (Yale graduate students used the catalog more than undergraduates, according to the survey, and faculty used it least): it sounds better to say that you want to take a second look at some curious laudanum stains on the endpapers of the Surtees Society's *Catalogi Veteres Librorum Ecclesiae Cathedralis Dunelm* than to say that you've got to quick get some call numbers for a whole bunch of books under the heading of "Feudalism." Subject searches are obvious confessions of ignorance; author-title searches aren't, or aren't so straightforwardly.

After online catalogs began appearing, though, it was possible to analyze searches without interviews, by studying the computer's transaction logs. And scholars like Pauline Atherton Cochrane, of Syracuse University, found that people were *very* interested in subject searches—more interested now, possibly, because they (erroneously) thought that the computer would be better at them than cross-referenced card catalogs were. Sadly, online catalogs are still terrible at subject searches; their noise level, in the informational sense, is incredible. Card catalogs have the sense not to shuffle together alphabetically the myriad subheadings for "labor" in the medical sense and "labor" in the AFL-CIO sense; the online catalogs I've seen don't. Card catalogs don't lump subheadings for traffic control in Alexandria, Virginia, together with ones for the lost library at Alexandria, Egypt, either. The "See also" card at the beginning of a set of subject entries in a card catalog didn't yank you to another part of the catalog, and abandon you there; it just suggested that you might want to expand your search in various directions if you didn't find enough where you stood. There is nothing like this yet in any but the best online catalogs, and even these have peculiarities. (If you look up "Greyhounds" on HOLLIS you won't be advised to see also "Dogs"; and if you look up "Dogs," and choose selection 1, which "retrieves information on the use of the above headings," you will puzzle over this brief note: "subdivision Dogs under groups of Indians, e.g., Indians of North America—Dogs.")

Nor is there an equivalent for guide cards—those beauties that stick up above the rest, with typed headings—which form a sort of loose outline of knowledge built into the trays, and help you to keep your bearings, and teach you as you go. Card catalogs are "precoordinated," whereas online catalogs are still almost entirely "postcoordinated," which means that the burden of figuring out how the universe of subjects ought to be organized has been shifted away from the cards and onto you, the user, who must now master Boolean "AND NOT" filters and keyword trickery and crabwise movement by adjacent call numbers merely in order to block avalanches of irrelevancies.

I have no doubt that it will all get better. That's the wonderful thing about software: it gets better. Soon it will be possible to browse big subjects like the Bible or Film or the Mafia or Pollution in a productive way, as we formerly could, instead of despairing when we get a message saying YOUR SEARCH RETRIEVED 1,028 RECORDS. A thousand records, remember, is only a little more than one card drawer. My fingers could arpeggiate Lisztlessly through them, the lead hand's fingers feeding card clumps to the trailing hand, scanning, rejecting, repositioning, in a minute or two. But online, a thousand records is instant death right now. "Studies of online catalog use and users have uncovered a pair of problems that seem to be endemic in today's online catalog systems," Ray Larson, a professor at Berkeley's library school (or, as it is now called, the School of Information Management and Systems), wrote conclusively in 1991:

> These are: (1) a large percentage of subject searches fail to retrieve any bibliographic records; and (2) when subject searches succeed in retrieving records, they often retrieve too much material for the user to evaluate effectively.

Larson cites an earlier study of his own in which he found that the average number of online records retrieved in his sample was 77.5, whereas the average number that users actually took a look at was 9.1. The "futility point" in online searches—the point at which you give up and go with what you have—is, because of screen fatigue and the sequential lethargy of system response, much lower than in card-catalog searches. The life of the mind suffers as a result.

Not so for experienced onliners, you may contend—those who have developed a feel for Library of Congress subject headings, and may even have the now indispensable four-volume *Library of Congress Subject Headings* open beside their keyboard—but if this is the case it is because, as Professor Larson neatly points out, "part of the experience acquired by 'experienced users' is frequent search failure and information overload when subject searching." Larson goes as far as to say that online catalogs "are, in effect, conducting a program of 'aversive operant conditioning' against subject searching by their users." You could, in fact, go Larson one better by hypothesizing that online catalogs are acting to reinforce the tendency toward mindless academic hyperspecialization, since any attempt to venture into areas in which one is a novice, using the library's basic search tool, is met with the sharp electric shock of a long search warning. Certainly it is truer now than ever that if you want your scholarship to be read, you had better find a way to maneuver it into the early letters of the alphabet, because online, nobody's getting much past the "G"s and "H"s.

Software engineers are clever and adaptable people. They have, more than most of us, profited speedily from their mistakes. We have leaped ahead from, say, the late-seventies computer catalog at the University of Toronto Library, which reportedly included a program to rotate any "Sir" beginning a name entry to the end of the name: the program not only moved all the stand-alone "Sir"s but bestowed involuntary knighthood on writers like Ernest Sirluck (who was a professor at the University of Toronto at the time and an editor of, among other things, Milton's *Areopagitica*), turning him into "Luck, Ernest Sir." Any day now, information retrieval will be a new and amazing experience: "For the first time the catalog user will be freed from the tyranny of the linear sequences of A-Z and 0-9," Michael Gorman headily writes, in an anthology called *Closing the Catalog*. We will cast off our letter fetters, he seems to promise, and soar. Envisioning what Gorman calls the "New Jerusalem" of the online catalog, I can fantasize about one that would include an aging-and-fading component, so that the older a given database record is, the yellower (or pinker, or ocean-bluer) the screen would be at its corners, thereby offering us some of the instantaneous secondary information that cardboard offers us now. (Word-processing packages would also benefit from what might be called AGE or OLD utilities— for Advanced Geriatric Engine and Optional Latent Dogearing, respectively.) And the more times a bibliographic record is called up by the users of the database, the darker will be

the accumulation of random "grime pixels" in the top margin—though never so dark that they would interfere with
legibility, of course, and every tenth retrieval might remove
one grime dot rather than add one, since handling wears
away previous deposits, too. We will be able to tour mind
rooms full of three-dimensional representations of catalog
cabinets by gesticulating with our data gloves like armchair
Shivas, so that we will have some intuitive sense of the size
of the collection we are interrogating, just as we do now
when we walk into the lobby of a library we haven't visited
before and size up its rows of card cabinets; we will have
ways to maintain a sense of where we are in the database, as
we do now through drawer and cabinet labels, through
guide cards, and through our subconscious feel for where
the rest rooms and the circulation desk are; we will have
screens whose resolution will be the equal of Library of
Congress printed cards, or even of handwritten cards; we
will be able to look at five or six records at a time, and to
move forward and backward through 826-unit clusters of
retrieved records with the rifflingly variable speeds we now
attain over semi-pliant paper. All this and more will be ours
in the years to come, assuming there is money to pay for it.
But it isn't ours yet, and Michael Gorman and his colleagues
in *Closing the Catalog* were foretelling the ways that online
techniques would free information retrieval from various
alphanumeric tyrannies almost fifteen years ago. Today, if I
take a stool in front of a University of California MELVYL
screen and type, for instance, BROWSE SU CENSORSHIP (meaning "Please show me the subject headings relating to Censorship"), this is what I get back:

> LONG SEARCH: Your search consists of one or more very common
> words, which will retrieve over 800 headings and take a long time
> to complete. Long searches slow the system down for everyone on

the catalog and often do not produce useful results. Please type HELP or see a reference librarian for suggestions.

If I type in BRO SU ROME—HISTORY, I get the same thing. So, too, if I'm curious about AIR POLLUTION or BIRTH CONTROL or PHILOSOPHY OF HISTORY or HISTORY OF PHILOSOPHY, or BIBLE—HISTORY, or even INFORMATION STORAGE AND RETRIEVAL. If I need some books on LINGUISTICS or FOLKLORE and ask MELVYL what it has, and I do so during normal working hours, I get a slightly different message:

> PEAK LOAD RESTRICTION: Your search consists of a common word which would retrieve over 6,400 headings and would slow down the system. During peak load periods, your search cannot be completed. You may reissue your search to make it more specific, or try again during the evening or early morning.

And if I try to narrow the search by typing, say, FI XS ROME—HISTORY (meaning "Please show me only those subject headings that *begin* with the words 'Rome—history' "), I will be sure to miss many excellent books, including Robert Brentano's *Rome Before Avignon,* which is cataloged under "Rome (Italy)—History—476–1420." Nor will title-keyword searching solve my Roman history problems with MELVYL: to get one possible sample of things I will miss if I place too much confidence in keywords and exact subject headings, I can type FI SU (ROME HISTORY) AND NOT XS (ROME HISTORY) AND NOT XS (ROME ITALY HISTORY) AND NOT TW (ROME) AND NOT TW (ROMAN) AND LANG ENGLISH, which translated means, "Please show me all the books with subject headings that contain 'Rome' and 'history,' but whose subject headings do not *begin* either with 'Rome—history' or 'Rome (Italy)—history' and that do not contain either the word 'Rome' or 'Roman' anywhere in the title, and that are in English." Even after this narrowing-down (which takes 97 search cycles and should only be performed after midnight, when few are roaming the system), I will see over 130 books, among them Peter Brown's *Power and Persuasion in Late Antiquity* and Gillian Clark's *Women in the Ancient World*—books I would have missed had I been too uncritical a keyword devotee. And MELVYL is, in fairness, a much more flexible and powerful system than many, especially in its ability to marshal long chains of Boolean exclusivity: if you do an analogous FI KSH search (KSH refers to Keywords of the Subject Heading) on Harvard's catalog (which cheats by defaulting to a limited, initial-word subject search very similar to MELVYL's XS, and which disallows commands longer than one line), HOLLIS too will choke on topics like ROME—HISTORY, or ETHICS—HISTORY, or AGRICULTURE—HISTORY, or COSMOLOGY, or BOOKS AND READING, or COINS, or TEXTILE (but not TEXTILES), or TOBACCO, or LIBRARIES, or our friend INFORMATION STORAGE AND RETRIEVAL. Each time, HOLLIS comes back with its HELP OVERFLOW screen, saying in boldface: "Your search retrieved more than the maximum number of items the system can display."

None of those general headings deserve a system rebuff. All of them are eminently reasonable ways to begin a search—a search that we who have research papers, or dissertations, or mere essayistic tirades due might like to begin in the next few days, not two or five years from now, when the online catalog has been improved to the point where it can comfortably accommodate this sort of inquiry. If there is already a big wooden machine in the library that is able to point us quickly in a few directions without calling us users of "common" words and thereby hurting our feelings, maybe we should keep it. The fact that the card catalog is no longer the necessary first stop in a visit to the library shouldn't doom it. If nobody uses it for months at a time, stuff it away in the rare-books wing, or sequester it on a seldom visited subbasement floor, crowded humbly among the Z shelves (Z is the call letter for bibliography and library science), like Mike Mulligan's obsolete steam shovel. Or it could be pushed off to the far end of the reference room (one row of cabinets bolted on top of another to halve its footprint, the entire structure festooned with warnings that its information is not current), where it will gather exactly the same amount of dust as other big and usefully out-of-date library catalogs: Cutter's, or the British Museum's *General Catalog of Printed Books,* or the magnificent pea-green-and-gold wall of the 756-volume *National Union Catalog, Pre-1956 Imprints.*

There are still some librarians who do what they can to save the card catalogs under their care. The librarian of the small, separate library-school library at Berkeley, Patricia Vanderberg, stores her two card cabinets in the stacks, out of range of the administrative eye, but she has kept them. They were edited by a now retired librarian named Virginia Pratt. Ms. Pratt "did some special things to that catalog," Patricia Vanderberg told me. The university, however, which is in a self-mutilating mood these days, plans to merge the library-school library with the main library, and before the merger there will be a severe culling; the card catalog will almost certainly be thrown out. But for the time being, if some afternoon, depressed by thoughts of cardnage now in progress, you were to travel to the stacks of the library-school library, you could restore your good spirits by contemplating an unharmed, unshrunk, fully operational (though frozen) subject catalog.

Fifty drawers compose it. They are made of blond wood. Pull out one of the "C" drawers, the one labeled "Catalogs." Here are several guide cards: one for "Catalogs," one for "Censorship," one for "Children's Literature." Before you have read or touched a single card, you have learned something important about the library-school library, and even possibly about librarianship in general: the edges of the cards following the guide cards for "Censorship" and "Children's Literature" are dark with handling, whereas the ones following "Catalogs" are not. Thus "Censorship" and "Children's Literature" have over the years been of more interest to library-school students than "Catalogs" has. This is a surprise—at least, it was a surprise to me. Maybe it's one reason we're in this pickle.

And abruptly you realize, looking at these expressive dirt bands, that even the libraries, like Harvard and the New York Public Library and Cornell, who microfilmed or digitized some of their cards prior to destroying them, have—by failing to capture any information at all about the relative reflectivity of the edge of each card—lost something of real interest, something eminently studiable. Who knows what a diligent researcher who photographed (from above, on a tripod) each close-packed drawer of Harvard's Widener catalog with a high-contrast camera might find out, were he to correlate his spectrographic dirt-band records with the authors that, as distinct clumps, exhibited some darkening? Of course the "Kinsey" cards would be thoroughly dirt-banded—but which others? This is, or was, a cumulative set of scholarly Nielsen ratings for topics at twentieth-century Harvard that is perhaps more representative than any other means of surveying we have. Instead of tossing its catalog out, Harvard ought to have persuaded a rich alumnus to endow a chair for dirt-band studies.

If, though (back at Berkeley's library-school library), you now take a glance at those two other major subjects in the still-extant subject catalog, the ones more popular than "Catalogs," and begin by flipping the "Censorship" guide card toward you, you will note that Virginia Pratt has prepared some helpful "See also" material, typed with a red typewriter ribbon on several different models of typewriter:

Censorship
SEE ALSO
Libraries—Censorship
Liberty of the press
Expurgated books
Prohibited books
Condemned books
Books and reading for youth—Censorship
Government information
Children—Books and Reading—Censorship
Book burning
Pornography

A second card goes on, still in red:

Censorship (continued)
SEE ALSO
Freedom of information
Audio-visual materials—Censorship
Libraries—₁Place name₁—Censorship
Young adults—Books and reading—Censorship
Textbooks—Censorship
School libraries—Censorship

And then in black there follows:

For additional material on this subject see:
   Vertical file: Intellectual freedom

MELVYL will retrieve all the subject headings in this helpful
list that have the word "censorship" in them, because that is
what it mechanically does, but it will not give you any of the
others, since their access relies on the perceived relationship
between two categorical concepts rather than on rote text
strings. As a result, once this subject catalog is thrown out,
Milton's *Areopagitica,* a work of brilliance and occasional
syntactic impenetrability protesting the 1643 act of Parliament that required the seizure of "scandalous, unlicensed,
and unwarrantable" books and pamphlets—a work, surely,
of some small importance to the history of political censor-

ship—will, because MELVYL lists it under "Liberty of the Press" and "Freedom of the Press" instead of under "Censorship," not come to the attention of a library-school student, or any student, interested in writing a paper on the topic.

Similarly, the "See also" card that Virginia Pratt wrote for "Children's Literature" lists sixteen sensible cross-references, including pointers to "Fairy Tales," "Storytelling," "Bibliotherapy," and "Juvenile Literature"; MELVYL, on the other hand, offers an unmanageable and indiscriminate list of 745 subject headings, none of which is "Fairy Tales" or "Storytelling"—though MELVYL will obligingly refresh your screen with another disorderly list of 306 subject headings for "Fairy Tales" if you think to ask it to. Ms. Pratt's card catalog is good, it is smart, it knows what we need to know—it wants to help us be better librarians. Before we junk it, forcing students to depend instead on subject headings bought in bulk from pooled databases that have been edited not by minds but by iterative software routines, perhaps we should read a little of *Areopagitica,* since the cards were kind enough to refer us there:

> We should be wary therefore what persecution we raise against the living labours of publick men, how we spill that season'd life of man preserv'd and stor'd up in Books; since we see a kinde of homicide may be thus committed, sometimes a martyrdome, and if it extend to the whole impression, a kinde of massacre, whereof the execution ends not in the slaying of an elementall life, but strikes at that ethereall and fift essence, the breath of reason it selfe, slaies an immortality rather than a life.

It is not just crankish and extreme to say that a "kinde of massacre" is going on in libraries right now. There is the exuberant recycling of the card catalogs themselves; and then there is the additional random loss of thousands of books as a result of clerical errors committed in disassembling each card catalog, sorting and boxing and labeling its cards, and converting them en masse to machine-readable form—a kind of incidental book burning that is without flames or crowds and, strangest of all, without motive. If a great research library, in the process of converting two million cards, loses track of one tenth of 1 percent of them, say, severing our access to two thousand books that offend nobody, we can only shake our heads in astonished perplexity. "A few things"—i.e., cards—"that weren't converted got dumped, but, you know, that's the nature of life," Judith Brugger, of Cornell, said to me; and every cataloger and technical-services person I asked admitted that there are now books in their library that, owing to inevitable slipups of one sort or another, aren't in the online catalog that is supposed to help you find them. Or there is an online record, but the book isn't on the shelf where the computer says it is. Barbara Strauss, formerly of OCLC, told me that the flaws in online catalogs have created a whole new class of in-house dislocation specialists: people who, like the editors of corrupt codices or of early editions of Shakespeare, are able to divine from the existing computer record what sort of text-entry mistake might have been made, and hence where they should begin to look in the stacks for those ghost books that they know they own but just can't find.

The current situation is not without a few hopeful signs. Cornell's Judith Brugger was nearly ready, I felt when I talked to her, to recognize why her own university's card catalog—whose brutal pollarding proceeds apace—deserves to be spared. Ms. Brugger has degrees in Russian and English as well as in library science, is capable of a passing reference to Derrida, and is full of ideas about how to modify the Anglo-American cataloging rules so that librarians can venture forth and catalog the Internet, which needs it. Twice, she startled me by using the words "art form" in reference to card catalogs, something that nobody else had done. And she mentioned, as an example, the Library of Congress catalog, so "brown and beautiful and round" that it could "bring tears to your eyes." She spoke reverently of the tiny catalog at the Keats-Shelley Memorial House in Rome, which is "quaint and perfectly specific and completely comprehensive." She has even kept some handwritten cards as souvenirs of an earlier job. And yet, amazingly, of her own library's cards she said simply, "They have to be burned." Cornell possesses what is, in her estimation, "the Velveteen Rabbit of card catalogs." It has *mismatched cabinets*. It has *broken drawers*. It is *incorrect*.

Mightn't it, I asked, develop a hint of saving quaintness over the next fifty years? Mightn't there be ways that future historians could extract unexpected insights about life and thought and prevailing mental taxonomies by analyzing how Cornell once classified books, and how it revised its classifications over time? "We don't see any research value in archaic card practice," Ms. Brugger told me. "User studies are the thing now, not particularly strategies for recording data." (A few days later, she called to be sure I understood that she was speaking on her own behalf, and not on behalf of Cornell, which, it seems, has no official policy vis-à-vis its card catalog—although it's hard to see how a dumpster can be construed as a value-neutral storage site.)

But when Ms. Brugger said that user studies were the thing now, I thought I heard her waver: Woopsie, she seemed to be thinking, maybe user studies won't always be the thing? Maybe paper database strategies will be very hot in twenty-five years? What I took to be a truly hopeful sign, though, was Ms. Brugger's unexpected metaphor: Cornell's card catalog equals Velveteen Rabbit. That beat-up, brown-and-white spotted, sawdust-stuffed hero of Margery Williams's book for children is a *sympathetic* figure, who becomes more precious and indispensable to the Boy who owns him the more his fur wears away and his tail comes unsewn and his boot-button eyes lose their luster. The only way for a possession, a toy, to become "Real," the Skin Horse explains to the Velveteen Rabbit, is for it to be loved:

> "Generally, by the time you are Real, most of your hair has been loved off, and your eyes drop out and you get loose in the joints and very shabby. But these things don't matter at all, because once you are Real you can't be ugly, except to people who don't understand."

When the Boy falls ill with scarlet fever, and the doctor orders the gardener to burn the threadbare, germy Velveteen Rabbit, the Velveteen Rabbit grows sad and sheds a tear on the ground. Out of the tear, a flower grows, and out of the blossom of the flower there appears a magic fairy, who saves the Velveteen Rabbit from being burned by changing him into a real rabbit. This may or may not be a sappy story, but as an allegory of card catalogs it works fairly well. It goes something like this. The User loves his Velveteen Catalog so much that it begins to show signs of wear and tear: broken drawers, mismatched cabinets, out-of-date subject headings, worn cards. The User sickens financially, and he is unable to keep a watchful eye on the Velveteen Catalog. A Doctor of Technical Services orders the Velveteen Catalog burned for the User's own good, and replaced with a new, more antiseptic reference toy. Awaiting its fate, the Velveteen Catalog lets fall a single drawer, out of which blossoms a savioress, who helps the Velveteen Catalog escape into the stacks by transforming it from a Real catalog into an even Realer art form. A moment's reflection suggests that Judith Brugger secretly sees herself—

unbeknownst even to her—not as the cold-hearted torcher of Cornell's cards, but as their salvation.

And it's a good thing, too, since even non-Cornellians may remember one especially eminent, especially studied user of the Cornell catalog during its glory days: V. Nabokov. He and his fictive friend Timofey Pnin would regularly withdraw the heavy Slavic Literature card trays from the "comprehensive bosom of a card cabinet" back in the forties and fifties, and, on the wings of a hundred typewritten, time-and-space-spanning cross-references, would overleap the irrelevant ocean and return for an hour or two to green, mythic, pre-Revolutionary Russia, inhabited by lost leading lights like "Kostromskoy" and "Zhukovski," and Aleksandr Pushkin. The very cards that Nabokov turned and pondered while he worked on his translation of *Eugene Onegin* are, as far as I have been able to determine, still in place in Cornell's shabby-genteel catalog. The library would be well advised to keep them there.

But the real reason to protect card catalogs is simply that they hold the irreplaceable intelligence of the librarians who worked on them. Kathryn Luther Henderson, a professor at the library school of the University of Illinois at Urbana-Champaign, told me, "I've made catalogs I've been very proud of, or had a hand in making them." Her work, and Virginia Pratt's work, and the work of all those other people who spent every weekday thinking about the interconnectedness of the books around them, deserves praise and admiration, not clear-cutting. "It's going to be another generation before we realize that we've done this, and what we've done," Professor Henderson said. When I talked to her, she told me that she had some cards that were produced, she thought, in the 1850s for the Harvard catalog. "If somebody came into my office and I weren't here, they'd probably throw them out," she said.

There are other, higher-volume card hoarders, too. One of Maureen Finn's operators at OCLC worked on the retrospective conversion of chunks of a catalog from the University of Washington. The university didn't want the cards returned— they wanted OCLC to toss them out on the spot. But this operator (too reticent to consent to an interview with me) didn't go for that. He had looked carefully at the words on those cards; he had reached an understanding with them. He is, according to Maureen Finn, currently storing portions of the University of Washington's card catalog in his apartment.

But the biggest and most heroic hoarder of them all is Tom Johnston. Mr. Johnston is the painter and conceptual artist who, simply because he asked for them, is receiving hundreds of thousands of cards from Harvard's Widener Library. The real treasures, in a sense, of the now incoherent Widener catalog are or will be his, for he is currently being sent the cards representing, in part, seldom borrowed books that the library is moving to off-site storage. I reached Mr. Johnston in October of 1993, at a number in France, and asked what he plans to do with them all. He was spending several months at a huge, empty château in the Sauternes region; the pieces of the Widener catalog, however, were arriving steadily (much to the dismay of his secretary) at the Department of Art at Western Washington University, where Mr. Johnston teaches. Of course he could, he said, have them forwarded to France, and paper the rooms of the Château Suduiraut with them, or dig a trench a mile long and bury them there, but so much of contemporary art destroys things, and he has decided that he isn't interested, this time, in destruction for artistic ends. Still, he does want to "get them in front of the public," somehow. There is a beautiful museum in Bordeaux; he was considering writing a proposal to create a "really nice" conceptual installation with the cards there.

Exactly what sort of installation he hasn't figured out yet. (He has the cards, but Harvard, with its finely tuned sense of relative worth, kept the cabinets.) Mr. Johnston's previous work has often played with bibliographic themes: he made, for example, a series of large, geometric paintings that were hung in pairs. "If you look at them a certain way, you might see a book," he told me. More recently, he solicited pieces of hair—strands, braids, and dreadlocks—from strangers and acquaintances and taped them onto selected pages of a Gallimard edition of Camus's *L'Etranger*. (The book still closes, but not completely.) When one of the "C" boxes arrived from Harvard, just before Johnston left for France, he looked up the cards for Camus. "There's no rod holding them in. You just pull it out, read it, turn it over, sometimes there's notes on the back. . . ." He doesn't think, however, that he will be taping hair to the Camus cards, because of his personal vow to do no harm. He is a graduate of the University of California at Santa Barbara. (UCSB, incidentally, finished throwing out its main catalog in the summer of 1993.) The Harvard cards come packed in old memos from OCLC's RETROCON folks announcing softball games, potluck dinners, and paper-airplane contests, and Johnston is saving these crumpled communiqués, too, true antiquarian that he is.

He is weighing the possibility of inviting international artists and "thinkers" to send him their ideas about what should happen to his sizable collection. Though he is pleased to have it—"Think of all the people who have touched those cards!"—he is concerned about how much of his studio it will eventually occupy, about the hundreds of boxes getting out of order, about whether he'll go crazy having taken on this responsibility, and about the substantial cost of postage, which he, rather than Harvard, is voluntarily bearing. "I think I owe them money," he said. He wonders what the reaction will be when the world learns what he now legally owns. Maybe Harvard will suddenly decide that it misses this large, conveniently packaged core sample of its history and will ask for it back. "That would be fine, too," Mr. Johnston said.

Maybe, in fact, the riskiest, most thought-provoking piece of conceptual art that anyone could create out of these found materials is the original card catalog, enclosed in its own cabinets, sitting undisturbed somewhere within the library it once described.

(1994)

Books as Furniture

On the cover of a recent mail-order catalog from a place called The Company Store, a man and a woman in white pajamas are posed in the middle of a pillow fight. But there isn't one feather in the air, because The Company Store, of La Crosse, Wisconsin, sells new pillows—not stale, corrupt, depopulated pillows from some earlier era of human insomnia, but fresh, unashamedly swollen dream-bags corpulent with clean, large-cluster white goose down of a quality that only European white polar geese can grow. The Company Store also sells things like new flannel blankets, new bed wedges, and new baffled-box comforters. They are not in the business of selling beat-up editions of forgotten nineteenth- and early-twentieth-century books.

But in another way The Company Store is in fact a used-bookseller—or at least the people there are committed book propagandists—since more than twenty old volumes appear in the pages of the catalog. On top of a pile of five folio-folded Wamsutta sheets in Bluette, Black Cherry, Ivory, Sunset, and Onyx, there sits a worn oblong shape that looks to date from about 1880, with a pair of wire-rimmed glasses resting on it—glasses that might be used to read the pages they surmount. Sadly, it isn't quite possible to make out the title on the book's spine. But the title in another picture in this catalog—a very small photograph on page 66—does, just barely, cross the threshold of decipherability. The catalog designer has reversed the negative, so that the letters are backward, and the words they spell are partly covered by a finger, but if you look closely you can still identify which book, out of all the books that have ever been published, is lying open facedown on a white-pajamaed thigh—the thigh, it seems, of the woman who was first seen pillow-fighting on the cover. Now she is alone, lost in a fiction-inspired reverie, leaning against a vertical pillow prop with low, stumpy arms that is helping her sit up in bed: one of those readers' pillows that my wife and her college friends used to call "husbands." The woman is in the middle of reading *The Wood-Carver of 'Lympus,* published in 1904 and written by someone named Mary E. Waller.

I went to a big library and took the elevator to the lowest level of the underground stacks, and found there a copy of *The Wood-Carver of 'Lympus* identical with the one in the picture. The novel is about an unsophisticated high-altitude apple farmer named Hughie, who lives in the Green Mountains of Vermont, on Mt. Olympus—or Mt. 'Lympus, as the locals call it. A falling log has left Hughie crippled in some serious and vaguely Hemingwayesque way, so Hughie, with marriage now out of the question, teaches himself wood carving, aided from afar by cultured friends. They forward him trunkfuls of books and reproductions of European art: he reads Carlyle and George Sand and Browning and Bret Harte, and he stares attentively at a photograph of Michelangelo's *David;* and, little by little, under this mail-order tutelage and influence, Hughie succeeds in elevating himself from limping amateur whittler to Olympian panel artist and wainscoteur. One of his correspondents, Madeline, on her way through northern Italy, sends him a set of carved black-oak bookshelves. She writes him, "I like to imagine all those books you have been gathering and making yours on these special shelves."

I've been thinking about bookshelves myself lately, and imagining the shelves one might fill by searching through mail-order catalogs for the books they use as props (often searching at extremely close range: part of the delight comes in figuring out, with the aid of tiny clues and keyword computer searches, the identity of a book whose title at first seems totally illegible), and I've been thinking, too, about what our mail-order catalogs and our bookshelves, those two affiliated regions of cultural self-display, reveal about the sort of readers we are, or wish we were. We are not, clearly, whatever The Company Store would have us believe, casual bedtime consumers of the novels and travel books of Mary E. Waller. *The Wood-Carver of 'Lympus* went through at least twenty-three printings after 1904, according to the copyright page—which would have made it a big book for Little, Brown—but my copy was last checked out on January 19, 1948, and was returned on January 20: too promptly, one suspects, to have been read. The model in the white pajamas and I could be the only two people who have read, or pretended to read, this work in several decades. And yet a very small image of it has been delivered by bulk-rate mail to thousands of households. In another picture in the catalog, the pajama woman is asleep, embracing a seventy-two-inch-long body pillow: she is dreaming, needless to say, of disabled mountain men and the bookshelves full of Carlyle that taught them everything they know; *The Wood-Carver of 'Lympus* waits on her bedside table.

Nor is The Company Store alone among mail-order catalogs in giving prominence to the old or little-known work of literature. I counted thirty-six hand-me-down books, none with their original jackets on, in fifteen different settings, in the Crate & Barrel catalog for the spring of '95. The books lie open on chairs, on hammocks, on the floor, as if whoever was reading them had left off briefly to check the status of an earth-toned lentil soup; on their pages rest studiously haphazard placeholders—a shell, a twist of ribbon, an apple, a daisy. The Crabtree & Evelyn catalog for spring offers a pair of three-and-a-half-ounce containers of Southampton Rose Home Fragrance Spray, which is a kind of highbrow air freshener, for seventeen dollars; its dignity is enhanced, and its price defended, by its placement next to a fancily bound Italian biography of Queen Elizabeth from 1965, whose title, translated, is *Elizabeth I of England: The Virgin with the Iron Fist*—itself not such a bad name for an air freshener. On page 28 of the spring Tweeds catalog, a woman wearing a nice cotton sweater holds open an unidentifiable clothbound book bearing visible, and quite beautiful, mildew stains. In one of the latest J. Crew catalogs, there is a literary interlude on page 33: a man in shorts and plaster-dusted work boots, sitting in a half-remodeled room—on break, apparently, from his labor of hammering and gentrifying—is looking something up in what close inspection reveals to be a *Guide Bleu* to Switzerland, probably from the forties, in French.

What is it with all these books? Isn't the Book supposed to be in decline—its authority eroding, its informational tax base fleeing to suburbs of impeccably edged and weeded silicon? Five minutes with the tasteful Pottery Barn catalog of March 1995 may be somewhat reassuring. A closed universe of about fifty books circulates decoratively in its pages. The Pottery Barn catalog's library may have been selected for the alpha-wave-inducing beige and blue-gray and dull red of its bindings, but the actual titles, which are nearly but not quite unreadable, sometimes betray reserves of emotion. In the tranquillity of a cool living room, a cream-colored book entitled *Tongues of Flame* appears, minus its jacket, on a shelf of the Trestle Bookcase, near the Malabar Chair. Then it shows up in some peaceful shots of iron end tables. Next, on the page that offers what the Pottery Barn's furniture-namers call a Library Bed—"a bed whose broad panels suggest the careful woodworking found in old English libraries"—a historical novel called *A Rose for Virtue* makes its quiet entrance, underneath a handsome ivory-toned telephone. Three pages later comes the big moment, the catalog's clinch: for, lying at the foot of the Scroll Iron Bed, open facedown on the cushion of the Scroll Iron Bench, as if it were being read, is a half-hidden volume that can be positively identified as *Tongues of Flame,* and leaning fondly, or even ardently, against it, at a slight angle, is *A Rose for Virtue.* Whether the rose's virtue survives this fleeting flammilingus, we are not told; it's enough to know that the two books, after their photographic vicissitudes, are together at last.

So I went to the library again, and checked out *Tongues of Flame.* It's a collection of short stories, by Mary Ward Brown, which was published by Dutton in 1986. (There is also a novel called *Tongues of Flame,* by Tim Parks, set in England, that came out in 1985, but the large pale-gold letters on the binding of the Dutton edition are unmistakable.) The title story is about a married woman who wants to help a stuttering drunk reform his life by taking him to church. Her program seems to work at first, but one evening the preacher delivers a sermon so potent it sends the alarmed man right back to the bottle; in a matter of hours, his clumsy cigarette-smoking has set fire to the church. "Save the Bible!" hollers one of the parishioners as the flames rise from the roof, and it is eventually saved. The author writes:

The wet pulpit, with the Bible still on it, had been brought out into the churchyard. Pews sat haphazardly about. Songbooks, Sunday School books, and Bible pictures for children were scattered on the grass.

Were it not for the color-coordinating book lovers at Pottery Barn, I would never have read Mary Ward Brown's short story—and it's worth reading, more flavorful, perhaps, for having been found circuitously. Nor would I ever have troubled to determine which hymn it is that contains the simple but stirring phrase "tongues of flame." It's from "Father of Boundless Grace," by the prolific Charles Wesley (Methodist, brother of John Wesley, and inspirer of William Blake), and it was probably written sometime in the 1730s:

> A few from every land
> At first to *Salem* came,
> And saw the wonders of Thy hand,
> And saw the tongues of flame!

And if I hadn't read *Tongues of Flame,* I might never have been reminded of the story of another, bigger book fire. It took place in London on Saturday, October 23, 1731, at two o'clock in the morning. What was to become the library of the British Museum—a set of about a thousand books and manuscripts, which included the collection of the old Royal Library, along with the fabulous accumulation of Robert Cotton—was shelved, far too casually, in a room in a house in Westminster, and was overseen (according to Edward Miller's *That Noble Cabinet*) by the son of the by then aged classical scholar Richard Bentley. The room below the library caught fire; tongues of flame found their way up through the wainscoting and reached the backs of the bookcases—or book presses, as they were often called—and, as the conjoined libraries began to sigh and crackle, the Speaker of the House of Commons, who lived nearby and had hurried over when he heard the clamor, plucked warm and smoking bundles of ancient parchment off the shelves and tossed them out the window to save them. Like Chuck Yeager, smoke-smirched but ambulatory after his plane crash at the end of *The Right Stuff,* Dr. Bentley himself emerged from the conflagration with the Codex Alexandrinus, the priceless fifth-century manuscript of the Greek Bible, in his arms. He was dressed in his nightgown, but he had apparently taken a moment, in the name of scholarly dignity, to slap on his wig. A hundred and fourteen books were ruined or lost that night—some of them "burnt to a Crust," many of them irreplaceable—and a number of the ones that had been flung out the window to safety were swept together into heaps of shuffled and water-damaged pages and boxed away. Librarians didn't succeed in restoring order to some of the surviving fragments until a century later.

And if I hadn't been reminded of that British Museum fire I wouldn't have been moved to reread the great book-fire scene in Mervyn Peake's novel *Titus Groan,* published in 1946, which uses some of the elements from the mythical prehistory of the British Museum. Here's how Peake describes the passing of Lord Sepulchrave's library at Gormenghast:

> The room was lit up with a tongue of flame that sprang into the air among the books on the right of the unused door. It died almost at once, withdrawing itself like the tongue of an adder, but a moment later it shot forth again and climbed in a crimson spiral, curling from left to right as it licked its way across the gilded and studded spines of Sepulchrave's volumes. This time it did not die away, but gripped the leather with its myriad flickering tentacles while the names of the books shone out in ephemeral glory. They were never forgotten by Fuchsia, those first few vivid titles that seemed to be advertising their own deaths.

Fuchsia and the others escape out the window, and the next morning we view the library's desolate remains:

The shelves that still stood were wrinkled charcoal, and the books were standing side by side upon them, black, grey, and ash-white, the corpses of thought.

Umberto Eco seems to have been inspired by this scene, right down to its studded book spines, and inspired, too, by the story of the British Museum fire, in writing the description of burning books which ends his big book, *The Name of the Rose.* "Now I saw tongues of flame [*lingue di fiamma*] rise from the scriptorium, which was also tenanted by books and cases," says Eco's narrator. And then, revisiting the ruined abbey years later, he reports:

> Poking about in the rubble, I found at times scraps of parchments that had drifted down from the scriptorium and the library and had survived like treasures buried in the earth; I began to collect them, as if I were going to piece together the torn pages of a book. . . .
> Along one stretch of wall I found a bookcase, still miraculously erect, having come through the fire I cannot say how. . . . At times I found pages where whole sentences were legible; more often, intact bindings, protected by what had once been metal studs. . . . Ghosts of books, apparently intact on the outside but consumed within.

How thoughtful of the Pottery Barn catalog to send its customers back on this short but fiery thematic mission, and at the same time to rescue Mary Ward Brown's *Tongues of Flame* from the prospect of absentminded immolation— flinging it out the window, as it were, toward us, simply by photographing it. Bookstores and book reviews deal with new books, and even antiquarian booksellers can only align old books on their silent shelves, where they wait for buyers. But the junk-mail catalogs—sent out by the millions to people who never asked for them but nonetheless look through them from time to time and puzzle over the versions of life they present—go further, extending to past books the courtesy of present inclusion, and surrounding printed fiction with life-size fictional rooms that resemble our own real rooms except that they are a good deal neater, costlier, and more literate.

We know that it's a lie. One of the larger pieces in the Pottery Barn catalog is the Sierra Armoire, made of wormwood and machine-flagellated pine. The armoire, pictured with one of its double doors ajar, is stuffed with a miscellany of books whose bindings glimmer from its shadows: a textbook of pathology from before the Second World War, an original hardcover of Bellow's *Adventures of Augie March,* Paul Horgan's *Citizen of New Salem,* a bound German periodical from 1877, and also—so deeply shadowed that only its width and the faintest hint of a typeface give it away—*Tongues of Flame.* There isn't a self-help book or a current best-seller to be seen, because the men and women who live in the rooms of the mail-order catalogs never read best-sellers. In fact, they never read paperbacks. Next to the picture, the description says, "Long before there were closets to house clothing, linens and books, armoires did the job."

Well, this is true. Bookcases, or book cupboards, were called armaria as early as the first century, when some books were still published—that is, multiply copied—on rolls (*volumina*) and stored on their sides, with little tags hanging from their ends that bore their titles. Seneca, who died in the year 65, rather scornfully mentions book-bearing armoires inlaid with ivory in his essay "On Tranquillity of Mind." And in one of the earliest surviving pictures of a book armoire, found in a manuscript called the Codex Amiatinus, from the eighth century (but possibly copied from an earlier, now lost manuscript, the Codex Grandior), the books, large and bound in red, lie flat on the shelves, with the doors of the armarium open. The picture is reproduced in John Willis Clark's *The Care of Books,* a monumental history of the bookcase, first published in 1901. Professor Clark also quotes from the Customs of the Augustinian Order, which required that the armarium be "lined inside with wood, that the damp of the walls may not moisten or stain the books," and that it be "divided vertically as well as horizontally by sundry shelves on which the books may be ranged so as to be separated from one another; for fear they be packed so close as to injure each other or delay those who want them."

In English, the word "armarium" relaxed into "almery" or "aumbry," as in this sixteenth-century account of life at Durham Cathedral:

> And over against the carrells against the church wall did stande certaine great almeries of waynscott all full of bookes, wherein did lye as well the old auncyent written Doctors of the Church as other prophane authors with dyverse other holie mens wourks, so that every one dyd studye what Doctor pleased them best.

Eventually, armoires came to look more like modern bookshelves, shedding their cupboard doors, but thievery and misshelving led to the collateral invention of another deterrent: book chains. The books were flipped around, with their fore-edges rather than their bindings facing outward on the shelf; rings were clipped or riveted to their front covers; and these rings were linked to surprisingly thick, dangling, Jacob Marleyesque chains, some short, some several feet in length, whose other ends encircled iron rods that ran horizontally in front of a shelf or across the top of an angled lectern. Michelangelo designed a chained library. A bookcase historian named Burnett Hillman Streeter, who was a canon of Hereford Cathedral in the 1930s, and a loving restorer of its chained library, reports that libraries at Cambridge remained on leash until the early part of the seventeenth century, while at Oxford the practice persisted until 1799. Samuel Johnson would have read chained books; and when Coleridge somewhere laments the impossibility of escaping the fetters of language—when he says, "Our chains rattle, even as we are complaining of them"—perhaps he has the memory of book chains specifically in mind.

So the Pottery Barn catalog is invoking centuries of monastic and academic tradition when it observes that books were once stored in armoires, as were clothes and linens. But can its copywriter truly believe that anyone is now going to keep a book collection behind the closed pine doors of a $999 cupboard? No. Catalog designers long ago learned for themselves and put into earnest practice the observation that one of Anthony Powell's characters made when he drunkenly pulled a glass-fronted bookcase down on himself while trying to retrieve a copy of *The Golden Treasury* in order to check a quotation: "As volume after volume descended on him, it was asserted he made the comment: 'Books do furnish a room.' " Catalog designers know perfectly well that books, if we are fortunate enough to own any, should be out there somewhere, visible, shelved in motley ranks or heaped on tables as nodes of compacted linearity that arrest the casual eye and suggest wealths of patriarchal, or matriarchal, learnedness. Books entice catalog browsers, readers and nonreaders alike, into furnishing alternative lives for themselves—lives in which they find they are finally able to perform that contortional yoga exercise whereof so many have spoken, and can "curl up with a good book."

What, then, will the Pottery Barn's armoire hold in practice? The catalog copy quietly goes on to note that this piece of furniture is "roomy enough to hold a 20″-deep television or stereo equipment (holes must be drilled in back)." Now we see: it makes a nice decorative envelope for a TV—but it can't be pictured performing that primary and perfectly legitimate duty, because that would interfere with the catalog browser's notion of him- or herself. What will make the browser pause and possibly lift the phone is the promise, the illusion, that the armoire is magical, that the spirit of those beautiful shadowy books in the picture will persist after delivery, raising the moral tone of the TV—in other words, that the armoire's bookish past will give the TV a liberal education.

It's undeniable that books furnish a room, and it's nothing to be ashamed of. They require furniture, in the form of bookshelves, but they are themselves furniture as well. "No furniture so charming as books, even if you never open them, or read a single word"—so Sydney Smith, one of the founders of the *Edinburgh Review,* and a devoted Victorian reader, told his daughter as they had breakfast in his library. By chance, the book immediately to the right of *The Wood-Carver of 'Lympus* where I found it in the library was something called *Bits of Talk, in Verse and Prose, for Young Folks,* published in 1892, by Helen Jackson. She devotes a chapter to tips on making rooms pleasant to live in. She recommends sunlight first, and then color, especially the color red:

> In an autumn leaf, in a curtain, in a chair-cover, in a pin-cushion, in a vase, in the binding of a book, everywhere you put it, it makes a brilliant point and gives pleasure.

She goes on:

> Third on my list of essentials for making rooms cosey, cheerful, and beautiful, come—Books and Pictures. Here some persons will cry out: "But books and pictures cost a great deal of money." Yes, books do cost money, and so do pictures; but books accumulate rapidly in most houses where books are read at all; and if people really want books, it is astonishing how many they contrive to get together in a few years without pinching themselves very seriously in other directions.

Hunca Munca and Tom Thumb, the Two Bad Mice in Beatrix Potter, try their best to maneuver a dollhouse bookcase holding a faux *Encyclopædia Britannica,* bound in red, into their mousehole, but it doesn't quite fit. At the age of eighty and between Prime Ministerships, William Gladstone became fascinated with the problems of book storage, and during a visit to All Souls College, Oxford, he "launched out on his theme one evening in the Common Room," in the words of one observer, "and illustrated his scheme of bookshelves by an elaborate use of knives, forks, glasses, and decanters." Gladstone was not entirely sure how England was going to shelve all the books it produced without its citizens' being, as he writes, "extruded some centuries hence into the surrounding waters by the exorbitant dimensions of their own libraries." But one thing Gladstone was sure of: bookcases should be plain. "It has been a fashion to make bookcases highly ornamental," he says. "Now books want for and in themselves no ornament at all. They are themselves the ornament."

Books are themselves the ornament. A tenth-century Arabic-speaking scholar learned the truth of this proposition as he was browsing in the book bazaar in Córdoba, Spain. Córdoba was a literary capital; it held what was then the largest library in the world. Our scholar (whose name I don't know) was looking for a particular manuscript that he hadn't yet been able to find for sale. Finally, to his inexpressible joy, he came across a copy, written in an unusually fine script. He bid for it eagerly. "But," he writes,

> always the auctioneer returned with a higher bid, until the price far exceeded the actual value. Then I asked the auctioneer to show me the competitor who offered so much. He introduced me to a gentleman in magnificent garments and when I addressed him as Doctor, telling him that I was willing to leave the book to him if he needed it badly, as it was pointless to drive the price up higher, he replied: I am neither a scholar nor do I know what the book is about; but I am in the process of installing a library, in order to

distinguish myself among the notables of the city, and happen to have a vacant space which this book would fill.

Books fill vacant spaces better than other collectibles, because they represent a different order of plenitude—they occupy not only the morocco-bound spine span on the shelf, but the ampler stretches, the camel caravans of thought-bearing time required to read them through. If you amass a private library of hundreds of thousands of volumes, as the great Caliph Hakim II of Córdoba did before he died, in the year 976, you can feel confident that you have secured a kind of implied immortality: you die owning in reserve all the hours and years it would take those who outlive you to read, not to mention copy over, the words each book contains—and that bank of shelved time is your afterlife. And if you will your books to a cathedral library, or to a university, with the firm injunction that the books you give be chained in perpetuity (a stipulation that a number of English and Italian library benefactors included in their wills), you can't truly die, or so you may secretly believe: you can't sink to infernal sub-basement floors or float off to some poorly lit limbo, because your beloved delegation of volumes, the library that surrounded you in life, and suffered with you, and *is* you, is now tethered firmly to the present; you will live on, linked by iron and brass to the resonant strongbox of the world's recorded thought. One testator of 1442 asked that his rare books be chained in the library at Guildhall, so that, he says, "the visitors and students thereof be the sooner admonished to pray for my soul."

But no deterrent, including chains, is a guarantee of immortality. Books can burn, and they can suffer depredations under various kinds of zealotry, and they can simply get sold off for cash or mutilated by misguided conservators. The particular manuscript that the tenth-century Arabic scholar coveted and couldn't afford (he doesn't tell us what book it was) was very probably a casualty of several attendant centuries of civil war and turmoil in Spain. A satisfyingly heavy blue tome from 1939, called *The Medieval Library*, tells us that by the time Philip II of Spain was fitting out the library of the Escorial, not a single Arabic manuscript, nothing from the glory days of Córdoba, could be found anywhere in the kingdom. ("Fortunately, the capture of a Moroccan galley in which a considerable number of Arabic books and manuscripts was found relieved the royal librarian's embarrassment," writes S. K. Padover.) In England, tens of thousands of manuscripts—works that would have been dusted with foxtails by dynasties of whispering attendants in the Vatican if they had been fortunate enough to escape there—perished during the suppression of the monasteries in the sixteenth century. They died slowly in some cases: used to polish candlesticks and boots, to wrap pies, to press gloves flat, or to repair broken windows. Manuscripts of Duns Scotus, who later became Gerard Manley Hopkins's preferred scholastic philosopher, were nailed to the walls of outhouses and torn off page by page, forced to become, as one proud library purger wrote, "a common servant to evere man."

All this distant adversity has one positive effect, however: the books now on our shelves become more ornamental and more precious—regardless of their intrinsic worth—by the charged, Lindisfarnean absence of the books that could have influenced or improved them, directly or at many removes, but can't because they are lost. This explains why some of us, like eager high-school science students doing a unit on fruit flies, are drawn to study up close the short lived images in catalogs or magazines, in search of tiny, attractively arbitrary points of literary embarkation. These books happen to be the books we

have now. They've made it—made the leap from library catalog to mail-order catalog. They're survivors. I haven't yet
ordered one of the tall revolving-shelf bookcases that the
Levenger company, that very successful maker of "Tools for
Serious Readers," sells, but I did recently look up the multivolume *Biographical History of Massachusetts,* published in
1909, that Levenger has shelved for display in the revolving
bookcase shown on the cover of its early-summer catalog. I
found, in Volume II, the story of Henry Albert Baker (no relation), a nineteenth-century dentist and lecturer on oral defor-
mities, who in 1872 discovered the principle of the pneumatic
dental mallet, a device used for forcing wads of silver amalgam
into excavated molars. Baker, in the words of his biographer,

> happened to have in his hands a tube such as boys use for bean-
> blowers. At the same time he had in his mouth a round piece of
> candy which dissolved rapidly. He playfully put one end of the
> tube between his lips and accidentally the candy slipped into the
> tube. He covered the lower end of the tube with his finger to pre-
> vent it from dropping. As soon as he felt it touch his finger he
> sucked the candy back and to his surprise it flew up the tube with
> such force that he thought he had fractured one of his front teeth.
> He lay awake nearly all the following night trying to evolve a plan
> to utilize the force so mysteriously concealed. The next morning he
> was at the machine-shop bright and early and within three days he
> had the pneumatic mallet complete.

What could be more worth knowing than this? We could do
worse than accept the reading suggestions that fall unsolicited
through our mail slots.

There is a surprising further development in the history of
the book and the bookcase. Not only is the book the prop
of commonest resort in the world of mail order; but objects
that resemble books—nonbook items that carry bookishly
antiquarian detailing—are suddenly popular. The book as a

middle-class totem is in fashion to a degree not seen since Joseph Addison in 1711 encountered a private library containing dummy books of "All the Classick Authors in Wood," along with a silver snuffbox "made in the Shape of a little Book." ("I was wonderfully pleased with such a mixt kind of Furniture," he wrote.) Catalogs now offer book-patterned ties, book brooches, and settees covered in trompe-l'oeil-bookshelf fabric. Pier 1 recently advertised a round glass-topped table whose base is a fake stack of nine large leather-bound books. The latest Horchow Home collection includes, for $869, an entire coffee table made in the image of two immense faux books hewn from chunks of beechwood; the top one is pretending to be Volume I of an Italian edition of Homer. The catalog for See's candies sells the Chocolate Classics, a book-shaped box of candy bars. The Paragon gift catalog offers a fairly awful table clock with one fake gold-tooled book perched on top and two fake books underneath, bearing the legend, in gold script, "Times to Remember." Paragon also has an ex-libris frame for snapshots, in printed fabric, showing many shelves of black- and red-bound books—black and red being the colors, we remember, of the poor scholar's books in *The Canterbury Tales*. A catalog called *Ross-Simons Anticipations* has a three-hundred-dollar mirror whose frame consists of several "shelves" of artificial old-style book spines, so that when you check your tie you'll be thronged with literary feelings.

And then there is the *Eximious of London* catalog, which began appearing in American mail pouches several years ago. ("Eximious" is an archaic word meaning "distinguished" or "select.") It carries a four-volume set of book coasters (water-resistant), and a book pencil pot covered with precise replicas of Volume IV of an old edition of the collected works of Racine. I spoke with Cricket, of Customer Service, who told me that the Racine pencil pot was probably their best faux-book seller. And there is the so-called "scholarly magnifying glass with faux bookspine handle." The handle is a vividly lifelike mold taken from a book called *Ramsay's Poetical Works*. It's a provocative choice. Allan Ramsay wrote verse in what to an American ear is intolerable Scottish dialect, but he also has the distinction of having opened, in Edinburgh, in 1725, the first circulating library—a place where, as in a modern video store, you rent what you can't afford to buy. Ramsay thus initiated the great change in the demography of readership that takes us from eighteenth-century Gothic chambers of sensationalism to the nineteenth-century corona- tion of the novel as the preeminent literary form, and, even- tually, to the complete subordination of leather-bound books of poetry like Ramsay's own.

Finally, there is the Faux Book Cassette Holder. Several companies sell false fronts for cassettes, CDs, and videotapes, but this is the only one that made me want to read some Shakespeare. The product turns "an unsightly situation into a stunning bookshelf asset," Eximious says. "The mellow row of books looks exactly like a set of leather-bound antique vol- umes, because the resin mould was actually taken from such a set." What set is it? It's the Pickering's Christian Classics collection, published in the 1840s by the bibliophilic William Pickering, who had a thing for miniature books, or what librarians call "tinies." His tiny of several Latin poets drew the attention of Gladstone himself, who noted with approval that it weighed only "an ounce and a quarter." I couldn't put my hands on a copy of Saltmarsh's *Sparkles of Glory,* the eleventh volume in Pickering's row, or on Hill's *Pathway to Piety*, but I did read some of the ninth volume—Christopher Sutton's *Learn to Die,* a reprint of a work first published in 1600, in black-letter type. Those embarrassing multicassette pop-music anthologies you may have bought (or, rather, I

may have bought) on impulse, by phone, while watching
Court TV—the ones with titles like *Forever '80s,* or *The Awesome '80s,* or *Totally '80s*—can now reside, shielded from
inquisitors, behind the binding of a book that contains mor-
bidly helpful thoughts such as this:

> Seeing therefore, that on every side, wee have such urgent occa-
> sion, to passe the dayes of this wearysome Pilgrimage in trouble,
> and pensivenesse of minde, may wee not thinke them thrice
> blessed, who are now landed on the shoare of perfect Securitie,
> and delivered from the burden of so toilesome a labour: May wee
> not bee refreshed, in calling to minde, that this battaile will one
> day be at an ende, and wee freed from the thorowes of all these bit-
> ter calamitites?

As for beauty, Sutton writes:

> Doe not some few fits of a feaver, marre all the fashion? The incon-
> stancy of all worldly glory! All this stately and pageantlike pompe
> shall vanish away, and come to nothing, as if it never had bene.

Just the right note to strike in a cassette holder. As I read
Learn to Die, I began wondering whether Christopher Sutton
had been spending time at the Globe Theatre: variations on
phrases and metaphors from Shakespeare's late plays, especially from soliloquies in *Hamlet,* kept cropping up. Even the
opening words of the book—"That religion is somewhat out
of joynt"—recall Hamlet's announcement that "the time is
out of joint." So I got down a copy of *Hamlet,* and soon saw
that I was mistaken. It wasn't that Christopher Sutton had
been hearing Shakespeare; it was that Shakespeare had been
reading Christopher Sutton: *Learn to Die* came out in 1600,
while *Hamlet* wasn't produced until about 1602. And yet Sutton isn't listed in any study of Shakespeare's sources that I
checked, or in the Arden *Hamlet,* or in the nineteenth-century
variorum edition of *Hamlet* by Horace Howard Furness.
Could the Eximious catalog be giving us, for only $51.50 plus

shipping, an admittedly minor but nonetheless significant and as yet undissertationed source for Hamlet's death-fraught inner sermons? Could a mail-order catalog be sending us to graduate school?

It is a little disorienting, though—the wish to disguise one's cassettes or one's videotapes behind this extreme sort of leathery surrogacy. Better, truer, braver it would have been for Eximious to market a set of faux Penguin paperbacks, intermingled with a few faux Vintage Contemporaries. Our working notion of what books look like is on the verge of becoming frozen in a brownish fantasy phase that may estrange us from, and therefore weaken our resolve to read, the books we actually own. Hamlet, who was tolerant of bad puns, might have been tempted to point out that when a book turns faux it may cease to be a friend.

If we momentarily resist the gold-filigreed leather archetype, we may discover that the essential generous miracle of the bound book—which is the result of its covert pagination (that is, its quality of appearing to have only two surfaces when closed but in fact fanning forth dozens or hundreds of surfaces when opened)—is, right now, undergoing more technical experimentation and refinement and playful exaggeration than at any other time in its history. The book, considered as a four-cornered piece of technology, bound on one side, is still surprisingly young. Signs of its youth are to be found, naturally, in the children's section of the bookstore, where a brilliant corps of paper-engineers have lately made their mark. The children's section has third-generation pop-up books that arch and pose under the stress of page-turning like protégées of Isadora Duncan. There are lift-the-flap books, which carry subordinate pages on their pages, offering further surprises of surface area, and yet allow their flaps to be torn off without protest. (My son, who is one and a half, spends an hour each day reviewing his now flapless lift-the-flap books.) On these shelves you'll find letter-pouch books, like *The Jolly Postman,* and up-to-date variations on the old textural pat-the-bunny and feel-daddy's-scratchy-face theme; you will encounter rows of miniature, stiff-paged Chunky or Pudgy books, and the foam-padded Super Chubby series from Simon & Schuster, and the patented double-wide House Books from Workman Publishing, all of which boldly make a virtue of the necessary thickness of the non-virtual page. Even *Goodnight Moon* is now a board book. And there are books here with neo-medieval tabs to hold them closed, and real wheels to roll on, and books that have a hole in every page and a squeaking pig in their heart. There are books that are really toy kits with pamphlets, like *Build Your Own Radio,* published by Running Press, which when opened reveals circuitry, not words; or the *Make Your Own Book* kit, with paper and binding glue; or consummations like *The Mystery of the Russian Ruby,* which includes its own Sherlock Holmesian hinged bookcase disguising a secret stairway and a disappearing high-heeled foot; or the folio-size construct that calls itself a book, and is published by St. Martin's, a reputed book publisher, but that upon opening burgeons into a 360-degree two-story Victorian dollhouse. Upstairs, near the fireplace, there is a small lift-the-flap book cupboard holding six weighty, untitled volumes.

Several times lately, encouraged by this foliated ferment in the children's section, or by the confident bibliophilia to be found in the bulk-mail catalogs, I have stood before my own six undistinguished bookcases, and regarded the serried furniture they hold with a new level of interest and consideration. The best bookcase moment, I find, is when you reach up to get a paperback that happens to sit on one of the higher shelves, above your head. You single it out by putting a fingertip atop the block of its pages and pulling gently down, so that the book rocks forward and a triangle of cover design appears from between the paperbacks on either side. The book's emergence is steadied and slowed by the mild lateral pressure of its shelved peers, and, if you stop pulling just then, it will hang there by itself, at an angle, leaning out over the room like an admonishing piece of architectural detail; it will not fall. Finally the moment of equilibrium passes: the book's displaced center of gravity and the narrowing area it has available for adjacent friction conspire to release its weight to you, and it drops forward into your open hand. You catch the book that you chose to make fall. And, with any luck, you read it.

(1995)

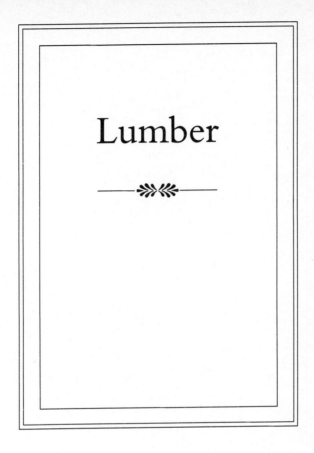

Lumber

Lumber

(i)

Now feels like a good time to pick a word or a phrase, something short, and go after it, using the available equipment of intellectual retrieval, to see where we get. A metaphor might work best—one that has suggested itself over a few centuries with just the right frequency: not so often that its recovered uses prove to be overwhelming or trivial, nor so seldom that it hasn't had a chance to refine and extend its meaning in all kinds of indigenous foliage. It should be representatively out of the way; it should have seen better days. Once or twice in the past it briefly enjoyed the status of a minor cliché, but now, for one reason or another, it is ignored or forgotten. Despite what seems to be a commonplace exterior, the term ought to be capable of some fairly deep and marimbal timbres when knowledgeably struck. A distinct visual image should accompany it, and yet ideally its basic sense should be easily misunderstood, since the merging of such elementary misconstruals will help contribute to its accumulated drift. It should lead us beyond itself, and back to itself. And it should sometimes be beautiful.

The mind has been called a *lumber-room,* and its contents or its printed products described as *lumber,* since about 1680. Mind-lumber had its golden age in the eighteenth century, became hackneyed by the late nineteenth century, and went away by 1970 or so. I know this because I've spent almost a year, on and off, riffling in the places that scholars and would-be scholars go when they want to riffle: in dictionaries, indexes, bibliographies, biographies, concordances, catalogs, anthologies, encyclopedias, dissertation abstracts, library stacks, full-text CD-ROMs, electronic bulletin boards, and online electronic books; also in books of quotations, collections of aphorisms, old thesauruses, used-book stores, and rare-book rooms; and (never to be slighted, even if, in my own case, a habitual secretiveness limits their usefulness) in other living minds, too—since "Learned men" (so William D'Avenant wrote in 1650, when the art of indexing was already well advanced) "have been to me the best and briefest Indexes of Books"; or, as John Donne sermonized in 1626, "The world is a great Volume, and man the Index of that Booke."

Boswell, for example, said, in the last pages of his biography, that Johnson's superiority over other learned men "consisted chiefly in what may be called the art of thinking,"

> the art of using his mind; a certain continual power of seizing the useful substance of all that he knew, and exhibiting it in a clear and forcible manner; so that knowledge, which we often see to be no better than lumber in men of dull understanding, was, in him, true, evident, and actual wisdom.

Logan Pearsall Smith, in an essay on the sermons of John Donne, asserts that the seventeenth-century divines, "with all the lumber they inherited from the past, inherited much also that gives an enduring splendour to their works." Michael Sadleir, in his *The Northanger Novels: A Footnote to Jane Austen* (1927), writes: "There are probably no items in the lumber-rooms of forgotten literature more difficult to trace than the minor novels of the late eighteenth century." One of those minor novels was Charles Johnstone's *Chrysal* (1760–65), in which a bookseller named Mr. Vellum stores surplus copies of books by a dead self-published author for seven years in the "lumber garret" so that he can pass them off as new creations. Laurence Sterne mentions "the lumber-rooms of learning" in Book IV of *Tristram Shandy* (1761).

Goethe revered Sterne, and he might have read *Chrysal* (which was translated into German in 1775); and Goethe's learned yearner, Faust, calls the spirit of the past, as it is reflected in the minds who study it, a *Kehrichtfaß* and a *Rumpelkammer,* in a line that has been variously Englished as a "mouldy dustbin, or a lumber attic" (Philip Wayne), "a junk heap, /A lumber room" (Randall Jarrell), "Mere scraps of odds and ends, old crazy lumber, / In dust-bins only fit to rot and slumber" (Theodore Martin, revised by W. H. Bruford), "A very lumber-room, a rubbish-hole" (Anna Swanwick), "A heap of rubbish, and a lumber room" (John Stuart Blackie), "A rubbish-bin, a lumber-garret" (George Madison Priest), "A trash bin and a lumber-garret" (Stuart Atkins), "An offal-barrel and a lumber-garret" (Bayard Taylor), "a trash barrel and a junk room" (Bayard Quincy Morgan), "A lumber-room and a rubbish heap" (Louis MacNeice and E. L. Stahl), and "A mass of things confusedly heaped together; /A lumber-room of dusty documents" (John Anster). Lord Francis Leveson Gower's early translation (John Murray, 1823) may be, for this particular passage, the best:

> Read but a paragraph, and you shall find
> The litter and the lumber of the mind.[1]

---

[1] Gower's translation offers a bonus *lumber* earlier that is almost as inspiring:

> Hemm'd round with learning's musty scrolls,
> Her ponderous volumes, dusty rolls,

Master Humphrey has lumber dreams in the first chapter of Dickens's *Old Curiosity Shop:*

> But all that night, waking or in my sleep, the same thoughts recurred and the same images retained possession of my brain. I had ever before me the old dark murky rooms—the gaunt suits of mail with their ghostly silent air—the faces all awry, grinning from wood and stone—the dust and rust, the worm that lives in wood— and alone in the midst of all this lumber and decay, and ugly age, the beautiful child in her gentle slumber, smiling through her light and sunny dreams.

Hazlitt does not refer to the lumber of scholarship where you would expect him to, in his Montaignesque "On the Ignorance of the Learned," but he does so, affectionately, in "On Pedantry," an essay that also contains his helpful circular definition of learning as "the knowledge of that which is not generally known." Of a character named Keith in *South Wind,* Norman Douglas writes, "He had an encyclopaedic turn of mind; his head, as somebody once remarked, was a lumber-room of useless information."

Norman Douglas's "somebody" was probably Lord Chesterfield, who in 1748 advised his son that "Many great readers load their memories without exercising their judgments, and make lumber-rooms of their heads, instead of furnishing them usefully." Sir Thomas Browne, though he was one of the greatest of readers, and of indexers, claimed to have avoided this pitfall: "I make not therefore my head a grave, but a treasure, of knowledge," he writes, in *Religio*

Which to the ceiling's vault arise,
Above the reach of studious eyes,
Where revelling worms peruse the store
Of wisdom's antiquated lore,—
With glasses, tools of alchemy,
    Cases and bottles, whole and crack'd,
    Hereditary lumber, pack'd.
This is the world, the world, for me!

Medici (1642), finding no use here for the word "lumber,"[1] but getting some mileage instead out of the Greek root of *thesaurus*—"treasure-house"—a word associated with dictionaries long before Roget,[2] and employed in passing in an eighteenth-century Latin poem written by Johann Mencke (and edited by a collateral descendant, H. L. Mencken) called *The Charlatanry of the Learned:*

> The bookshops are full of Thesauruses of Latin Antiquities which, when examined, turned out to be far less treasuries than fuel for the fire.

Mencken himself, in his autobiographical "Larval Stage of a Bookworm," said that

> At eight or nine, I suppose, intelligence is no more than a small spot of light on the floor of a large and murky room.

This is Mencken's elegantly spare version of John Locke's *dark room,* from *An Essay Concerning Human Understanding* (1690), which is illuminated by shafts of external and internal sensation:

> These alone, as far as I can discover, are the windows by which light is let into this *dark room.* For, methinks, the understanding is not much unlike a closet wholly shut from light, with only some little opening left, to let in external visible resemblances, or ideas of things without. . . . [Locke's italics.]

And Locke's unlit closet may be an irreligious revision of the room of despair, "a very dark room, where there sat a man in an iron cage," in Bunyan's *Pilgrim's Progress* (1678).[3]

---

[1] Not every passage quoted herein will actually contain the word; that would be obsessive.

[2] Cf. Thomas Cooper's *Thesaurus Linguae Romanae & Britannicae,* 1565.

[3] Both Locke's and Bunyan's *dark rooms* may owe something to a sermon by John Donne delivered on Christmas Day, 1624: "God does not furnish a roome, and leave it darke; he sets up lights in it; his first care was, that his

Practicing architects had tired, by the 1890s, of dark seventeenth-century rooms of the soul, and had developed as a result an antipathy to the closet. Russell Sturgis, in an article on "The Equipment of the Modern City House," appearing in *Harper's Magazine* in April 1899, mentions one architect who wanted to rid domestic life of closets altogether, arguing that they were

> extremely wasteful of space, and in every way to be shunned; that they were places where old lumber was stored and forgotten, dust-catchers, nests for vermin, fire-traps.

But one has to store things somewhere; and Sherlock Holmes in 1887 compared the brain in its untutored state to a "little empty attic," which should be properly stocked:

> A fool takes in all the lumber of every sort that he comes across, so that the knowledge which might be useful to him gets crowded out, or at best is jumbled up with a lot of other things, so that he has a difficulty in laying his hands upon it. (*A Study in Scarlet.*)

Holmes warns Watson that "it is a mistake to think that that little room has elastic walls and can distend to any extent." Montaigne, however, disagrees: when considering the question whether (in Florio's translation, "Of Pedantisme") "a mans owne wit, force, droope, and as it were diminish it selfe, to make roome for others," he at first appears to hold that it does, and then he decides that, no, on the contrary, "our mind stretcheth the more by how much more it is replenished."

These preliminary examples and semirelevant corollaries, having stretched the elastic walls of the preceding paragraphs nearly to the point of tissue damage, must now draw back to

---

benefits should be seene; he made light first, and then creatures, to be seene by that light. . . ."

reveal, in a kind of establishing quotational shot, the one really famous piece of lumber we have. It was published in 1711, the work of the twenty-three-year-old Alexander Pope. (Youth is often a time of lumber: "An ever increasing volume of dimensional lumber is juvenile wood," as Timothy D. Larson pointed out in 1992, in his "The Mechano-Sorptive Response of Juvenile Wood to Hygrothermal Gradients," indexed in the *Dissertation Abstracts* CD-ROM.[1]) Pope's *An Essay on Criticism* describes a bad critic:

> The Bookful Blockhead, ignorantly read
> With Loads of Learned Lumber in his Head.

This is a very good couplet: *ignorantly* fills its alloted verse-hole with a lumpy tumultuousness, like a rudely twisted paper clip, and the three capital Ls on the next line halt in their places one after another as remuneratively as a triplet of twirling Lemons in a slot machine just before the quarters start spraying out. Pope's jingle has stayed with us: it is included under the heading "Reading: Its Dangers" in *The Home Book of Quotations;* it appears in *Bartlett's* and *The Oxford Dictionary of Quotations.* Even in extrapoetical contexts it continues to find advocates: as recently as 1989 (so the *Wilson Library Literature* CD-ROM index points out), Peter A. Hoare contributed a chapter to *The Modern Academic Library: Essays in Memory of Philip Larkin* that was called "Loads of Learned Lumber: Special Collections in the Smaller University Library." Hoare writes that specialized collections, regardless of whether they are directly related to

---

[1] Juvenile wood is wood near the pith of the tree; it has a "larger longitudinal hygrocoefficient of expansion than mature wood," writes Larson, who is concerned that the expansion-habits of juvenile wood will lead to "an increase in the frequency and severity in spatial deformation of wood subjected to hygrothermal gradients."

any "immediate academic programme," nonetheless "contribute, not always in an easily definable way, to the quality of the whole institution"; and he mentions Larkin's useful distinction between the "magical value" and the "meaningful value" of literary manuscripts.

Where in *his* library, though, one wants to ask, did Pope find his *lumber*? Pope was an artful borrower, a mechanosorptive wonder, as generations of often testy commentators have shown; many of his finest metrical sub-units have an isolable source. (E.g., Pope's "Windsor Forest" mentions a "sullen Mole, that hides his diving Flood," which rodent is, says commentator Wakefield, a borrowing, or burrowing, from Milton's "Vacation Exercise," where there is a "sullen Mole that runneth underneath.") Is *learned lumber* from Milton, too, then?

No, it isn't. Milton didn't use *lumber* in any poem, and you will find it (with the aid of Sterne and Kollmeier's *Concordance to the English Prose of John Milton,* 1985) only once in all his prose works: "When Ministers came to have Lands, Houses, Farmes, Coaches, Horses, and the like Lumber," he says in *Eikonklastes* (1649), "then Religion brought forth riches in the Church, and the Daughter devour'd the Mother." Is Pope's *lumber* from Shakespeare, then, or Spenser, or Marlowe, or Urquhart's translation of Rabelais? Can it really be that he coined the phrase himself? The critical editions of Pope—even the great Twickenham series that came out piecemeal while Nabokov was working on *Pale Fire* (1962) and his Pushkin commentary—suggest no specific sources in this case; E. Audra and Aubrey Williams, the Twickenham editors of *An Essay on Criticism,* confine themselves to a footnote citing the *Oxford English Dictionary:* "*Lumber*] 'useless or cumbrous material' (OED)." Is it from Horace or Quintilian, in the original or in translation? (Lady Mary Wortley

Montagu: "I admired Mr. Pope's Essay on Criticism at first, very much, because I had not then read any of the antient critics, and did not know that it was all stolen.") Is it from Jonathan Swift?

Swift does indeed have a passage in his early "Ode to Sir William Temple" that goes

> Let us (for shame) no more be fed
> With antique Reliques of the Dead,
> The Gleanings of Philosophy,
> Philosophy! the Lumber of the Schools
> The Roguery of Alchymy,
>   And we the bubbled Fools
> Spend all our present Stock in hopes of golden Rules.

This was written around 1692—the *Oxford Dictionary of Quotations* quotes just its fourth line—but the ode remained unprinted until 1745, when it was included in one of Dodsley's *Miscellanies;* it isn't likely that Pope read it until after he had published *An Essay on Criticism* (1711, 1711—I must try to remember that date) and had befriended Swift. Swift's first published poem, his "Ode to the Athenian Society" (1692), is a potential influence; it praises the efforts on the part of the Athenian Society[1] to strip Philosophy, that "beauteous Queen," of her old lumber:

> Her Face patch'd o'er with Modern Pedantry,
>   With a long sweeping Train

---

[1] Samuel Johnson, in his "Life of Swift," described the Athenian Society as "a knot of obscure men." They were Samuel Wesley (whom we will meet again later), Daniel Defoe, and the publisher John Dunton, among others; they published Swift's flattering "Ode" in their *Athenian Gazette,* vol. 5, supplement, 1692. Dunton wrote that Swift's "Ode" was "an ingenious poem" (See John Nichols, *Literary Anecdotes of the Eighteenth Century,* ed. Colin Clair, p. 122), but Pat Rogers (*Jonathan Swift: The Complete Poems,* p. 604) reports that Joseph Horrell's harsh verdict—that this is Swift's "worst poem by odds"—is "shared by many critics."

> Of Comments and Disputes, ridiculous and vain,
> All of old Cut with a new Dye,
> How soon have You restor'd her Charms!
> And rid her of her Lumber and Her Books,
> Drest her again Genteel and Neat,
> And rather Tite than Great,
> How fond we are to court Her to our Arms!
> How much of Heav'n is in her naked looks.

Despite the naked looks, this setting of *lumber* (which I found using the *Concordance to the Poems of Jonathan Swift,* edited by Michael Shinagel, 1972) is also comparatively hum-drum—not capable on its own of inspiring Pope's magnifi-cently punched-up lumber-couplet. And Swift's early prose is no help, either. In *Tale of a Tub* (1704) there is the interesting brain-recipe for distilling calfbound books in an alchemical solution of *balneo Mariae,* poppy, and Lethe and then "snuffing it strongly up your nose" while setting to work on your critical treatise, whereupon (in another variation on the notion of the brain as a treasure-house and thesaurus)

> you immediately perceive in your head an infinite number of *abstracts, summaries, compendiums, extracts, collections, medulas, excerpta quaedams, florilegias* and the like, all disposed into great order, and reducible upon paper.

Amid these rudenesses about modern erudition, however, not one lumbered disparagement, perplexingly, appears. We can be sure of the absence, since there is nothing listed between *ludicrously* and *lungs* in Kelling and Preston's computer-generated *KWIC Concordance to Jonathan Swift's A Tale of a Tub, The Battle of the Books, and A Discourse Concerning the Mechanical Operation of the Spirit* (1984). (KWIC stands for Key Word In Context.) It could be that Swift felt less inclined to use the word "lumber" after he showed Dryden his Athenian "Ode" and Dryden said to him (as Johnson tells it), "Cousin Swift, you will never be a poet." Dryden, after all, had himself been a lumberer of some prominence in his day: "We bring you none of our old lumber hither," the Poet Laureate promised the King and Queen, on behalf of a newly consolidated dramatic company, in 1682; and in his prologue to *Mr. Limberham* (1680) he complains that

> True wit has seen its best days long ago;
> It ne'er looked up, since we were dipt in show;
> When sense in doggrel rhymes and clouds was lost,
> And dulness flourished at the actor's cost.
> Nor stopt it here; when tragedy was done,
> Satire and humour the same fate have run,
> And comedy is sunk to trick and pun.
> Now our machining lumber will not sell,
> And you no longer care for heaven or hell;
> What stuff will please you next, the Lord can tell.

("Machining lumber" means clunky theatrical supernaturalism and personification, *deus ex machinery*.) To Swift the word would have felt like a piece of Dryden's proprietary vocabulary, and, wounded by Dryden's brutal assessment of his literary future, he purged it from his speech for over twenty years.[1] Or maybe not.

Either way, Swift and Dryden don't look to be convincing sources for Pope's durable phrase. Is it from Samuel Butler's *Hudibras,* which Swift had by heart, or did Pope get it from Francis Bacon's *New Atlantis,* or from a sermon by Donne or Jeremy Taylor, or from John Locke? ("Locke's reasoning may indeed be said to pervade every part of the *Essay on Criticism,*" writes Courthope, another nineteenth-century Pope commentator.) And, more elementarily—before we get too

---

[1] There is no *lumber* in *Gulliver's Travels* (1726). The word resurfaces in Swift's "The Progress of Poetry," written c. 1719 but not published until the *Miscellanies in Prose and Verse* (1728), which was edited by Pope: "To raise the lumber from the earth." Pat Rogers subjoins a note to this line: "*lumber* one of Pope's favourite terms of opprobrium."

carried away in our snuffing for sources—what exactly does the word "lumber" *mean* in Pope's poetry, and in poetry generally? Do we really understand what Pope has in mind, metaphorically, when he refers to "Loads of Learned Lumber"? What might these loads look like? Edwin Abbott's *Concordance to the Works of Alexander Pope* (1875) helpfully gives, in addition to the "learned" line, three later settings for "lumber," all from *The Dunciad,* two of which employ the word nominatively, in the relevant anti-pedantic sense:

Lumber.
Dropt the dull *l.* of the Latin store *D.* iv. 319
With loads of learned *l.* in his head *E.C.* 613
Thy giddy Dulness still shall l. *on D.* iii. 294
A l.-house *of books in ev'ry head D.* iii. 193

Edwin A. Abbott writes, in his introduction to the concordance his father compiled, "I venture to commend the following pages to all those who wish to be able to know at any moment how Pope used any English word in his Original Poems." And who would not want to know at any moment how Pope, of all poets—one of the most skilled word-pickers and word-packers in literary history—used any English word? Who does not feel an inarticulate burble of gratitude toward the senior Mr. Abbott (1808–1882; headmaster of the Philological School, Marylebone) for the enormous manual labor he expended in copying and sorting Pope's lines, creating a book that, though few will read it cover to cover, selflessly paves the sophomore's strait path to pedantry? Concordances are true triumphs of what Michael Gruber, a pseudonymous thriller writer and marine biologist, recently called "siftware"[1]—they are quote verifiers and search en-

---

[1] See the WELL's "Info" Conference ("A Conference About Communication Systems, Communities, and Tools for the Information Age"), Topic 641 ("Internet Encyclopedia"), Responses 15 (Oct. 26, 1993): "Your hyperency-

gines that in an ardent inquirer's hands sometimes turn up poetical secrets that the closest of close readings would not likely uncover.[1]

But grateful though we must always be to Edwin Abbott, the truth is that in the case of *lumber,* at least, his grand Victorian concordance fails us—fails us because it indexes only from the revised, final version of *The Dunciad* (1743). It does not include a more revealing use of *lumber* that appears in the first, and at times superior, *Dunciad* of 1728.

The searcher *will* find this particular couplet, though, in the beautiful, blue *Concordance to the Poems of Alexander Pope,* in two volumes, by Emmett Bedford and Robert Dilligan, produced in 1974 with the help of a Univac 1108 and an IBM 370 computer, using optically scanned microfilm images of the Twickenham edition.[2] Alternatively, you can find the cou-

---

clopedia software (or 'siftware') would direct you toward a basic article on spiders, analogous to the FAQ files placed in many newsgroups." The WELL is an electronic conferencing system: (415) 332-8410; http://www.well.com.

[1] Inspired by Kent Hieatt's numerical analysis of Edmund Spenser's "Epithalamion" (*Short Time's Endless Monument,* 1960), a sophomore in college, in 1975, wrote a paper on the numerical structure of Book I of *The Faery Queen,* in which he pointed out that the word *seven* appears for the first time in the poem on line seven, stanza 17, Canto vii of Spenser's poem ("For seven great heads out of his body grew"), and appears in precisely the same context (a mention of the seven-headed beast that carries the Whore of Babylon) as surrounds the word *seven* in Revelations chapter 17, verse 7. Without Osgood's concordance to Spenser (1915) and several concordances to the Bible open before him, the student would never have noticed this further tiny instance of Spenserian numerology. And it was so incredibly *easy,* too, once I (for it was I) had decided what to look up: "Index-learning," Pope himself pointed out, reworking some earlier snideries of Charles Boyle and Dean Swift,

> turns no student pale,
> Yet holds the Eel of science by the Tail.

[2] Soberingly, the editors of the concordance write that "this optical scanning proved to be the phase of the project that caused the most problems and it seemed for a time that we had traded a tedious but straightforward

plet that Abbott omitted as I first found it, by peering into the greatest lumber-room, or lumber-ROM, ever constructed: the all-powerful, manually keyed *English Poetry Full-Text Database,* released in June of 1994 on four silver disks the size of Skilsaw blades by the prodigious Eel of Science himself, Sir Charles Chadwyck-Healey.

Chadwyck-Healey's forces are responsible for a variety of CD-ROM power-tools: they have brought us the National Security Archive Index of previously classified documents; the catalog of the British Library to 1975; full texts of *The Economist, The Times, The Guardian, Il Sole 24 Ore,* and works of African-American literature; indexes of periodicals, films, music, and French theses; the full text of the nine-volume *Grand Robert de la Langue Française;* United Nations records indexed or in full text, auction records, Hansard's record of the House of Commons, a world climate disk, and British census data; all 221 volumes of Migne's *Patrologia Latina;* on and on. But nothing can remotely compare, in range and depth and tantric power, with their *English Poetry Database,* which promises, and moreover delivers, something like 4,500 volumes of liquidly, intimately friskable poetry by 1,350 poets who wrote between A.D. 600 and 1900.

Not that it is all English poetry: "all" is a meaningless word to use in connection with so sprawling a domain. "Nowhere in our publicity do we say that we are including every poem ever written or published in the English language," writes

---

task [i.e., manual text-entry] for an exasperatingly complicated one. . . . But these difficulties were related to the fact that the technique of direct optical scanning, the claims of computer and data processing houses to the contrary, is still in the developmental stage. Our experience with this method makes us feel that for most purposes literary scholars had best regard it as in the realm of the possible as contrasted with the practical."

Alison Moss, Chadwyck-Healey's editorial director, in a news-letter; and the project consciously sidestepped certain squishy areas: American poetry, drama, verse annuals and miscellanies (with some important exceptions), and poems by writers not listed or cross-referenced as poets in the *New Cambridge Bibliography of English Literature*. The project's heavy reliance on this last-mentioned work has led to some puzzling exclusions. While the *English Poetry Database* includes a truly astounding and thrilling number of minor poems by minor poets, it is unreliable in its coverage of minor poems, and in some cases major poems, by major prose writers.

"I shall not insult you by insinuating that you do not remember Scott's *Lay of the Last Minstrel,*" wrote Vladimir Nabokov in the top margin of page 37 of his teaching copy of *Madame Bovary*[1]; but Walter Scott's poem is not to be found in the *English Poetry Database*.[2] The poem by the nineteenth-century *Erewhon*-man, Samuel Butler, about a plaster cast of a Greek discus-thrower kept prudishly in storage,

> Stowed away in a Montreal lumber room
> The Discobolus standeth and turneth his face to the wall

is not in the *Database,* even though it was good enough for Auden's *Oxford Book of Light Verse* and for a number of editions of *Bartlett's Familiar Quotations*. (Inexplicably, *Bartlett's* doesn't index it under "lumber" or "room" in the current edition, as it has in the past, but it is still stowed away

---

[1] Reproduced in *Lectures on Literature*, p. 137.

[2] There is an ode *to* Walter Scott in there, by one Horatio Smith, that mentions the "minstrel's lay" and "lordly *Marmion,*" and there is even the text of an entire anthology that Scott edited, *Minstrelsy of the Scottish Borders*. There are 227 poems by William Bell Scott, a painter in the circle of Rossetti. But Sir Walter's own poetry, which, as Francis Jeffrey wrote in a review of the *Lay* in 1805, "has manifested a degree of genius which cannot be overlooked," was overlooked.

in there.) George Meredith is listed as a mid-nineteenth-century novelist in the *New Cambridge Bibliography of English Literature* and not cross-referenced as a poet, so none of his poetry is on Chadwyck-Healey's disks, though Meredith is part of nearly every anthology of Victorian poetry. Benjamin Disraeli's blank-verse epic, called *The Revolutionary Epic,* conceived, according to *The Oxford Companion to English Literature,* as a "companion to the *Iliad,* the *Divina Commedia,* and *Paradise Lost,*" was skipped over by the databasers, evidently simply because Disraeli is classed as a novelist; while five poems by his less famous father, author of *Curiosities of Literature,* made the grade, including these lines from the end of "A Defence of Poetry" addressed to James Pye, the poet laureate:

> Thou, who behold'st my Muse's rash design,
> Teach me thy art of Poetry divine;
> Or, since thy cares, alas! on me were vain,
> Teach me that harder talent—to refrain.

They make a nice table-grace for minor poets of all ages.

There are other mystifying prose-poetry juxtapositions, too. The poems that Goldsmith inserted into *The Vicar of Wakefield* are in the *English Poetry Database* ("When lovely woman stoops to folly"), as is the "chair-lumbered closet" that Goldsmith mentions in his poem "The Haunch of Venison," but not the poems Charles Dickens put in *The Pickwick Papers* ("Creeping on, where time has been, /A rare old plant is the Ivy green"[1]), or any of Dickens's other poems or prologues:

> Awake the Present! Shall no scene display
> The tragic passion of the passing day?

---

[1] It was set to music several times and in song form sold tens of thousands of copies.

Leigh Hunt's poetry is here, but not one poem by Thackeray.[1]
There are eighty religious poems by a certain Francis William
Newman, including the interestingly abysmal antipollution
tract "Cleanliness" (1858), which staggers to its Whitman-
esque peak with

> The workers of wealthy mines poison glorious mountain torrents,
> Drugging them with lead or copper to save themselves petty trouble;
> And the peasant groans in secret or regards it as a "landed right,"
> And after some lapse of time the law counts the right valid.

The work of this Newman is included because the *New Cambridge Bibliography* lists him as a minor poet of the period
1835–1870. Not a hemistich, however, by the man's older
brother, John Henry, Cardinal Newman, finds its way in, since

---

[1] "During almost his whole literary career he had been a sparing but an
exquisite writer of a peculiar kind of verse, half serious half comic, which is
scarcely inferior in excellence to his best prose," says George Saintsbury, in
A History of Nineteenth-Century Literature. I couldn't find any *lumber* in
Thackeray's poems, but I did find a good poem about a garret, called "The
Garret." Here are two middle stanzas:

> Yes; 'tis a garret—let him know't who will—
>   There was my bed—full hard it was and small;
> My table there—and I decipher still
>   Half a lame couplet charcoaled on the wall.
> Ye joys, that Time hath swept with him away,
>   Come to mine eyes, ye dreams of love and fun;
> For you I pawned my watch how many a day,
>   In the brave days when I was twenty-one.
>
> And see my little Jessy, first of all;
>   She comes with pouting lips and sparkling eyes:
> Behold, how roguishly she pins her shawl
>   Across the narrow casement, curtain-wise;
> Now by the bed her petticoat glides down,
>   And when did woman look the worse in none?
> I have heard since who paid for many a gown,
>   In the brave days when I was twenty-one.

See Thackeray's *Ballads and Tales*, Scribners, 1904, pp. 103–4.

the *New Cambridge Bibliography* categorizes Cardinal Newman as a mid-nineteenth-century prose writer. Yet Cardinal
Newman's poems are both better and better known ("Lead,
kindly light"); two were chosen by Francis Turner Palgrave for
his *Golden Treasury, Second Series*.[1] Emily Brontë's poetry
was reached by Chadwyck-Healey's rural electrification program, but Charlotte's and Anne's was not, despite the fact that
all three women published a book together in 1846: *Poems, by
Currer, Ellis and Acton Bell*. "It stole into life," wrote Mrs.
Gaskell of the book: "some weeks passed over without the
mighty murmuring public discovering that three more voices
were uttering their speech." It got a decent review in the
Atheneum, and while many will concede that Emily's poetry
shows the most talent, Charlotte's is not embarrassing:

> The room is quiet, thoughts alone
> People its mute tranquillity;
> The yoke put off, the long task done,—
> I am, as it is bliss to be,
> Still and untroubled.
> ("The Teacher's Monologue")

> Warm is the parlour atmosphere,
> Serene the lamp's soft light;
> The vivid embers, red and clear,
> Proclaim a frosty night.
> Books, varied, on the table lie,
> Three children o'er them bend,
> And all, with curious, eager eye,
> The turning leaf attend.
> ("Gilbert")

And if you search the *English Poetry Database* for the
words *join* and *choir* and *invisible* together you will retrieve

---

[1] It is a comfort to know, though, that two hundred and ninety of Palgrave's own poems are on these disks. Reading the poetry of people famous
for their anthologies is a melancholy but instructive task.

sixty-four nineteenth-century efforts by such fixtures of the poetasters' pantheon as Atherstone, Bickersteth, Caswall, Coutts-Nevill, Mant, Smedley, and Mary Tighe (and Byron and Keats and Coleridge, too)—but you won't pull up George Eliot's

> O may I join the choir invisible
> Of those immortal dead who live again
> In minds made better by their presence

or any other poetry she wrote. (I found two instances of "rubbish-heap" in Eliot's 488-page *Collected Poems,* edited by Lucien Jenkins, but discovered no *lumber.*)

Finally, if you want to read about "hope's delusive mine" in Samuel Johnson's verses on the death of Dr. Levet, your hopes will be dashed; in fact if you browse for any "S. Johnson" in the database's name index you will browse in vain. (You will find "L. Johnson," "R. Johnson," and "W. Johnson," though.) Still, the actual texts of Johnson's two best poems, "London" and "The Vanity of Human Wishes," are hidden within, retrievable not by poet's name but by title or search-word, since they were republished in Dodsley's *Collection* of 1763, one of the compendia that Chadwyck-Healey's editors (rightly) shipped off to the Philippines for keypunching.[1] Dodsley's *Collection* fortunately also happens to contain one version of Richard Bentley's only poem (he isn't listed in the name index, either), a poem itemizing the tribulations of the scholar:

---

[1] Optical scanning isn't feasible for old typefaces and foxed paper, and even when the material is in a modern edition and hence legible to scanning software, the raw output still demands, just as it did for the disillusioned Pope concordancers in the seventies, a considerable amount of labor-intensive "markup"—to distinguish things like titles, epigraphs, footnotes, and side-notes from text, for instance, and stanza breaks from page breaks—not to mention the inevitable manual fiddling afterward to fix small errors, like dashes that were read as hyphens.

> He lives inglorious, or in want,
> To college and old books confin'd;
> Instead of learn'd he's call'd pedant,
> Dunces advanc'd, he's left behind.

Samuel Johnson could recite Bentley's poem from memory, as H. W. Garrod reminds us in *Scholarship: Its Meaning and Value,* before he (Garrod, that is) goes on to praise A. E. Housman (a Bentley worshipper himself) as a "great scholar and, as I shall always think, a great poet," which is a remarkably generous assessment, since Housman had, in a preface to his edition of Manilius,[1] viciously dismissed Garrod's earlier Manilian emendations as "singularly cheap and shallow" and judged Garrod's apparatus criticus "often defective and sometimes visibly so."

Housman would probably say similarly rude things about the holes, minor and major, in the *English Poetry Database* (no Jonathan Swift at all, anywhere?[2]) since Housman spent most of his life absorbed in "those minute and pedantic studies in which I am fitted to excel and which give me pleasure," and was intolerant of grand schemes and mechanized shortcuts. Moreover, his own 1896 volume, *A Shropshire Lad,* is missing from the disks, possibly for copyright reasons, a fact that would have nettled him, although he would have pretended not to care.

---

[1] Manilius being the Roman astrological poet who gave Johnson the tag he applied to Cowley and the rest of the Metaphysicals, *discordia concors* (not to be confused with Horace's *concordia discors,* or Gratian's *Concordia discordantium canonum*): you can find the Manilian reference in a footnote to the life of Cowley in G. Birkbeck Hill's 1905 edition of Johnson's *Lives of the Poets,* a lovely example of old-fashioned scholarship, or you can search the Saturnian rings of the Latin CD-ROM published by the Packard Humanities Institute and Silver Mountain Software, which takes about five minutes.

[2] No Macaulay's *Lays of Ancient Rome?* Only one of Daniel Defoe's poems? Nothing by Lewis Theobald?

But we, on the other hand, shouldn't say rude things. This database may be, as John Sutherland pointed out in the *London Review of Books* (vol. 16, no. 11, 9 June 1994), the most significant development in literary scholarship since xerography. And even Sutherland's high praise is insufficient. The *EPFTD,* as some refer to it, is a mind-manuring marvel, and we are lucky that a lot is left out (provided that no university libraries, tempted by its aura of comprehensiveness, "withdraw"—which is to say, get rid of—the unelectrified source books themselves); we don't want every corner of poetry lit with the same even, bright light, for such a uniformity would interfere with what Housman himself called the "hide-and-seek" of learning. The god of scholars, Housman pointed out in his "Introductory Lecture," "planted in us the desire to find out what is concealed, and stored the universe with hidden things that we might delight ourselves in discovering them." And the fact is that Chadwyck-Healey's demiurgic project comes so much closer than anything else in paper or plastic to the unattainable *om* of total inclusion (containing, by my estimate, several thousand times more poetry than *Great Poetry Classics,* itself a fine shovelware CD-ROM published by World Library, Inc.) that hunter-gatherers of all predilections can pretend, some of the time, when it calms their research anxieties to do so, that no obscurity of consequence will be left unfingered. After all, the disks hold (on top of hymns before 1800, and nursery rhymes) many verse *translations* from other languages into English, if they were published before 1800—a very useful subcategory for the lumber-struck.

(ii)

Having borrowed a copy of the *English Poetry Database* from Douglas Roesemann, manager of Chadwyck-Healey's U.S. base in Alexandria, Virginia, with the rash pledge that I would review it for *The New York Review of Books,* I stuck the tip of my index finger in the center hole of Disk 2 on a summer afternoon in 1994. This is one of the safer ways to handle a CD-ROM, especially one with a suggested retail value of over ten thousand dollars. (The whole multidisk kit goes for $47,500 in the U.S., according to the last price list I saw.) I was thus able to flourish, to flaunt, around the first joint of a single finger, like one of those living collars certain reptiles unfurl to frighten away predators, "all" of English poetry from 1660 to 1800.

On the point of popping open my computer's spring-loaded tray and laying the Pierian pancake in its circular bed—about to enclose its infinite riches in a little CD-ROM drive[1]—I

---

[1] Marlowe's "Infinite Riches in a Little Room" is, by the way, the motto used in a nineteenth-century advertisement for Scribner & Armstrong's

noticed that my finger was a little unsteady, and so too was the iridescently flared CD-reflection of my overbooked room. I was aware of the possibility that my private quote-stash, my typewritten cullings, my heaps of coffee-splashed and ant-jaywalked photocopies on the floor, some of which I had grown quite fond of, would appear embarrassingly skimpy and unmethodical when ranked against the neat, single-sourced lumber-list I knew I would get in minutes using the *English Poetry Database.* Would the speed and thoroughness of one-stop searching overwhelm my project with easy erudition (*airudition,* perhaps) and inhibit my will to finish? Dilettante and scholar-pretender though I was content to remain, I didn't like the idea that readers of *The New York Review of Books* would assume, merely because I was an admitted Chadwyck-Healeyan, that I had read even less than I had read in the paginal sprints and leg-stretches I had performed to lumber up for my chosen task. I was reminded of A. E. Housman's contemptuous footnote about a German classicist:

> Wolf, like all pretenders to encyclopedic knowledge, had a dash of the impostor about him, and we have no assurance that he had read the book which he thus presumes to judge.

Of Housman, D. R. Shackleton-Baily wrote in 1959:

"Bric-a-Brac Series" of literary reminiscences, edited by Richard Henry Stoddard. The ad appears in the back of the American edition of Leslie Stephen's *Hours in a Library,* which contains two essays on Pope. *Infinite Riches: Gems from a Lifetime of Reading* (1979) is the title of a 588-page "garnering" by Leo Rosten, which excludes quotations from poetry, novels, Shakespeare, and the Bible. Under "Books" Rosten offers a précis of a relevant Hebrew legend: "Whenever the shelves in the Library of Heaven were entirely full, and a new, worthy book appeared, all the books in the celestial collection pressed themselves closer together, and made room." The *English Poetry Database* is the most efficient compression of the celestial collection yet.

I have always suspected that the animus which he sometimes seemed to show against the great German dictionary, the *Thesaurus Linguae Latinae,* had partly to do with a feeling that such compilations help lazy scholars to conceal their lack of reading.[1]

In literary history as elsewhere, a find is valuable to the degree that it is hard to come by, and the frightening thing about a huge full-text poetry stockpile like Chadwyck-Healey's is that any word or phrase in it, regardless of the bespidered and dust-fledged remoteness of the book from which it was taken, is as easily unearthed as any other. Barring variant spellings, or typos in the original poem or in the transcription, which may help it elude literal searching, no thought, no image anywhere in it is out of the way. Richard Bentley (whom the hard-to-please Housman praised for the "firm strength and piercing edge and arrowy swiftness of his intellect, his matchless facility and adroitness and resource"), when compelled to defend his *Dissertation on the Epistles of Phalaris* from an attack by Charles Boyle and friends, wrote:

> I am charg'd with several faults; as first, for citing Passages *out of the way.* An Accusation I should wish to be True, rather than False. For I take it to be a Commendation, to entertain the Reader with something, that's *out of the common way;* and I'll never desire to trouble the World with *common Authorities,* as this Gentleman would have me do.

But on the level playing field of the CD-ROM, Amhurst, Bickersteth, and Smedley are "common Authorities" equal in weight to Butler, Dryden, and Pope: the scholar gets no earned learnedness credits for quoting them. And yet there they are up on the screen even so—blandly, blindingly obscure, insisting on assimilation.

---

[1] Quoted in Norman Page's *A. E. Housman: A Critical Biography* (1983), p. 175.

Unsure of my ability to digest the sudden hairball of new fascinations that Disk 2 was sure to deposit at my feet,[1] I postponed the worrying search, and turned instead to my stereo system. Removing the Suzanne Vega CD that was slumbering in my Magnavox portable CD-player (featuring Dynamic Bass Boost circuitry), I replaced it with Chadwyck-Healey's silver poemage. I listened.

It may not be universally known that you can play CD-ROM software disks on ordinary audio CD-players. The digital sequence is misread as an analog signal. Eighteenth-century English poetry, as interpreted by my Yamaha stereo receiver and peripherals, generated an edgy square-wave buzz, around a low E-natural, a *discordia concors* lower than a table saw (except when it is cutting a piece of wood with a split end), more like one of those neck hair trimmers that the stylist pulls out of a drawer in the final phase of a haircut, but with excellent spatial separation and some gratuitous conch-shell oceania on top. Disk 3 (1800–1900, poets A–K) sounded much the same. Every so often the power-substation effects would let up a little and there would be some short-lived but lyrical swooshing, as of several cooling hoses playing over the mind at once, although this was not nearly as pronounced as in the excellent *Library of the Future* CD-ROM, Version 3 (which offers the complete texts of "over

---

[1] Bentley said of Warburton, one of Pope's early annotators, that he had a voracious appetite for knowledge, but a poor digestion; fifty years earlier Hobbes wrote that "it is an argument of indigestion, when Greek and Latin sentences unchewed come up again, as they used to do, unchanged." In an Easter sermon in 1619, John Donne said, "The memory, sayes St. *Bernard,* is the stomach of the soul, it receives and digests, and turns into good blood, all the benefits formerly exhibited to us in the particular." And Ovid refers to Chaos, embryon Nature, as a "rudis indigestaque moles"—"a rude and indigested mass" in Dryden's interestingly literal translation, 1693.

1,750 historical, classical, and cultural titles" for $149.95): this has some very well-defined swooshing intervals that put me in mind of the circular-sander finishes that David Smith used for his big minimalist sculptures, finishes that as you stare into them become three-dimensional, and yet, like some works of science fiction, yield little in real brain-nourishment.

The CD-ROM that works best under this sort of auditory misprision, though, is *Compton's Encyclopedia*. As a beginner's encyclopedia, played on a computer, it has its uses (offering black-and-white pictures of lumber mills, for instance), but as a found John Cage for headphones, as a multimedia dramatization of James Russell Lowell's phrase about "the omniscience of superficial study,"[1] it's perfect. The first track is given over to the usual vagrant digital buzzing and swooshing. But in track two, the left and right channels split, and each carries a separate inventory of audio clips. In your right ear you hear an intelligent woman reading alphabetized words like *abdominal cavity, adrenal, algae, brackish, bronchial tree, catastrophic, cephalothorax, conflicting,* and *contour feathers,* while in your left, a Ted Baxtery voice booms out political clichés. ("Give me liberty or give me death!" "The British are coming!" "Don't shoot until you see the whites of their eyes!") The woman quietly continues with: *massive collapse, minute food particles,* and *mucous membrane,* while Roosevelt angrily declares war on "the Japanese empire." You'll hear *potential energy, prolonged, protective coloration, pyroclastic rocks, receptors, rectangular grid, residues, rhythmic pulsing, savage,* and *serrated bristles,* over

---

[1] "His [Dryden's] mind was growing to the last, his judgment widening and deepening, his artistic sense refining itself more and more. He confessed his errors, and was not ashamed to retrace his steps in search of that better knowledge which the omniscience of superficial study had disparaged." (*Among My Books,* 1870, "Dryden.")

Martin Luther King's "I have a dream" speech. *Stoloniferous, structural defects, taxonomic order,* and *tentacles* accompany Kennedy's "Ask not" speech. *Underground burrows, vulcanism,* and *voluntary muscle* are superimposed over a moment from Tchaikovsky's *Nutcracker. Water-dwelling species* comes in over the bark of a dog, a mosquito whines over the Equal Rights Amendment. A third didactic man intones *fingerlike projection* over some hooting monkeys, and he enunciates *encroaching* and *engorgement* over the casual grunts of a pig. The experience is hypnotizing, draining, and not to be missed: it is like living through four years in a suburban high school in forty-five minutes.[1]

But even the antiphonal disROMtion of Compton's audio files couldn't distract me forever from the duties and temptations of high-speed eighteenth-century retrieval, and two days after my initial failure of nerve I found I was prepared to open my clone-tower's drive once again and awaken Chadwyck-Healey's Disk 2 from its dogmatic lumber. I performed a "Standard Search" across the entire disk, and immediately discovered something of value (to me): an additional lumber-couplet from Pope's first version of *The Dunciad,* a version I had never read. In *Dunciad I,* Pope trains his metered hate on Lewis Theobald, the unfortunate critic and minor poet who doomed himself by venturing some acute criticisms of Pope's edition of Shakespeare. Theobald sits surrounded by books in his study: "He roll'd his eyes that witness'd huge dismay," Pope writes (and this happens to be a mock-epic echo of a line

---

[1] Compton's is also a more intelligently conceived encyclopedia in some ways than the flashier *Encarta '95*—if you search for the word "concordance" on Compton's, you retrieve a passage about Bible concordances; if you perform the same search on *Encarta,* you get every article that includes the shortened text-string *concord:* the town in Massachusetts, Henry David Thoreau (who was born there), the supersonic Concorde, and so on.

from *Paradise Lost,* as Pope tells us in a footnote—Theobald, like Milton's Satan eyeing Hell, glances in misery over the gilded prison of his library)—

> He roll'd his eyes that witness'd huge dismay,
> Where yet unpawn'd, much learned lumber lay.

Notice the "Where yet unpawn'd" clause: probably Pope revised this couplet out of *Dunciad II* because he had second thoughts about pawning off his earlier and better use of *learned lumber,* in *An Essay on Criticism,* on this new placement. But to me the passage was of interest mainly because it proved, as none of the other concordanced lumber-quotations directly did, that Pope was (like Samuel Butler before him) consciously aware of the pawnbrokerly undermeaning of *lumber.*

For in English prose and poetry, *lumber* doesn't mean what most Americans think it means ("felled timber"); rather it means, roughly, *old household goods, slow-selling wares, stuff,* or *junk*—junk of the sort you might find at a junkshop, or even, figuratively, at Yeats's foul rag-and-bone shop of the heart. The bookful blockhead's head is not filled with fresh, sap-scented New England plywood, ready for postdoctoral carpentry, but rather with broken, sprung, pawed-over, and possibly pawned Old World trinkets and bric-a-brac. "Lumber, old stuffe" is the concise definition given by Robert Cawdrey, author of the first English dictionary, *A Table Alphabeticall . . . of hard usuall English wordes* (1604).

Only recently did we lose this meaning in the United States. When William Faulkner, in a class at the University of Virginia in 1957, described the writer "reaching into the lumber room" to find the plots and images he needs, he was referring to what he moments earlier had called his "junk box."[1] But

---

[1] *Faulkner in the University,* Frederick L. Gwynn and Joseph L. Blotner, eds., University of Virginia Press (1959), pp. 116–7.

by 1987, that old drossy sense of "lumber" was sufficiently dormant in American usage that Donald Duclos could write an interesting paper (published in *The Eugene O'Neill Newsletter* and listed in the MLA CD-ROM Index) entitled "A Plank in Faulkner's 'Lumber Room': *The Emperor Jones* and *Light in August.*" The paper calls attention to some telling verbal similarities between Faulkner's book and O'Neill's play. "I suggest," Duclos writes, "that that play became a significant plank in [Faulkner's] lumber room of building materials."

We shouldn't be surprised that Duclos mistook Faulkner's meaning. There has always been confusion over *lumber-room* in America—and in Mississippi, Faulkner's state, the existence of a nineteenth-century Natchez firm called the R. F. Learned Lumber Company left matters especially ambivalent.[1] Faulkner himself, being American, used *lumber* often enough in the familiar building-supply sense—for instance, a character pauses "among the mute soaring of the moon-blond lumber-stacks" in "Pantaloon in Black," a pleasant surprise I found via volume 1 of Jack L. Capps's 1977 concordance to *Go Down, Moses,* one of the series of concordances overseen by The Faulkner Concordance Advisory Board at the U.S. Military Academy at West Point. H. L. Mencken, in *The American Language,* writes that "*Lumber,* in England, means articles left lying about and taking up needed room, and in this sense it survives in America in a few compounds, e.g., *lumber room*"; but even if the compound hadn't survived in America when Mencken was writing,

---

[1] Charles W. Crawford wrote a history of the R. F. Learned Lumber Co. as his dissertation for the University of Mississippi in 1968. Though he never went to college, Rufus Frederick Learned, whose father was a lawyer and whose mother ran a boarding school for girls, could easily have known of Pope's couplet; Pope was a pedagogical staple.

Faulkner could have found it easily in the junk box he reached into most often and most helpfully, *Ulysses*. Near the beginning of Joyce's novel, Stephen Dedalus stands in front of his students thinking about storytelling and memory. ("For them too history was a tale like any other too often heard, their land a pawnshop"; Pyrrhus and Julius Caesar, being stories, "are not to be thought away"—"they are lodged in the room of the infinite possibilities they have ousted.") Stephen then dismisses his students from class:

> Quickly they were gone and from the lumberroom came the rattle of sticks and clamour of their boots and tongues.

On the next page, "Hockeysticks rattled in the lumberroom." And then, on page 714, we find a "lumbershed with padlock for various inventoried implements." You can collect these passages[1] by reading *Ulysses,* of course, or, if you've already read it and can't face reading it again, or if you don't want to read it at all, you can arrive at them as I did, with the help of Miles L. Hanley's *Word Index to James Joyce's Ulysses* (1937), a manually typewritten volume that was the result of gluing Joyce's words onto 220,000 cards[2] and alphabetizing

---

[1] Cumulatively reminiscent, perhaps only to me, of the lines

> While yet I groped
> Within the darkened lumber-room
> Of memory

in one of John Davidson's *Fleet Street Eclogues,* "Michaelmas" (1893). It's in the *English Poetry Database,* Disk 3. Joyce read John Davidson.

[2] A mere 20,000 cards shy of the rude and indigested mass of cards that Guy Montgomery produced from all of Dryden's poetry and plays and left alphabetized but unpublished on his death in 1951. Mary Jackman and Helen S. Agoa used Professor Montgomery's fearsome legacy to create an early computer-generated punch-card concordance (1957): it may look a little crude, but it's very useful. It led me to the "machining lumber" in the Prologue to *Mr. Limberham* (quoted above), which, since it was part of a play, wasn't included in the *English Poetry Database.*

them into six wooden racks of post-office pigeonholes. (Theresa Fein, notes Hanley in his acknowledgments, is the person who did most of the actual work of typing, alphabetizing, proofreading, and verification—I hope Joyce wrote her a thank-you.)[1] The *Word Index*'s page references don't exactly match the pagination of the familiar Random House edition, but they are close enough that you can eventually spot what you're looking for, and when you do, you feel (because you had to hunt a little harder than usual) that you've done some real scholarly work.

So when Pope in *The Dunciad* neatly describes a row of owlish scholars—

> A Lumberhouse of Books in ev'ry head,
> For ever reading, never to be read

—the lumber-house he has in mind is not a moon-blond, plank-ranked lumberyard at all, as I used to think, but a "Lombard-house," or a pawnshop. He wants us to understand that scholars are borrowing from the past, cashing in on and taking credit for things they don't own. He hasn't forgotten that he was himself born on or just off Lombard Street,

---

[1] Was *Finnegans Wake* an attempt to write an unconcordanceable book? If so, the attempt failed: see Clive Hart, *A Concordance to Finnegans Wake* (1963). Hart, of the University of Lund, persuaded his wife to type *Finnegan* out on three-by-two-and-a-half cards and together they sorted it into a "Primary Index," an index of "Syllabifications," and an index of "Overtones." (The word *Propellopalombarouter,* for example (p. 314), is separately indexed under *Propellopalombarouter,* and its syllabifications *pellopalombarouter, lopalombarouter, palombarouter, lombarouter, barouter, router,* and *outer.*) With Hart's help, I found one *lumber closet* and a slurred version of *Lombard Street:* ". . . she rapidly took to necking, partying and selling her spare favours in the haymow or in lumber closets or in the greenawn *ad huck* (there are certain intimacies in all ladies' lavastories we just lease to imagination) or in the sweet churchyard close itself . . ." (p. 68). "I wouldn't miss her for irthing on nerthe. Not for the lucre of lomba strait" (p. 207).

so named because thirteenth-century Lombard pawnbrokers (cf., *Longobardi,* "long-beards"[1]) collected there to do business, replacing persecuted Jews. (Pepys called it "Lumber Street" in 1668; Wycherley spelled it "Lumbard Street" in 1675.)[2] It is a street "still familiar to the public eye," writes De Quincey in one of his essays on Pope, and important

> first, as the residence of those Lombards, or Milanese, who affiliated our infant commerce with the matron splendours of the Adriatic and the Mediterranean; next, as the central resort of those jewellers, or "goldsmiths," as they were styled, who performed all

---

[1] Du Cange's *Glossary,* "Langobardi," cites "Guntherus lib. 2. ex Ottone Frising. lib. 2. cap. 18. de Gestis Friderici," which proves to be a bearded-lady anecdote by Bishop Otto of Freising (c. 1110–1158): "For to increase their army [by the drafting of women] they twisted the women's hair about the chin in such a way as to imitate a manly and bearded face, and for that reason they were called Lombards (*Longobardi*), from their long beards." (Otto of Freising, *Deeds of Frederick Barbarossa,* tr. by Charles Christopher Mierow, p. 127.) Eric Partridge, however, in his *Origins* (1958), under "Lombard," cites a private letter to him in which Ernest Weekley speculates that *Longobardus* refers to long axes (*barta* in Old High German), and not long beards. Whatever it was that was long, beards or axes, their owners came to be called Lombards. Perhaps it was both: one thinks of Tolkien's blade-wielding, ore-loving dwarves, with their beards tucked under their belts. (Tolkien himself does not seem to be interested in the dwarvish etymology of Lombardy, but he does use *lumber*. Pamela Blanpied, author of a book about dragons, has kindly called my attention to Gandalf's description of Butterbur, the innkeeper, in Tolkien's *The Fellowship of the Ring,* ch. 10: "A worthy man, but his memory is like a lumber-room: thing wanted always buried.")

[2] Pepys's *Diary,* September 16, 1668; William Wycherley, *The Country Wife,* IV, iii., modernized as "Lombard Street" in some editions. The *u*-spelling was common: University Microfilms offers *Aqua Genitalis,* a sermon by Simon Patrick on baptism, which was preached "at Alhallows Lumbard-street," October 4, 1658, and published in 1670, and a collection of *Farewell Sermons* by various hands (1663), including "Mr. Lyes summary rehearsal at the conclusion of the last morning exercise at All-hallows Lumber-street." *A True Narrative of the Proceedings at the Sessions-House in the Old-Bailey* describes a "yound [young] lad" who was tried and convicted for stealing one hundred and forty pounds "out of a goldsmiths shop in Lumbard Street" in 1678.

the functions of modern bankers from the period of the Parlia-
mentary War to the rise of the Bank of England,—that is, for six
years after the birth of Pope. . . .

Lumber seems originally to have meant possessions pawned
to a Lombard, or money received in exchange for articles
pledged to a Lombard; a *lumber-room* or *lumber-house* or
lumber-office was a pawnbroker's establishment, or, more
broadly, a storeroom in a bank where a debtor's possessions
were held as collateral. During Pope's childhood, there were
several proposals for the founding of charitable, semi-public
lumber-houses, on the model of church- or state-funded
monts-de-Piété in Paris, Amsterdam, and Rome—one
prospectus, circa 1708, entitled *The New Lombard Houses*,
proposed to lend money "in a manner most cheap and easie
to the Industrious Poor" at the rate of about 5 percent—
nonetheless, pawnbroking remained a private enterprise in
England. Elisha Coles's long-running *English Dictionary*
listed the various spellings in 1676:

> *Lombard, Lombar, Lum-, D.* a bank for ufury or pawns, alfo as
> *Lombardeer,* an Ufurer or Broaker, fo called from the
> *Lombards, Longobards,* Inhabiting the hither part of *Italy,* and
> much addicted to Ufury.

(*D.* stands for "Dutch.") The successor to Elisha Coles was
Nathan Bailey; his *Universal Etymological English Dictionary* (1721) became, according to Gertrude Noyes, "the most
popular and representative dictionary of the eighteenth century."[1] Its fourth edition appeared in 1728, the year of Pope's
first use of "Lumberhouse"; it has:

> LOMBAR-*Houfe* [*of* **lumpe** or **lompe**, *Du.* a Rag] a Houfe in
> which feveral Sorts of Goods are taken in as Pawns: Alfo where
> they are expofed to Sale.

---

[1] De Witt T. Starnes and Gertrude E. Noyes, *The English Dictionary from
Cawdrey to Johnson,* 1946, p. 107.

LOMBARD-*Street* [fo called, becaufe the Refidence of the *Lombards,* who were great Ufurers, &c.] a Street near the *Royal Exchange, London.*

This sense of *lumber-house* is obsolete now, although *Brewer's Dictionary of Twentieth-Century Phrase and Fable* (1991) includes a related entry for *LOMBARD:* "An acronym for Loads of Money but a Real Dickhead." Skeat's *Etymological Dictionary* half seriously includes Minsheu's onomatopoeic derivation from 1627: "*Lumber,* old baggage of houshold stuffe, so called of the noise it maketh when it is remoued, *lumber, lumber,* &c." (Skeat comments: "If any reader prefer this fancy, he may do so.") The *Pocket Dictionary, or Complete English Expositor* ("A Work entirely new, and defign'd for the Youth of both Sexes, the Ladies and Persons in Business"), published in 1753, defined *Lumber* as "Old, heavy, ufelefs furniture"; and Samuel Johnson, two years later, influentially but too narrowly defined it as *Any thing ufelefs or cumberfome: any thing of more bulk than value,* adducing a wonderful sentence from one "Grew," who is, I assume, Nehemiah Grew (1641–1712), a plant-microscopist and Royal Societitian:

> If God intended not the precife ufe of every fingle atom, that atom had been no better than a piece of *lumber.*

Johnson also gives Pope's "*lumber*-house of books in ev'ry head" as an illustrative quotation—without, however, any hint of banking or brokering in his definition: the usurious sense of *lumber* had always been slightly slangy, and Johnson held "modern cant" in low regard. (He was "at all times jealous of infractions upon the genuine English language, and prompt to repress colloquial barbarisms," said Boswell of him.)[1]

---

[1] "... such as *pledging myself,* for *undertaking; line,* for *department,* or *branch,* as, the *civil line,* the *banking line.*" (*The Life of Samuel Johnson,* Dent, II, 143, A.D. 1777.)

Latham's dictionary, in 1866, sticks very close to Johnson's definition: "Cumbersome matters of more bulk than value; old stuff." Noah Webster's *An American Dictionary of the English Language* (1828) also echoes Johnson:

> LUM′BER, *n.* [allied to Sax. *leoma,* utensils, or to *lump, clump,* a mass, or Dan. *lumpe,* a rag; *lumperie,* trifles; Sw. *lumpor,* rags, old cloths; D. *lomp;* G. *lumpen;* Fr. *lambeau.* In French, *lambourde* is a joist.]
> 1. Any thing useless and cumbersome, or things bulky and thrown aside as of no use.
>> The very bed was violated—
>> And thrown among the common *lumber.*
>>> *Otway.*

But Webster adds the woody meaning that was by then widespread in the U.S. and Canada:

> 2. In America, timber sawed or split for use; as beams, joists, boards, planks, staves, hoops and the like.

Webster was prone to fanciful etymology, and we should be careful not to be swept away by it; still, his hint that the American and (French-)Canadian logger's meaning of *lumber* could be related to or influenced by the French word "lambourde" (joist) is more helpful than the entry in *The Oxford Dictionary of English Eytmology* (1966), which doesn't attempt to explain the transatlantic shift of meaning at all; and it has more pith than the conjecture offered by Joseph T. Shipley, in his personable *Dictionary of Word Origins* (1945), which seems a little too neat:

> In American pioneer days, when the land was cleared for farming, there were many felled trees lying around; these, being discarded material, were *lumber*—which later was put to good use.[1]

---

[1] Edward Henry Brooke Boulton, president of the Institute of Wood Science in Sussex, offers an interesting, although unsubstantiated, alternative theory in the article on "Lumbering" that he contributed to the new revised *Chambers's Encyclopaedia* (1973): "A 'Lombard' was . . . a man who

American writers from time to time use the word in the English way (Poe, in his "The Rationale of Verse," wrote that metrical quantity "is a point in whose investigation the lumber of mere learning may be dispensed with, if ever in any"); but the reverse is seldom true: Adam Smith is the only writer from Great Britain I can come up with who used our sort of *lumber* several times.[1] In *The Wealth of Nations* (1776), he writes:

> In a country quite covered with wood, where timber consequently is of little or no value, the expense of clearing the ground is the principal obstacle to improvement. By allowing the colonies a very extensive market for their lumber, the law endeavours to faciliate improvement by raising the price of a commodity which would otherwise be of little value, and thereby enabling them to make some profit of what would otherwise be a mere expense.

---

kept a pawnbroker's shop, and the word 'lumbering' arose in the early days of the North American settlers when timber was used as a medium of exchange." And the *Century Dictionary and Cyclopedia* (1911) notes, under "limber," that *limar* (plural of *lim*) means "boughs" or "branches" in Icelandic. One is tempted to propose that Viking explorers left the Indians of North America with some *lim*-lumbery Icelandic wood-word, which then persisted for six centuries or so in one or more Indian languages, until the Indians passed it on to the tree-felling colonists. The difficulty with this theory is that I have been able to find only one such word in my hasty check of Native American dictionaries. *Li•me-* is a noun-stem meaning "woods," "brush," or "branch" in the tongue of the Northern Sierra Miwok people, who ate acorn meal, grizzly bears, and yellowjacket larvae in the mountains not far from Sacramento, California. Sacramento is a very long way from Leif Ericsson's Vinland, wherever it was exactly. See Catherine A. Callaghan, *Northern Sierra Miwok Dictionary,* 1987, p. 132.

[1] The English seem for the most part to have been unaware of the competing sense. Dickens, describing a raft of logs on the St. Lawrence River near Montreal, felt obliged to introduce the novel word to his readers: "All the timber, or 'lumber,' as it is called in America, which is brought down the St. Lawrence, is floated down in this manner." (*American Notes,* 1842, Vol. II, p. 198.) Similarly the *OED* cites Trollope's observation in *North America* (1862) that "Timber in Canada is called Lumber."

Incidentally, the Poe and the Adam Smith I found by searching the *Library of the Future* CD-ROM, Version 3, which
gives forty-five competent *lumber*ians (not Alexander Pope,
though), from Harriet Beecher Stowe ("The garret of the
house that Legree occupied, like most other garrets, was a
great, desolate space, dusty, hung with cobwebs, and littered
with cast-off lumber"), and Oscar Wilde ("The middle-aged
are mortgaged to Life," says Lord Illingworth, in *A Woman
of No Importance;* "The old are in Life's lumber-room"), to
Johann Wyss's *Swiss Family Robinson* in translation ("The
stairs served afterwards for a kind of lumber-room").

Webster's Second (1934), the dictionary Nabokov loved,
includes the obsolete pawning sense of *lumber* as its first definition for the word; its one quotation comes from the prologue to *The Scarlet Letter*—

> The heap of Customhouse *lumber.*   *Hawthorne*

—which refers to the yellowing documents and the torn piece
of scarlet cloth in the second story of the Custom-House that
betray Salem's guilty secret.[1] *Webster's Third* (1961) scraps the
Hawthornian lumber and replaces it with a bit of forward-
looking table-thumpery halfway between timber-cutting and
encumbrance-clearing—"<get rid of the useless ~ that blocks
our highways of thought—John Dewey>"—substituting

---

[1] There are affinities (perhaps Updike reviewers have already pointed
them out?) between the old men in their chairs on the porch of the Poorhouse, in the beginning of Updike's first novel *The Poorhouse Fair,* and
those "venerable figures," the Custom-House officers, in the entry of
Hawthorne's Custom-House, "sitting in old-fashioned chairs, which were
tipped on their hind legs back against the wall." Conner, Updike's young
administrator, has an office in the cupola, up four flights, and his job is similar in flavor to Hawthorne's narrator's job (Custom-House Surveyor).
Updike was, it appears, deliberately linking his book to *The Scarlet Letter,*
as he did again later in *Roger's Version.*

Dewey because (as Herbert Morton shows in his valuable history of *Webster's Third*) its unsentimental editor, Philip Gove, wanted quotations that pulled their weight of definitional meaning, not ones which merely demonstrated that a famous name had employed the word. "The hard truth is that literary flavor in a dictionary quotation represents a luxury of a bygone age," Gove wrote, heartbreakingly[1]—and it is true that Hawthorne's Custom-House context doesn't get you very far if you don't already understand what he's talking about.

Funk & Wagnalls New Standard Dictionary (1963), however, manages to quote Hawthorne[2] *and* convey meaning:

> 2. Discarded household goods; disused articles put aside.
> Happy the man who in a rainy day can betake himself to a huge garret, stored, like that of the Manse, with *lumber* that each generation has left behind it from a period before the revolution.
> HAWTHORNE *Mosses, The Old Manse* p. 26. [H. M. & CO. 1891.]

(Notice that *Funk & Wagnalls* gives specific page references, like the *OED*. *Webster's* doesn't.) Isaac Funk and his heirs also call our attention to a couplet from Cowper's "Table Talk" (1782) about poetry in the time of Cromwell:

> 3. Hence, worthless stuff; rubbish.
> Verse, in the finest mould of fancy cast,
> Was *lumber* in an age so void of taste.
> COWPER *Table Talk* 1. 627.

The rest of Cowper's passage (one of three by him, according to the *English Poetry Database,* that have *lumber* in them) is good:

> But when the second Charles assumed the sway,
> And arts revived beneath a softer day,

---

[1] *The Story of* Webster's Third: *Philip Gove's Controversial Dictionary and Its Critics,* Herbert C. Morton, 1994, p. 99.

[2] Who, like Poe, wanted to use *lumber* in the English sense as evidence of his unprovinciality.

Then like a bow long forced into a curve,
The mind released from too constrain'd a nerve,
Flew to its first position with a spring
That made the vaulted roofs of pleasure ring.

(But Cowper is not at all pleased, as he goes on to say, with the "dissolute and hateful school" of indecent poets that surrounded Charles II, by whom he means men like John Wilmot, Earl of Rochester, appointed a Gentleman of the Bedchamber in 1665, and author of the most beautiful piece of lumber-poetry extant, which I plan to quote in a moment.)

The last meaning in the *Funk & Wagnalls* entry, flagged by a dagger to indicate that it is obsolete, is "6†. A pawnshop," and there follows a generous quotation from Trench's *On the Study of Words* about *lombard-rooms*. *Webster's Third,* by contrast, entirely eliminates the debtor-creditor meaning, except to allude to it in a capsule etymology: "perh. alter. of ¹*lombard;* fr. the use of pawnshops as storehouses of disused property."

Yet *Webster's Third* is much better about the modern sense of *lumber-room* than either *Webster's Second* or *Funk & Wagnalls:* besides furnishing a primary meaning ("a room in which unused furniture and other discarded articles are kept: STOREROOM"), it gives a separate figurative submeaning that includes the following ungrudgingly long but apt citation: "<go through life . . . filling the *lumber room* of their minds with odds and ends of a grudge here, a jealousy there— J.L.Liebman>."

Who was J. L. Liebman? Joshua Loth Liebman was a Boston rabbi and "one of the leading radio preachers in America," according to the author's note at the back of his *Peace of Mind* (1946)—"his sermons over NBC, ABC and CBS coast-to-coast networks have been heard by millions." He is dead and forgotten now, as so many are. *Dead, wee become the Lumber of the World,* wrote the Earl of Rochester, around 1674, immortally translating a chorus from Seneca's *Trojan Women:*

> After Death, nothing is, and nothing Death,
>   The utmost Limit of a gaspe of Breath;
> Let the Ambitious Zealot, lay aside
> His hopes of Heav'n, (whose faith is but his Pride)
>   Let Slavish Soules lay by their feare;
>   Nor be concern'd which way, nor where,
>   After this Life they shall be hurl'd;
> Dead, wee become the Lumber of the World,
> And to that Masse of matter shall be swept,
> Where things destroy'd, with things unborne, are kept.[1]

Rabbi Liebman's style—psychotherapeutical uplift pitched in an exalted Emersonian key—isn't easy to skim, but I was interested in his relatively late American use of "lumber room" in its traditional sense, and I didn't think I could put it to etymological use having only seen it laid out on the sheeted gurney of a dictionary page. That would be lazy; not up to A. E. Housman's exacting standard. Housman singles out for praise the scholar who is willing to spend

---

[1] *Bartlett's Familiar Quotations* gives just the lumber-line from this extraordinary passage, with spelling modernized, on the same page as it proffers a small falsehood by La Bruyère: "We come too late to say anything which has not been said already"—a sentiment imported, as *Bartlett's* notes, from Terence. (Robert Burton, who quoted Terence's thought in his *Anatomy of Melancholy,* was, unlike La Bruyère, careful to cite his source: "I make them pay tribute, to set out this my *Macaronicon,* the method only is mine own, I must usurp that of *Wecker e Ter. nihil dictum quod non dictum prius, methodus sola artificem ostendit,* we can say nothing but what hath been said, the composition and method is ours only, & shows a Scholar.") When Charles Blount, a friend of Rochester's, read the Senecan translation, he was understandably moved: "Indeed," he wrote Rochester, who was by this time raving with neurosyphilis, "the hand that wrote it may become lumber, but sure the spirit that dictated it can never be so." See Jeremy Treglown's *The Letters of John Wilmot, Earl of Rochester,* p. 234.

much of his life in acquiring knowledge which for its own sake is not worth having and in reading books which do not in themselves deserve to be read.

Housman could of course be wrong in his conception of scholarship: Edmund Wilson, who was hit hard by Freud, thought that "there was an element of perversity, of self-mortification, in Housman's career all along."[1] But Housman's self-denying intensity appealed to me in my outward-bound lumber-quest. And Liebman certainly qualified as a test of scholarly dedication: his book did not, in itself, deserve to be read, at least as literature. (As self-help, however, it is better written, certainly more allusive, than, say, Deepak Chopra's *Ageless Body, Timeless Mind,* which is something.) I spent about two hours paging impatiently through *Peace of Mind.* I thought—for you begin to develop an instinct for where a sought word can hide when you have looked for it long enough—that my prize would be middened in the section called "Inferiority Complex May Hide Self-Hate." It wasn't. I looked for it in the vicinity of "Let us learn, then, not to take the depression of the day or the month as the permanent state of our life." I expected to run into it as I came to: "When we are tired, every pinprick becomes the stab of a knife and every molehill becomes a mountain." But I didn't find it anywhere, and as I scanned steadily, feeling the marshmallow-sized minutes tumble by, occasionally tricked by two nearby words (*number* and *plod,* say), which my overeager stare united as the absent object of research—just as in adolescence my eyes would fuse an innocent word on one line (*full*) with another just below it (*knuckle*) into a

---

[1] E. M. Forster disagreed: "*Passion and Scholarship* may enhance each other's effects. A. E. Housman." (E. M. Forster, *Commonplace Book,* ed. Philip Gardner, p. 32.)

short-lived neutrino of an obscenity that I would invariably hurry back to reread—I became troubled by the knowledge that this was *not Rabbi Liebman's only book:* in other words, that I might have to scan *Hope for Man* or *Psychiatry and Religion* just as closely; and the suspicion that I was wasting my irreplaceable afternoon of research time got in the way of my attempt to concentrate on what I was looking at, so that several pages would rise in the east and set in the west without my being sure I had properly reviewed them. I flunked this test of scholarship: I couldn't make myself thoroughly skim *Peace of Mind.*

I flunked, also, in the case of T. D. Weldon's *Introduction to Kant's Critique of Pure Reason,* which I checked out because *Webster's Third* included, as part of its entry for *lumber,*

> <useless words . . . dropped as worthless linguistic ∼
> —T. D. Weldon>

Here I really tried: I took off my glasses so that I could be on closer terms with the page, and I braked the pace of my scanning by running a fingertip down each margin (the type was small, so it took me about three seconds), but again I kept blanking on the phrase that I was looking for; I had to whisper it to myself to keep my retinas primed for it. As the sense of my fallibility grew, I began to have fantasies of paying Text Busters, a local optical scanning service, the dollar or two per page it would take to put the whole book on a disk so I could search it electronically, even though that would take all the fun out of any finds I would make; and I remembered a *New York Times* article about Xerox's invention of an automatic page-turning system for scanners and copiers that employed an electrostatically charged sliding glass plate. Was it true that only the books that didn't deserve to be read deserved to be scanned, or only the books that did?

T. D. Weldon's book was not a masterpiece—it was a careful work of explication, not merely a tissue of "useless words," but not piercingly beautiful, either. George Herbert's line, about how speech

> Doth vanish like a flaring thing,
> And in the eare, not conscience ring

chased its tail in my conscience as I skimmed doggedly along, until I realized that for an indeterminate number of pages I had been unwittingly looking for "flaring thing" rather than "worthless linguistic ～." I didn't have the fortitude to go back. Nonetheless, although no *lumber* forthcame that afternoon, I did find this variation on Locke's *dark room* passage:

> This completes the catalogue of the kinds of furniture which are constantly being conveyed by the senses into the empty room of the mind's consciousness. (p. 31)

And I found this:

> It is unlikely that any philosopher has ever produced a more unutterably tedious work on metaphysics than Baumgarten's *Metaphysica;* or combined so successfully the pedantry of a dying scholasticism with the illusory clearness of a pseudo-geometrical demonstration. (pp. 40–41)

How exciting to be given a fresh touchstone of unutterable tedium! Alexander Gottlieb Baumgarten it would be, then: I immediately looked him up. His earliest work, a set of poetic precepts and theorizings that appeared in Latin in 1735, was annotated and translated by Karl Aschenbrenner and William Holther in 1954 as *Reflections on Poetry*. At first there looks to be a sort of lumber-room in it, when Baumgarten discusses the definitions of *poem, poetry,* and *poet:* "For rehashing these scholastic terms by nominal definitions, the overstuffed cupboards of the Scaligers, the Vosses, and many others are there to be pilfered." But "overstuffed cupboards" is only an anachronistic translation of "refertissima scrinia." A *scrinium* is a scroll-box,[1] or, in Baumgarten's modern extension of the word, a bookcase. The phrase just means "crowded shelves," then. Baumgarten does offer, however, a sensible note of warning some pages later:

> § 76. It is advisable to omit certain elements from a poem, § 75. If one were to try to present every interconnection of a historical theme, he might wonder if he should not include a substantial part of the world, not to say all the history of the ages: it is poetic to omit certain details and more remote connections.

And yet if I followed Baumgarten's advice here, in this non-poem, I would have to leave him out altogether, and that I could never do.

---

[1] "When a number of rolls had to be carried from one place to another, they were put into a box (*scrinium* or *capsa*). This receptacle was cylindrical in shape, not unlike a modern hat-box. It was carried by a flexible handle, attached to a ring on each side; and the lid was held down by what looks very like a modern lock. The eighteen rolls, found in a bundle at Herculaneum, had doubtless been kept in a similar receptacle." John Willis Clark, *The Care of Books*. 1901, p. 30.

(iii)

The *point* was—getting back to T. D. Weldon—that Weldon had possessed the self-discipline (assuming of course that he was not "something of an impostor," as Housman had called Wolf) to read a great deal of Baumgarten's *Metaphysica*—enough to judge it unworthy of wider notice, which discrimination is one of the public services that scholars perpetually perform. I'm very glad I spent several hours with Weldon's book (he contributed two pieces of mental furniture to my "empty room" or "overstuffed hatbox"—whichever it is), even though my time with it humblingly demonstrated my own inability to carry out the elementary postgraduate duty of checking it for a quotation. At times a feeling of inferiority does hide, as Rabbi Liebman suggests, something like self-hate, and it is true that many failed scholars, turning on the books that formerly absorbed them, rail at pedantry; Montaigne, De Quincey, and Hazlitt were guilty of this, as was Pope in *The Dunciad:* Maynard Mack, in his great study of Pope's library, describes the quibbling annotations the poet made as he read, and describes him "as a young man too close for comfort to the literary pedant."[1] And Pope's late collaborator, Bolingbroke, was "contemptuous in his language about men of learning," writes Leslie Stephen, in his life of Pope: "He depreciated what he could not rival."

But sometimes, contra Liebman, a feeling of scholarly inferiority may hide nothing so dramatic and colorful as self-hate, and may simply betray a wish for heroes and heroines. Some of us, falling short of what De Quincey called "massy erudition," retreat for a period to cultivate light learning about learnedness. We satisfy our craving for the emotions of intense study at second hand, by consuming gee-whiz stories about the omnilegent and omnilingual. "A learned man is the most venerable of all," Virginia Woolf wrote, in *Jacob's Room*—

> a man like Huxtable of Trinity, who writes all his letters in Greek, they say, and could have kept his end up with Bentley.

And in her essay on Bentley, she wrote: "Of all men, great scholars are the most mysterious, the most august":

> Since it is unlikely that we shall ever be admitted to their intimacy, or see much more of them than a black gown crossing a court at dusk, the best we can do is to read their lives—for example, the *Life of Dr. Bentley* by Bishop Monk.

What Woolf really meant here, though she was too proud, or perhaps too subtle, to say it, was: Since we will never have the evergreen knowledge of ancient texts they had, since their inner-espaliers are off limits to us, we must content ourselves with the vicarious flutter that comes from reading their heroic, or (in the case of Bentley) shameful, life-exploits.

---

[1] Mack loses restraint altogether when he writes: "I will make no secret of my belief that in his younger days Pope shows signs of the interest in word-catching that he scorned in others." (" 'Books and the Man': Pope's Library," in *Collected in Himself*, 1982, p. 318.)

So naturally Woolf was interested in the notion of a mental lumber-room. She entitled her essay on Hakluyt's *Voyages* "The Elizabethan Lumber Room"; she closes it with a sentence of appreciation for the prose of Sir Thomas Browne, whom she regarded as Hakluyt's noble broker:

> Now we are in the presence of sublime imagination; now rambling through one of the finest lumber rooms in the world—a chamber stuffed from floor to ceiling with ivory, old iron, broken pots, urns, unicorns' horns, and magic glasses full of emerald lights and blue mystery.

Browne may be responsible for one of the finest lumber-rooms in the world, but I have yet to find one *lumber* in Browne's own prose—not even in *Urne Buriall,* where I was certain it was waiting for me; nor any *lumber* for that matter in Donne's sermons or meditations, which were important wells of metaphor for Browne. And, though I badly wanted to come across some learned lumber in *Orlando,* I only spotted (besides the irrelevant "lurching and lumbering traffic") *lumber*-substitutes: "plate, cruets, chafing dishes and other movables," "a perfect rag-bag of odds and ends within us," "old iron," a starling "on the brink of the dust bin," a mind like a traveler's suitcase containing "something contraband for which she would have had to pay the full fine,"[1] the mind "a meeting-place for dissemblables," and a modern bookshop in which "the works of every writer she had known or heard of and many more stretched from end to end of the long shelves" or were "piled and tumbled" on tables and chairs. I wasn't too disappointed, though: *Orlando* as a whole is

---

[1] Compare Nabokov: "A book is like a trunk tightly packed with things. At the customs an official's hand plunges perfunctorily into it, but he who seeks treasures examines every thread." (*Lectures on Literature,* "Charles Dickens," p. 89.)

Woolf's lumber-*Room of One's Own:* in it she imagines an anthropomorphized anthology of the literary tradition that leads up to her. With touching, almost American naivete, her preface to the novel politely thanks Defoe, Browne, Emily Brontë, De Quincey, and Walter Pater for their help,[1] as well as nearer-and-dearers like Roger Fry and Julian Bell. It doesn't mention the Rev. George Croly (1780–1860)—author of a two-hundred-some page Byronesquerie called *The Modern Orlando,* published in 1846, which one wants to imagine the young Virginia Stephen reading in her father's library, and even copying bits of into one of her early commonplace books—a poem I found on Disk 3 of the *English Poetry Database.*[2] In it you will find the story of Isidore, a count who runs out of money and who applies for relief to a pawnbroker of sorts in the Roman ghetto. He and his companion enter the "Hebrew's ancient Store," a chamber rather like Woolf's Elizabethan lumber-room:

> The room was piled with all strange kinds of lumber;
> ·
> Huge folios, by the world long sent to slumber;
>   Arms on the walls, and pictures on the ground;
>   Cracked china; lutes, long guiltless of a sound;
> Furred mantles, missals, tarnished antique plate;
> ·
> A sepulchre of *things*—dim reliques of the great.

---

[1] As Harold Bloom points out in his thoughtful *The Western Canon,* 1994.

[2] There are fifty-five instances of *lumber* on Disk 3 (1800–1900, A–K) and forty-five on Disk 4 (1800–1900, L–Z): a total of one hundred *lumber*-uses for the nineteenth century. Compare this with the 129 *lumbers* on Disk 2, for the period 1660–1800, A–Z: much more poetry in the nineteenth century, less lumber. Yet *lumber* and *lumber-room* often feel overused in nineteenth-century contexts, and don't in the eighteenth century. Word-frequency studies, then, can't tell you whether something is more or less of a cliché.

But, speaking of dim relics of the great, the greatest of Orlando's "favourite heroes" never used the word "lumber." He came close. In *Henry IV, Part II,* Shakespeare has Mistress Quickly say that Falstaff is "indited to dinner to the Lubber's Head in Lumbert Street, to Master Smooth's the silkman." Who Master Smooth is, and what is the precise social tone of the "Lubber's Head," or "Leopard's Head," no glossator will divulge, but financial transactions are not far off, since moments later Mistress Quickly laments that she has loaned so much money to Falstaff that she may be forced to pawn her plate and even her gown.

Shylock's pound of flesh in *The Merchant of Venice* is probably not an equivoque on *lumber,* though. Never mind that one of the word's submeanings, aside from "money loaned," is, in the words of *Webster's Second,* "sometimes, specif., superfluous flesh"—the phrase "pound of flesh" predates Shakespeare in English, and Shakespeare, a punculsive, probably wouldn't have passed up the chance of making some sort of outright *Lombard-lumber-lump-of-lard* association if he had seen it.[1] The first example in the *OED* of this sense is from 1806–7, in Beresford's *Miseries of Human Life* ("With all my fleshy lumber about me"); Thomas Traherne contributes an apposite seventeenth-century line found in the *English Poetry Database:*

> A Body like a Mountain is but Cumber.
> An Endless Body is but idle Lumber.[2]

---

[1] Thomas Hood includes a defense of puns in the prefatory matter to the second edition of his *Whims and Oddities* (first ed. 1826): "I am informed that certain monthly, weekly, and very every day critics have taken great offence at my puns,—and I can conceive how some Gentlemen with one idea must be perplexed by a double meaning. To my own notion a pun is an accommodating word, like a farmer's horse,—with a pillion of an extra sense to ride behind;—it will carry single, however, if required."

[2] From Traherne's "In Making Bodies Lov could not Express."

William Trevor's *Reading Turgenev* (1991) has another example: "It seemed to her that her own flesh and bones were so much lumber, real but without real interest." (My wife is the source of this quotation.) Partridge's *Dictionary of Slang* has "live lumber," meaning "soldiers or passengers on board ship . . . ca. 1780–1910." But later fleshy meanings seem most often to refer to horses and dogs, not people, as in this instance from the *OED*:

> 1891 H. S. CONSTABLE *Horses, Sport & War* 15 Good thorough-bred horses have also lost what goes by the name of 'lumber'—such as lumps of flesh and fat . . . on the top of the neck.

And this from *The Century Dictionary and Cyclopedia*:

> A fine slashing dog, of good size, possessing plenty of bone without *lumber*, and excellent legs and feet.
> *Dogs of Great Britain and America*, p. 104.

Despite Shakespeare's disappointingly low keyword turnout, we shouldn't forget that his folios were themselves esteemed as pawnable lumber. In T. H. White's *Mistress Masham's Repose,* the underfed and word-hungry Professor, having misplaced his copy of Du Cange's *Glossary,* wonders for a salivary moment whether he should trade in one of his first-folio Shakespeares so he can buy a fishhook and snag some perch in one of the lakes of Malplaquet. Happily, Cook brings a packet of bloaters and the Professor can keep his Shakespeare. At the end of the novel, he receives *The Medieval Latin Word-List,* a gift that the Lilliputians have financed by "pawning their sprugs" (their gold coins), and he can finally look up the word that has been troubling his thoughts, the ambiguous *Tripharium.* (Though learned, T. H. White's book lacks *lumber.*)[1] Isaac D'Israeli, in his essay on

---

[1] Which makes no sense, since *Mistress Masham's Repose* takes place in Malplaquet, where *lumber*-users congregated. The Professor (who is, in

the recovery of manuscripts in *Curiosities of Literature,* tells how a lawyer in the papal court gave Petrarch two books by Cicero on Glory. Petrarch in turn

> lent them to a poor aged man of letters, formerly his preceptor. Urged by extreme want, the old man pawned them, and returning home died suddenly without having revealed where he had left them. They have never been recovered.

"Usurers," D'Israeli recounts, considered manuscripts

> as precious objects for pawn. A student of Pavia, who was reduced, raised a new fortune by leaving in pawn a manuscript of a body of law; and a grammarian, who was ruined by a fire, rebuilt his house with two small volumes of Cicero.

Medieval monastic libraries frequently demanded the deposit of a pledge before they loaned out books, and booksellers, or stationers, in university towns "had transcripts made, bought, sold and hired out books and received them in pawn."[1]

Fritz Eichenberg's illustrations, longobarded) recalls that "Dr. Swift was at Malplaquet, as we know, in 1712. He came here straight from Twit-nam, with the poet Pope." In White's Malplaquet there are "larders, laundries, cupboards, closets, still rooms, coal cellars, outward rooms frequented in his early days by Dr. Johnson, servants' halls, sculleries, harness rooms, pantries, dairies, cloakrooms, storerooms, and so forth," but no *lumber-room.* Did I miss it? The word *lumbago* jumped out at me several pages from the end (p. 249), but then I realized my error. (*Lumbago* makes you *lumber* because it hurts your back to walk normally.) When my mother read White's book to me, I assumed that "bloaters" were large pale German hot-dogs, but the *Concise Oxford Dictionary* says, incredibly, that they are smoked herrings. Listening to her read, I aspired to be the Professor—to live in a small booky shack in an overgrown garden. And in fact my office at this moment bears some resemblance to the Professor's *Rumpelkammer:* "As he was one of those unfortunate people who leave the book open at the quotation in some accessible place, all the window ledges, oven-shelves, mantel-pieces, fenders, and other flat surfaces were stocked with verified quotations, which had long been forgotten."

[1] *Old English Libraries,* Ernest A. Savage, 1912, p. 200. Savage quotes (pp. 202–3) from Henry Anstey's description (in his introduction to the *Munimenta Academica*) of the "ponderous iron chests, eight or ten feet

So Pope's unmannerly crack about Theobald's plagiariz-able library, "Where yet unpawn'd, much learned lumber lay," had an important literal meaning, too: Pope made a small fortune from his Homeric translations (jobbing out pieces of *The Odyssey* to junior poets and selling it all under his name), but Lewis Theobald was poor, clerkish, "supper-less" (so Pope cruelly calls him in *The Dunciad*), and in a pinch he would have relied on the possibility of pledging some of his sizable book collection as his bond. As late as 1731 Theobald was in serious financial distress: he wrote Warburton (who would later edit Pope) that "at present, when I should set down with a Mind & Head at ease & dis-embarrass'd, the Severity of a rich Creditor (& therefore the more unmercifull) has strip'd me so bare, that I never was acquainted with such Wants, since I knew the Use of Money."[1]

Poor in purse Theobald may have been; but he was not invariably a poor poet. *The Cave of Poverty* (1715) is a Gothic surprise—it describes the wicked Queen of Poverty in her cave, gloating over the misery she has wrought:

> Ten Thousand Doors, like Flaws in mouldring Earth,
> Led to the Center of the Gloomy Den;
> And each to streaky Gleams of Light gave Birth,
> That shot a-thwart the Dusk, and seem'd a-kin:
> > Pale as the Fire that on Night's Visage glows,
> > Serving alone her Horrors to disclose.

There are many stricken poets down in the cave—"Clusters of Bards" that lie in penury in "small silent Dormitories," trying to subsist:

---

in length and about half that width" that were kept by the university sta-tioner at Oxford in the late fifteenth century, holding "as many as a hundred or more large volumes, besides other valuables deposited as pledges by those who have borrowed from the chest."

[1] *Lewis Theobald*, Richard Foster Jones, 1919, p. 280.

With wild Profusion these consume their Store,
And rack Invention, lab'ring to be poor.[1]

And Theobald's *Shakespeare Restored* is an impressively rich work of textual criticism, too; the first of its kind on an English poet (as Theobald himself can't resist pointing out on the second-to-last page): its tone has some of Bentley's joshing roughness and show-offy annotative exuberance. As with many tractatuses, the supplemental material is more interesting than the main text—the sixty-one dense pages of Theobald's Appendix are full of insights and connections, some of them damaging to Pope. For instance, Pope had endorsed a change from "Aristotle thought" to "graver sages think" in a passage from *Troilus and Cressida*. In scandalized response, Theobald heaps up Diogenes Laertius, Cicero, Iamblichus, Strabo, Aullus Gellius, *King Lear, Coriolanus,* Beaumont and Fletcher's *Humorous Lieutenant,* Dryden and Lee's *Oedipus,* Sophocles, Anaxandrides, Alexis, Diphilus, Athenaeus, and others on the quarto page—invoking all these authors merely to prove that Shakespeare's anachronistic mention of Aristotle, in a play set in Troy, was "the Effect of Poetick Licence in him, rather than Ignorance" and that Pope's meddling was unwarranted, literal-minded, and indeed pedantic, which it was. Embarrassed, embittered by the exposure of his scholarly shortcomings, Pope adapted the premise of Theobald's

---

[1] Jones points out (p. 14) that Johann Jacob Bodmer (1698–1783), translator of *Paradise Lost* into German prose and author of an influential pre-Romantic treatise on the wonderful in poetry, was a fervent enthusiast of *The Cave of Poverty*. Theobald and Bodmer (a professor of history at Zurich) corresponded. Thus Pope's piddling arch-pedant, of all people, is a distinct English impulse behind German Romanticism, and German Romanticism in turn feeds back into English Romanticism. This pre-Romantic influence-laundering through a Swiss account makes more understandable a tiny but odd resemblance between the "Ten thousand doors" that lead to Theobald's gloomy cave and the "twice ten thousand caverns" reached by the tidal swell in Keats's sea-sonnet.

Cave of Poverty, swapping the Queen of Dulness for the Queen of Poverty and making Theobald himself the Queen's supplicant, and in this way came up with the first version of *The Dunciad,* which, over time, irreparably and wrongfully damaged Theobald's reputation. Theobald was without question a pedant[1]—but his is the good kind of pedantry, the kind in which playful fierceness and a motley flutter of cognate or merely ornamental references ("a Rhapsody of Rags," Burton or Donne would call it) colorfully and contentiously and self-parodically coexist. *The Cave of Poverty* is not dull, it's almost Dickensian, and *Shakespeare Restored* isn't dull, either, as Pope knew: the entertaining war between Bentley and Boyle over the authenticity of the letters of Phalaris had shown would-be pamphleteers that few things will get the readerly pulse racing like the spectacle of well-read scholars

---

[1] "It is hardly surprising that the phrase 'learned lumber' recurred to Pope's mind when describing Theobald's library in *Dunciad,* Book 1." (Maynard Mack, *Alexander Pope: A Life,* p. 429.) Peter Seary's superb *Lewis Theobald and the Editing of Shakespeare* (Oxford, 1990) devotes an appendix to Theobald's (vanished) library, which was auctioned over four evenings in 1744. Seary also shows that Theobald became increasingly sensitive to the *Dunciad*'s charge of pedantry, and therefore, in his edition of Shakespeare, suppressed his inclination to give tiny textual questions their discursive due: "Theobald's commentary established a new standard for editors of English texts and created new levels of expectation in the reading public, but a regrettable consequence of his fear of being considered a pedant is that often he fails to do himself justice in his accounts of his discoveries," writes Seary (p. 178). And Seary compellingly argues that Samuel Johnson, not Pope or even the despicable Warburton, was responsible for the conclusive defamation of Theobald as a scholar by the end of the eighteenth century: Johnson took over Theobald's methods and insights for his own edition of Shakespeare and for his *Dictionary* ("Theobald instituted the practice of citing parallels as a means of explicating obscure English words, and Johnson in the *Dictionary* followed his practice on an unprecedented scale," p. 207), while making unfair jabs at Theobald and failing to give him proper credit. Still, it is Pope's *Dunciad* that defames Theobald now—the fact that Johnson underappreciates him in his prefaces does no active harm to his reputation.

going after each other in the vernacular. (The *Poggio v. Filelfo*[1] and *Milton v. Salmasius* bouts were fought in Latin.) There was a market for learned strife in racy English. The same morning I read Theobald fume (rightly) at Pope's gratuitous "graver sages," I read this "Note upon the note" to an Englished version of Dr. Bentley's Horace, published by Lintot in 1712:

> In this *Ode* the Dr. makes a horrid Pother about the spelling of some proper Names; much Ink is spilt, many Pages consum'd, several old Parchments and Copies dusted, Commentators and Criticks quoted and confuted, various Lections settled, Indexes and Lexicons turn'd over, and a great deal of *Latin* and *Greek* squander'd away; and all to prove whether we must read, *Thyas,* or *Thias,* or *Thuas,* or *Thyias;* as also, whether we must say, *Rhacus,* or *Raecus,* or *Recus,* or *Runcus,* or *Rhucus,* or *Rhaetus,* or *Raetus. . . .*

But horrid Pothers over tiny cruces are exactly what we need from commentators: for they (the Pothers, I mean—and what an impossibly Anglican teacake of a word that is!) are hard evidence that someone has really grunted and sweated over this single lump of poetry. Some spelunker has stopped here, of all places, and sat down, and made this clammy side-grotto the temporary center of learning, toward which all else written impends; he has roamed as many of the "Ranks of subterranean Rooms" in the Cave of Poverty and poetry as he could, single-mindedly looking for antecedents; he has memorized, dated, compared and contrasted, triple-parsed, even dreamed about what he is elucidating—dreamed about it as Heinrich Heine's professor, in "The Harz Journey," dreams about

---

[1] Filelfo's orations and epithalamials were, writes John Addington Symonds, "conceived in the lumbering and pedantic style that passed for eloquence at that period." This is a *lumber* that mixes the sense of heavy footfalls and old vocabulary. (*Renaissance in Italy,* Modern Library, p. 456.)

walking in a beautiful garden where the flower-beds produced nothing but slips of white paper with quotations written on them, gleaming delightfully in the sunshine; and now and then he would pull up a handful and laboriously transplant them to a new bed, while the nightingales rejoiced his old heart with their sweetest notes.

So must have dreamed, I imagine, the far-darting commentator to Virginia Woolf's essays (vols. I–IV), Andrew McNeillie, who does not let go of one of Woolf's unattributed quotations until he has successfully located the unique floral attribution for its buttonhole; and on those rare occasions when he can't come up with a previous carnation, he sounds genuinely chagrined. Thus in her essay on Sir Walter Raleigh, Virginia Woolf mentions in passing the "vast and devouring space" of the centuries, and puts the phrase in quotation marks, without troubling to tell us where she got it. McNeillie searches everywhere, but for once he is stumped:

> The origin of this phrase, which VW also quotes in 'Papers on Pepys' below, has resisted all attempts at discovery.

Naturally I had to do a quick ROM-search for "vast and devouring space" in the *English Poetry Database;* I came up with half of it on Disk 3. In a verse drama called *Festus* (1877) by Spasmodic poet Philip James Bailey, a space-devouring work of 688 pages and over 31,000 lines that barely missed being excerpted in Palgrave's *Golden Treasury*[1]—a creation so vast, in fact, that the very word "vast"

---

[1] See "Some poems specifically considered but rejected" in the notes to Christopher Ricks's Penguin edition of *The Golden Treasury*, p. 511: "on whole too slight" was the final judgment in the manuscript of the anthology. In Edmund Gosse's *Critical Kit-Kats*, p. 145, there is this about the poem: "Mr. Bailey's *Festus* was really a power for evil, strong enough to be a momentary snare to the feet of Tennyson in writing *Maud*, and even of Browning."

appears in it 130 separate times (e.g., "Alp-blebs of fire, vast, vagrant")—you will find the phrase-fragment "devouring space" on line 15,772. Obviously this isn't Woolf's source—but since Bailey's *Festus* is a Faustian reworking, I felt some anticipatory giddiness at the possibility that the reference which had resisted McNeillie's researches might yield to my own, and that it would be waiting for me in Marlowe's *Dr. Faustus;* but when I hurried to the library to wash my hands in the milk of the excellent Marlowe concordance (Robert J. Fehrenbach, Lea Ann Boone, and Mario A. Di Cesare, 1982),[1] I determined that "vast and devouring space" wasn't to be found there (as *lumber* wasn't)—and how very presumptuous of me, anyway, to think that I could have divined the elusive source when McNeillie, who has devoted years of his life to this sort of maddening pursuit, could not. But someone someday, probably very soon (Chadwyck-Healey's *English Verse Drama Database* is out now),[2] will track it down. (*The Library of the Future* CD-ROM offers this from halfway through Dostoevsky's *Brothers Karamazov:* "The

---

[1] One of the dark-red Cornell Concordances that lure the eye here and there in the stacks—some of the others in the series sort the words of Ben Jonson, Herbert, Yeats, Blake, Skelton, Pascal's *Pensées,* Mandelstam, Racine, *Beowulf,* E. E. Cummings, and Swift. I can be sure I haven't missed any *lumber* in Samuel Johnson's poetry thanks to the Cornell *Concordance to the Poems of Samuel Johnson.* (A Latin epigram called "The Logical Warehouse: Occasioned by an Auctioneer's having the Groundfloor of the Oratory in Lincoln's-Inn-Fields" was the closest I got to *lumber-room:* it is printed as a poem of doubtful authorship in the Oxford edition of Johnson's poems.) One can easily become sentimental about these great series of concordances, since the more full-text material is available electronically, the less esteemed and understood they will be. They have magical as well as meaningful value, to use Larkin's dichotomy. "This person is worth studying," they affirm; "every word that this person wrote deserves its own private lanai of a line."

[2] I am avoiding it.

horses galloped on, 'devouring space,' and as he drew near his goal, again the thought of her, of her alone, took more and more complete possession of his soul. . . .") McNeillie is not alone; I am not alone: it is worth remembering that each lonely plodding footnoter is also an honorary citizen of the intergenerational federation of commentators. Virginia Woolf writes (in her essay called "Hours in a Library") that "a learned man is a sedentary, concentrated solitary enthusiast, who searches through books to discover some particular grain of truth upon which he has set his heart"; but he can draw comfort from the knowledge that other sedentary enthusiasts preceded him, and others will follow him—he can, if he wishes to wax eschatological, think of these as friends and colleagues of a sort, as Housman seems to have regarded Scaliger and Bentley, and "the next Bentley or Scaliger." Peter Lombard in his *Book of Sentences* built a useful central warehouse of theological quotation and analysis that developed, in the centuries after his death, a whole walled city and surrounding shantytown of secondary disputation and explication, as each hard-reading schoolman brought his trifles and trumpery to the great memorial Peter Lombard-room, to see what they were worth.[1] "A commentary must arise from the fortuitous discoveries of many men in devious walks of literature," wrote Samuel Johnson: I haven't read this quotation in its original context; I have plucked it from a paragraph by Pope's fussy Charles Kinbote of a commentator, the Reverend Whitwell Elwin, who includes it in his introduction to Pope's *Works*, on the same page that he announces his plan to cart off most of the "pedantic lumber" of previous commentators to appendixes.

---

[1] Maybe part of the reason scholastic learning was dismissed as "the lumber of the schools" was that Peter Lumber's *Sentences* occasioned so many heavy folio volumes.

And—to glance back at Lewis Theobald for a minute—one of the bits of pedantic lumber that *Shakespeare Restored* offers us is this note on *Hamlet*'s "bare bodkin" speech, which might have attracted Vladimir Nabokov's attention as he was imagining *Pale Fire*, since it supplies a missing connection (in the person of Theobald himself, Shakespeare's pedantic, moony worshipper, and Pope's antagonist) between Shakespeare, Pope, and the Kinbote-anagram, *botkin*:

> I can scarce suppose that he [Shakespeare] intended to descend to a Thought, that a Man might dispatch himself with a *Bodkin,* or little Implement with which Women separate, and twist over their Hair. I rather believe, the Poet designed the Word here to signify, according to the old Usage of it, a *Dagger.*

But *Pale Fire*'s Charles Kinbote—the Zemblan émigré who explicates an uneven neo-Augustan poem in rhymed couplets by John Shade—isn't only a stand-in for Pope's minor bodkin-toting foe, Lewis Theobald: he is all of Pope's eulogistic or crabby commentators superimposed. Here is how the Reverend Elwin describes an early editor, Warburton:

> He employed his sagacity less to discover than to distort the ideas of his author, and seems to have thought that the more he deviated from the obvious sense the greater would be his fame for inventive power. . . . The exuberant self-sufficiency of Warburton deluded him into the belief that [Pope's] text derived its principal lustre from the commentary. He selected for the frontispiece to his edition a monument on which were hung medallions of himself and the poet, and Blakey, the draughtsman, told Burke that 'it was by Warburton's particular desire that he made him the principal figure, and Pope only secondary, and that the light, contrary to the rules of art, goes upwards from Warburton to Pope.' (xx–xxi)

The lighting is very *Pale Fiery* indeed. But then another Pope editor, Mark Pattison, says this of Reverend Elwin:

> Mr. Elwin has adopted an opinion that Pope was engaged in a conspiracy with Bolingbroke for the writing down of the Christian religion, and the substitution of Bolingbroke's irreligious meta-

physics in its place. . . . To what Mr. Elwin has said of Warburton's commentary, we can make no objection. But he has sadly laid himself open to a *tu quoque* retort, by reproducing against Pope the same strained interpretation, the same imputation of meaning never meant, and the same inconclusive prosing on moral problems, which he objects to in Warburton.

Elwin reminds Pattison, in fact, of Richard Bentley's editing of *Paradise Lost:*

> Bentley first created a fictitious editor, who had corrected the poem for the blind author. Having set up this imaginary personage, he could attribute to his forgery every word or line which he wished to correct. Mr. Elwin sets up the hypothesis of an antichristian conspiracy, and deduces from it the meaning of particular passages.[1]

This is not so very far from Kinbote's paranoid pother over John Shade's wife's suppression of the Zemblan dimension of Shade's poem in its final version:

> [W]e may conclude that the final text of *Pale Fire* has been deliberately and drastically drained of every trace of the material I contributed; but we also find that despite the control exercised upon my poet by a domestic censor and God knows whom else, he has given the royal fugitive a refuge in the vaults of the variants he has preserved. . . . (*Pale Fire,* Vintage ed., p. 81)

And A. E. Housman—whose poems are referred to by Charles Kinbote as the "highest achievement in English poetry in the past hundred years"—is a fussing presence behind Nabokov's novel, too. There is one passage in particular from Housman's *Selected Prose* that could have opened an injector valve in Nabokov's Russian-gauge locomotive, if he saw it. It is from a snide review of a book of Lucilian fragments edited by Friedrich Marx:

> Mr Marx should write a novel. Nay, he may almost be said to have written one; for his notes on book iii (Lucilius' journey to Sicily)

---

[1] Pattison's *Essays,* vol. II (1889), "Pope and His Editors."

are not so much a commentary on the surviving fragments as an original narrative of travel and adventure.[1]

The twenty-year-old Nabokov, in the words of his biographer Brian Boyd, encountered, while at Cambridge, Housman's "glum features and drooping-thatch mustache . . . at Trinity's high table almost every night";[2] and Boyd quotes helpfully from *Speak, Memory,* where Nabokov admits

> the direct influence upon my Russian structures of various contemporaneous ("Georgian") English verse patterns that were running about my room and all over me like tame mice.

Mice are in their element in poetry's l.-room, by the way. Robert Louis Stevenson has a line in his *Child's Garden of Verses* about "mice among the lumber" (although he may well be talking about outdoor lumber—hay or stubble or brush, or even possibly wood—here);[3] and there are ten other nineteenth-century poems in the *English Poetry Database* that contain *lumber* and *mice* or *mouse* in them, including a read-aloud piece of sentimentalism by Mary Montgomerie Lamb (1843–1905), also known as Violet Fane. (She would not want to be confused with Mary Ann Lamb, Charles Lamb's matricidal sister.) It is called "The Old Rocking-Horse (In the Lumber-Room)":

---

[1] A. E. Housman, *Selected Prose,* ed. John Carter, p. 107. Carter's selection was published in 1962, however, the same year as *Pale Fire,* so that in order for this passage to have had some slight influential bearing on Nabokov's novel, we would have to assume that Nabokov read it in its original form in an issue of Oxford's *Classical Quarterly* from 1907, which is a sizable assumption.

[2] Brian Boyd, *Vladimir Nabokov: The Russian Years,* p. 171.

[3] Garden darkened, daisy shut,
　　Child in bed, they slumber—
Glow-worm in the highway rut,
　　Mice among the lumber.　(R. L. Stevenson, "Night and Day")

> The mice, in their frolicsome revels,
>   Sport over him night and day,
> And the burrowing moth
> In his saddle-cloth
>   Has never been flick'd away. . . .
>
> What a medley of eloquent lumber
>   Do his proud eyes lighten upon,
> From those drums and flutes
> To the high snow boots
>   And the mouldering stuff'd wild swan . . .

Yeats got the stuff'd wild swan of rhymed poetry to fly again at Coole a few decades later.[1]

It wasn't Housman's tame Georgian verse-mice, however, that swayed Nabokov in later years. Housman the critic (captious, haughty, ferulean) left his permanent mark on Nabokov's nonfictional style, just as Francis Jeffrey's harsh intelligence marked Housman. Here, for example, is Housman sounding sneeringly Nabokovian on the subject of translation:

"Scholars [Housman quotes] will pardon an attempt, however bald, to render into English these exquisite love-poems." Why?

---

[1] There is a mouse among the lumber of *Stultifera Navis: or, The Modern Ship of Fools,* by William Henry Ireland (1777–1835), once famous as a forger of Shakespeariana. Section XXXI, entitled "Of Foolish Antiquaries," has:

> Old stones, bones, coffins, without number,
> Pots, pipkins, pans, such kitchen lumber;
> Old chain, mail, armour, weapons rusty,
> Coins, medals, parchments, writings musty:
> Yet, after all antiques, not one compare I can
> To that most rare of all, an antiquarian.

("Mouse" comes earlier in the poem, in a footnote.) The *English Duden* (1960), a pictorial dictionary, gives an illustration for "lumber" in its two-page spread on "The Store Room" which shows an old umbrella, some cardboard boxes, a set of weightlifter's disks, and (no. 74) "the mouse."

Those who have no Latin may pardon such an attempt, if they like bad verses better than silence; but I do not know why bald renderings of exquisite love-poems should be pardoned by those who want no renderings at all. . . . Misrepresentation of Propertius is indeed the capital defect of this performance; good or bad, in movement, in diction, in spirit, it is unlike the original.[1]

Nabokov and Housman both used huge critical projects (Pushkin, Manilius) as ways of rationing self-expression—as counterweights to the trebuchet-flights of their lyricism.[2]

---

[1] "Tremenheere's 'Cynthia' of Propertius," in *Selected Prose,* pp. 91–93.

[2] The *lombard,* or *lombarda,* was a kind of military "engine," says the *OED,* used in sixteenth-century Spain. The first quotation the *OED* supplies for this separate meaning of *lombard* is from 1838. But Samuel Wesley uses artillery lumber in a metaphor in 1700, from his *Epistle to a Friend concerning Poetry:*

> A thousand trivial Lumber-Thoughts will come,
> A thousand Fagot-Lines will crowd for room;
> Reform your Troops [i.e., rewrite, cut], and no Exemption grant,
> You'll gain in Strength, what you in Numbers want.

It's tempting to think of the military *lombard* as a species of small trebuchet, turning dead lumbering weight into parabolic flight. (In the *Scientific American,* July 1995, Paul E. Chevedden, Les Eigenbrod, Vernard Foley, and Werner Soedel describe a modern reconstruction of a medieval trebuchet that successfully tossed a junk car, sans engine, eighty meters, using a thirty-ton counterweight. For a few seconds that car was not junk, it was science—it soared above all landfills.) But it may be that the *lombarda* wasn't in fact a portable trebuchet, but some sort of gun or cannon (cf. the *OED*'s ambiguous quotation of Zurita's *Annales,* 1610: "Começo se a combatir la ciudad con diuersos trabucos [trebuchets?] y lombardas")—or that Samuel Wesley (who was for a short time a chaplain on a man-of-war, according to the *Dictionary of National Biography,* and may have had some idea of what he is talking about, as I do not) is referring with his *lumber-thoughts* not to the *lombarda* at all, whatever it was, but the *limber.* The *limber* was a "two-wheeled carriage forming a detachable part of the equipment of all guns on travelling carriages," according to the *Encyclopaedia Britannica,* 11th ed., "Limber." The *limber-box* held ammunition. The notion of an army pulling its horse-drawn *limber*-carriages overland could have further helped the word "lumber" to load up on its heavy, hulking connotations. (*Limber* is still a word in use in the military sense, by the way. You can buy a Civil War

Naturally I looked semi-diligently in Housman's writing for the l. word, since any appearance of it would help me in my passing attempt to yoke him and Nabokov by violence to the same limber-load. But Housman, more power to him, prefers a quiet, beautiful word like *marl,* which collapses all the travertines of St. Peter's into its earthen fold, and yet escapes any charge of pedantry because no word so short was ever crabbed:

> In gross marl, in blowing dust,
>   In the drowned ooze of the sea,
> Where you would not, lie you must,
>   Lie you must, and not with me.   (XXXIII, *Last Poems*)

In prose he uses lumber-nyms like *dross-heap:* "Thinly scattered on that huge dross-heap, the Caroline Parnassus, there were tiny gems of purer ray." Where another writer might more gently speak of the lumber-room of Dryden's diction, Housman brutally calls it a "dungeon." The only real *lumber* I turned up in my hours with Housman was contained in a sentence by Francis Jeffrey, which Housman quotes disapprovingly in his review of *The Cambridge History of English Literature:*

> The tuneful quartos of Southey are already little better than lumber:—and the rich melodies of Keats and Shelley,—and the fantastical emphasis of Wordsworth,—and the plebeian pathos of Crabbe, are melting fast from the field of our vision.

"Little better than lumber" is a telling metaphorical choice for Jeffrey to have made, from the present vantage, since if

---

cannon and sixteen-inch limber for $130 from the *Art & Artifact* catalog, Fall Preview, 1995, p. 35: "The wheeled artillery limber with an opening trunk [that is, the limber-box] attaches to the back of the cannon.") Possibly *lumber-thoughts* was a simple typo for *limber-thoughts* (rather than a variant spelling of *lombard-thoughts*) in the one and only printing of Samuel Wesley's poem.

you search "Southey, R. OR Wordsworth, W. OR Crabbe, G. OR Keats, J. OR Shelley, P.B." for *lumber* in the *English Poetry Database* you will discover that none of them were lumberjacks, except for George Crabbe, once. (In a poem called "The Birth of Flattery," Flattery, the offspring of Poverty and Cunning, is able to revive the bloom of graceless forms, and "bid the lumber live.")[1]

Housman's and the Romantic poets' neglect didn't deter Nabokov, who, surprisingly enough, gives our chosen keyword a prominent setting in *Pale Fire*. The deposed Zemblan king, Charles, is imprisoned in a "dismal lumber room" (p. 121) in the royal palace. This "old hole of a room" contains a closet, and in the closet is a Zemblan translation of Shakespeare's *Timon of Athens,* as well as some "old sport clothes and gymnasium shoes," which will, for the ~-obsessed, recall Samuel Butler's lines (in "Religion") about the Sanctum of the Jews containing nothing but "lumber and old shoos," and will perhaps also bring to mind Dickens's mention of the old

---

[1] The quartos of Francis Jeffrey are little better than lumber now, but not the quartos of Southey: Southey brought us the story of Goldilocks and the Three Bears (in *The Doctor*), as well as one of the great poems about scholarship. Palgrave in his *Golden Treasury* titled it "The Scholar." Here are the first and last stanzas:

> My days among the Dead are past;
> Around me I behold,
> Where'er these casual eyes are cast,
> The mighty minds of old:
> My never-failing friends are they,
> With whom I converse day by day.

> My hopes are with the Dead; anon
> My place with them will be,
> And I with them shall travel on
> Through all Futurity;
> Yet leaving here a name, I trust,
> That will not perish in the dust.

shoes and fish baskets in Ebenezer Scrooge's lumber room.[1] A sliding door in the Zemblan lumber-room closet leads to a long secret passageway through which the King escapes; stumbling over "an accumulation of loose boards" (p. 133), he enters a second "dimly lit, dimly cluttered" lumber room, or *lumbarkamer* (this time Kinbote is good enough to supply us with the actual Zemblan-language equivalent),[2] a retreat that was once, as it happens, a dressing room in the Royal Theater, where Iris Acht, paramour of the King's grandfather, puffed and patched herself in preparation for her role in *The Merman*. All this is complicated and full of quadrupal playful para-meanings with short half-lives that I don't really follow, but it seems safe to say that the loose boards that block the door are Nabokov's nod to the preferred American meaning of *lumber*, which causes us pedestrians to stumble and mis-step in our comprehension of Anglicisms like *lumber-room*; and both ~rooms, linked by so "angular and cryptic" a passageway, could without too much symbolic tussling be taken to represent the two received linguistic traditions, the two dictionaries filled with ready-made verbal scenery, that the commentator king, and by inference Nabokov himself, must unite through painful acts of verbal and physical translation. Nabokov escapes one Russian *lumbarkamer* of second-hand literary heirlooms only to have to contend with the dust and sheets of an Anglo-American substitute.

---

[1] "Lumber-room as usual. Old fire-guard, old shoes, two fish-baskets, washing-stand on three legs, and a poker." (*A Christmas Carol*, "Marley's Ghost.") The detectable strain of anti-Semitism, or at least of raised Semitic consciousness, in some *lumber*-contexts can't be ignored. Jews are the heroic keepers of the past; that fact has amused or irritated some poets and novelists. Nabokov himself, however, wasn't anti-Semitic.

[2] The word (or *a* word, at least) for *lumber-room* in Russian is *kladovaia*. Vladimir Krymov wrote *Iz Kladovoi Pisatelia* (1951), which some online library catalogs translate as *From a Writer's Lumber Room*. In keeping with general European usage, a *lombard* in Russian is a pawnshop.

(iv)

And why was Nabokov so interested in the word? It may have caused him some memory-triggering linguistic trouble when he was teaching *Madame Bovary* in translation at Wellesley and Cornell. In the course he taught, partially published as *Lectures on Literature,* Nabokov worked over *Dr. Jekyll and Mr. Hyde* (which contains some "lumber of crates and bottles" and some "crazy lumber," although he didn't mention this fact to his students), and *Bleak House;* the scene at Krook's Rag and Bottle Warehouse, displaying "Kitchen-Stuff," "Old Iron," "Waste Paper," "shabby old volumes," and "Bones" (no *lumber*) Nabokov described in detail. Then he came to *Madame Bovary,* and dwelt on the "wonderful" jam-making scene (Part III, ch. 2) in which (and this is Nabokov, not Flaubert, speaking)

> little Justin, who having been told to fetch an additional pan for the jam, took one from the lumber room in the dangerous neighborhood of a blue jar with arsenic.

This is the same lumber-room arsenic that Emma later eats, having coaxed the key from Justin. Twice in his lecture notes

Nabokov mentions Flaubert's "lumber room"—it is the alchemical garret in which Homais, the self-important druggist, stores his apothecary materials and performs chemical putterings, pretending to be more of a man of science than he is:

> He often spent long hours alone there [writes Flaubert, as translated by Lowell Bair], labeling, decanting and repackaging, and he regarded it not as an ordinary storeroom, but as a veritable sanctuary from which issued all sorts of pills, boluses, decoctions, lotions and potions which he had made with his own hands and which would spread his fame throughout the countryside.

In the original French, the name that Flaubert has Homais give his upstairs sanctuary is not one of the cluster of basic alternatives for "warehouse" or "place of storage"—words like *depôt* or *magasin* or *debarras* or *grenier.* Rather it is the exotic-sounding (exotic at least to English-speakers) *capharnaüm.* Capernaum was the town in Galilee where such a press of spectators gathered to hear Jesus (Mark 2) that a palsied man had to be lowered in his bed through the roof to be healed, and it was the site of various other miracles and pronouncements, including the sermon Jesus preached (John 6) after the feeding of the five thousand with the magic loaves and fish-baskets. Hence "un vrai capharnaüm" came to mean (according to the stacked volumes of *Littré* and *Le Grand Robert* and *Trésor de la Langue Française*), a room in which lots of things are tumbled together pell-mell—a "lieu de désordre et de débauche." Harrap's dictionary and the *Oxford French Dictionary* offer *bear-garden* and *glory hole* as English equivalents, but these have an unsavory ring. "Lumber room" is the term that J. Lewis May supplies in his translation, the text that was imported into the *Library of the Future* CD-ROM. Translations by Mildred Marmur (Signet), Joan Charles (edited by Somerset Maugham), Alan Russell (Penguin Classics), Francis Steegmuller (Quality Paperback Book Club), and Paul de Man

(Norton) give *Capharnaum* without umlaut or explanation;[1] clearly, however, the English reader needs some interpretive help. Lowell Bair's translation for Bantam floats *depository* as an alternative, turning Homais's beakered retreat into a sperm bank, which may not be so far wrong, since it is the place where, in Flaubert's nudging phrase, he "se délectait dans l'exercice de ses prédilections." Gerard (not Manley) Hopkins, on the other hand, in his Oxford Classics edition, gives the burly and Father-Knows-Bestial *Den*.

Nabokov also addressed the problem of the best English equivalent. Although he uses *lumber room* in the published text of his lectures on *Madame Bovary,* it seems that he also at times tried *storeroom.* On a handwritten list of mistranslated words that he evidently read aloud to his students, in order that they might correct their copies of the Aveling translation—a facsimile of which, headed "Last Batch of Mistranslated Words," one may inspect in the *Lectures on Literature* paperback, p. 161—*Capharnaum* appears next to "storeroom (or house of confusion)." An additional hard-to-read note says "derived from the name of a [?devastated] city in Palestine." Maybe this list dates from a period following the first composition of the lectures: having encountered some American-undergraduate bewilderment when he used *lumber room,* Nabokov possibly fell back on a plainer word. But *Den, depository,* and *storeroom* are not good enough: they strip the faded splendor, the reverberantly umlauted plume of Carthaginianism, from *capharnaüm,* which in the

---

[1] Eleanor Marx Aveling, who was responsible for the version of *Bovary* that Nabokov assigned, did use an umlaut. She, we learn from Julian Barnes's *Flaubert's Parrot,* was the first English translator of the work, and, sunk in a *cafard*-naum of her own, she later killed herself with prussic acid.

mouth of a small-town pseudo-savant and freethinker like Homais is exasperating and ludicrous, and yet still preserves (as does *lumber room,* with its fitful gleams of old gold and Lombard wealth) a residue of its own original radical glory. "I can't accept the idea of a God who goes walking in his garden with his cane in his hand, lodges his friends in the bellies of whales, dies with a groan and comes back to life three days later," Homais tells Emma; his capharnaüm holds "acids and caustic alkalis" (which he sells on credit to Charles), rather than a prophet and a throng of converts. But it is nonetheless a place of novelistic transubstantiation, of course, in which Emma, driven to eat fistfuls of arsenic powder in Homais's chemical attic, an act without any of the classical panache of asps or hemlock, nonetheless manages to resurrect herself as an immortal tragic heroine, right on the powder-white page.

There is another beakerful of meaning in this seductive word, too. Gallic lexicographers suggest that *capharnaüm* may be influenced by a ruralism from the region of Berry, in central France. The Berry patois has *cafournion* or *cafourneau* or *caforgnau* (possibly a splice from *caverne,* "cavern," and *fourneau,* "stove"), meaning a little shack or side-room or shed or cabin. So the Eastern strangeness of one ancient biblical etymology merges with the hobnailed and humble country dialect of another. George Sand, soon to become Flaubert's esteemed correspondent, had called attention to the berrichon word in her pastoral novel *La Petite Fadette* (1848): her narrator takes a long sentence to explain that a schoolmaster would censure her for saying *carphanion* rather than *carphanaüm* [sic], but that she would have to teach *him* what it referred to: "the lumber room . . . the part of the barn next to the stables where we keep the yokes, chains, and tools of all kinds used with working beasts and for working the soil." (This English is taken from Eva Figes's

1967 translation, *Little Fadette*.) *Capharnaüm*, then, is an ideal word for Flaubert's purposes, which are to domesticate exoticism, to interleave realism with high romance, to confuse coarseness and exaltation. Homais's grandly named refuge may also, I note, be a fictionalization of what Flaubert called his "citadel" (*citadelle*). This was, George Sand writes in her diary for August 29, 1866, "a strange little old house built of wood that he uses as a wine store."[1] No doubt he exercised his predilections there, too.

Which carries us to Proust, who defended Flaubert's steely style late in his life from an attack in the *Nouvelle Revue Française*, but who listed George Sand as his favorite writer when he was fourteen. Readers of *Swann's Way* will remember Marcel's affection for Sand's "romans champêtres," and for the old forms of speech that his grandmother used, which were like old armchairs, on which

> we can still see traces of a metaphor whose fine point has been worn away by the rough usage [*usure*] of our modern tongue. As it happened, the pastoral novels of George Sand which she was giving me for my birthday were regular lumber-rooms full of expressions that have fallen out of use and become quaint and picturesque, and are now only to be found in country dialects.

One has to believe that *capharnaüm* was one of the worn-away words from Sand's pastoral dens that Proust had in mind here—and yet in the original, where we would hope to visit *un véritable capharnaüm* we confront, instead, a mere *mobilier ancien*, not a packed attic but something old packed away *in* an attic, as if Proust were deliberately obscuring his tracks by the Galilean lake, or as if he had

---

[1] See the Steegmuller-Bray translation of the Flaubert-Sand correspondence (1993), p. 18, and Anne Chevereau's edition of Sand's *Agendas*, vol. III (1992), p. 384.

interrupted his writing to think over "capharnaüm" and then had chosen to redirect his phrasing slightly, unwilling to dose his clause with Emma's arsenic, or unable to tolerate so thoroughly vulgarized a metaphor in his own prose, although he could love it and celebrate it in his grandmother's speech and in his mother's evening readings from Sand. Or Proust could here have fallen in step with some allied passage in an English book—possibly something from one of Ruskin's cathedral-threnodies (the mention of the fine points of ornament effaced by the rough usury of the modern tongue has a Lombardic stonemason's provenance that recalls Ruskin), flamboyancies that Proust's mother had diligently translated for him into "several red, green and yellow school exercise books" (see chapter 9 of Ronald Hayman's biography), as he, fired up with Ruskin-love despite his own TOEFL-unready English, wrote a series of essays about the church sites that Ruskin had so copiously empurpled. But I must resist the urge to page through the thirty volumes of Ruskin that Proust said he owned, or even through the French studies of Ruskin by Robert de la Sizeranne and J. A. Milsand whose translated passages Proust drew on for his essays before his English improved. I'm sure the lumber rests somewhere there; I'm sure that I would have to spend only four or five days holed up in the ornate 39-volume library edition by Cook and Wedderburn (1903) and—as in the story Ruskin tells in *Sesame and Lilies* (a work Proust translated) of some schoolboys throwing stones at their books, which they had piled on gravestones—the dead ~ would live again:

> So, also, we play with the words of the dead that would teach us, and strike them far from us with our bitter, reckless will; little thinking that those leaves which the wind scatters had been piled, not only upon a gravestone, but upon the seal of an enchanted vault—nay, the gate of a great city of sleeping kings, who would

awake for us, and walk with us, if we knew but how to call them by their names.

New lamps for old—that's what the novelist gives us: he beats the rugs, and with a bit of torn T-shirt he works the Old English petroleum distillate into the starved fleurette of the doubtful *fauteil,* and suddenly those huddled movables we always vaguely knew we owned and yet never gave their due seem worth hauling out into sunlit living rooms: the city of sleeping things and kings starts up, staggers in, and begins raving like Vault Whitman, who in 1855, ten years before Ruskin had imagined saying "Open Sesame" to the enchanted and encrypted city of the dead, in his thereafter suppressed Introduction to the first edition of *Leaves of Grass* (an edition that Malcolm Cowley calls, in his Penguin introduction, "the buried masterpiece of American writing"), wrote:

> The greatest poet forms the consistence of what is to be from what has been and is. He drags the dead out of their coffins and stands them again on their feet . . . he says to the past, Rise and walk before me that I may realize you.

Whitman, though, only uses *lumber* to mean *timber.*

Or, less hysterically, Proust could be remembering *Middlemarch.* During his tussles with the writing of *Jean Santeuil* he said in a letter: "There are moments when I wonder whether I do not resemble the husband of Dorothea Brook in *Middlemarch,* and whether I am not collecting ruins."[1] Of *Middlemarch*'s pasty and cold-fingered Mr. Casaubon—the collector of dead mythologies, whose promised Key to them all turns out to open nothing more than a cabinet of dry and worthless salvages from a lifetime of severe study—the impassioned Will Ladislaw says to Dorothea:

---

[1] *Proust: A Biography,* Ronald Hayman, p. 139. Either Proust or Hayman leaves off the terminal "e" in "Brooke."

"Do you not see that it is no use now to be crawling a little way after men of the last century—men like Bryant—and correcting their mistakes?—living in a lumber-room and furbishing up broken-legged theories about Chus and Mizraim?"

(I skimmed 165 pages of the Riverside edition before I found this; the fact that it was embedded in dialogue made it harder to spot.) Some pages earlier George Eliot lays out another lumber-room or curiosity-shop image. "The idea of this dried-up pedant," thinks Ladislaw as he falls in love with Dorothea,

> this elaborator of small explanations about as important as the surplus stock of false antiquities kept in a vendor's back chamber, having first got this adorable young creature to marry him, and then passing his honeymoon away from her, groping after his mouldy futilities (Will was given to hyperbole)—this sudden picture stirred him with a sort of comic disgust . . . (Riverside edition, p. 152.)

Eliot probably was thinking of Faust's line to Wagner about the spirit of the age being a *Rumpelkammer* when she had Will talk scornfully of living in a lumber-room. She translated Goethe and "read probably every word" by him, according to Gordon Haight, one of her biographers; and she helped G. H. Lewes with his once well-known biography, *The Life and Works of Goethe* (1855).

Mark Pattison, editor of Pope and biographer of Isaac Casaubon, was George Eliot's primary model for the character of Mr. Casaubon,[1] though Pattison is a more likable and (on paper, at least) a more complicated figure than the *Middlemarch* dry goods merchant. "To be mesmerized by a vast subject is a dilettante feature and a recipe for disaster," writes

---

[1] For some of the details of the link, see John Sparrow's *Mark Pattison and the Idea of University*. Gordon Haight strongly disagrees that Mr.

C. O. Brink, in his *English Classical Scholarship*. "It devitalizes activity and tends to cause such creative powers as there are to wither. I wonder," he adds, "if not something like it happened to Pattison."[1] And yet the last chapter of Pattison's best book, his biography *Isaac Casaubon,* is a frightening but inspiring portrait of a compulsive reader, a Greek-citation-hoarder, an urn-burier, who was (like all scholars, but especially those who spend a lifetime preparing themselves to write something that is too big for one brain to encompass) "greater than his books."[2] Books Isaac Casaubon did write, as Mark Pattison himself did, but they were never the Big Book, and instead he took Alp-blebs of notes. Unfortunately, the notes are useless without the mind they served:

> What he jots down is not a remark of his own on what he reads, nor is it even the words he has read; it is a mark, a key, a catchword, by which the point of what he has read may be recovered in memory.

"To this vast mass of material," writes Pattison of the real Casaubon, "his own memory was the only key." A sympathetic scrutineer, looking over Isaac Casaubon's shoulder with Pattison's help at his literary remains, sees only what Dorothea Brooke finally worked up the courage to examine in *her* fictional Mr. Casaubon's cabinet—he sees (again in Pattison's surprisingly lyrical and heartfelt words)

Casaubon was inspired by Mark Pattison, and devotes Appendix II of his biography to the "canard." But he isn't convincing.

[1] *English Classical Scholarship,* 1985, p. 132. To be mesmerized by a tiny subject can be a dilettante feature and a recipe for disaster, too. Brink goes on to quote from a letter of A. E. Housman to Lord Asquith asserting that Pattison was "a spectator of all time and all existence, and the contemplation of that repulsive scene is fatal to accurate learning."

[2] Mark Pattison, *Isaac Casaubon,* 2nd ed., Oxford: Clarendon Press, 1892, Section X, p. 434.

disjointed fragments, lying there massive and helpless, like the boulders of some abraded stratification.[1]

But the observer must nonetheless acknowledge, Pattison urges, that in the posthumous rubble of Isaac Casaubon (as in that of Mark Pattison, who abandoned his huge history of Renaissance scholarship) he is witnessing "the remains of a stupendous learning," which is something valuable and admirable, after all. Eliot called her *Middlemarch* notebook "Quarry," and this Ozymandian final chapter by Pattison, uninsistently autobiographical, was certainly one of the marmoreal desolations from which she prised chunks and cooked them for lime.[2]

Nor should we be surprised that Mark Pattison resorts to the word "lumber" himself, as he prepares to defend Isaac Casaubon's old-fashioned scholarship from the attacks of anti-pedants like Thomas De Quincey:

---

[1] *Isaac Casaubon,* p. 430. There are rhythms in this exciting sentence-fragment that remind one of Gibbon's translation of Poggio's description of fifteenth-century Rome: "The forum of the Roman people, where they assembled to enact their laws and elect their magistrates, is now enclosed for the cultivation of pot-herbs, or thrown open for the reception of swine and buffaloes. The public and private edifices, that were founded for eternity, lie prostrate, naked, and broken, like the limbs of a mighty giant; and the ruin is the more visible, from the stupendous relics that have survived the injuries of time and fortune." (*Decline and Fall,* vol. VIII, ch. 71.) The incoherent notes that survive a great classical scholar who has failed to complete his great work have, then, some of the sublimity and grandeur of Poggio's broken Forum. Still, I did not succeed in finding any *lumber* in Gibbon's descriptions of fallen Rome or sacked Constantinople.

[2] Latter-day Romans made cement by burning marble ruins for lime. A footnote by Dean Milman in the 1855 Milman, Guizot, and Smith edition of Gibbon, published by John Murray, says (vol. VIII, p. 277): "Ancient Rome was considered a quarry from which the church, the castle of the baron, or even the hovel of the peasant, might be repaired." Gordon Haight reports that George Eliot read *Decline and Fall* in 1855 and again in 1864; *Middlemarch* was written c. 1870.

De Quincey has endorsed the complaint that "the great scholars were poor as thinkers." De Quincey wrote at a time when "original thinking" was much in repute, and was indeed himself one of the genial race to whom all is revealed in a moment, in visions of the night. . . . A freshness and a vigour characterise the english and german literature of the fifty years 1780–1830, which are due to this effect [?effort] to discard the lumber of "unenlightened" ages.[1]

Looking up from this passage, which indirectly puts De Quincey and Pattison at antipodes, one can almost envision George Eliot conjuring up the figure of De Quincey as she worked out the character of Will Ladislaw—De Quincey being, like Ladislaw, a Lake-poet enthusiast, though not actually a poet, a follower of German esthetic philosophy, though not quite a philosopher himself, and above all, an extremely chatty and intelligent journalist. Why De Quincey himself resisted the temptation to use the word *lumber* in recounting his opium dreams or in writing about Pope I do not know.[2]

But to return to Proust momentarily, before we take leave for the time being of the confusingly crowded French tabernacle and return to the safe haven of Augustan English prose (since my French is sorrier than Proust's English, and Proust, says Hayman, "would have found it hard to order a chop in an English restaurant"[3])—the thing worth pointing out is that in *Swann's Way,* in the paragraph that follows Marcel's com-

---

[1] *Isaac Casaubon,* pp. 448–9.

[2] In his treatment of Pope's *Essay on Man,* however, De Quincey presciently describes Mr. Casaubon's *Key to All Mythologies.* The *Essay on Man* is a work, writes De Quincey, "which, when finished, was not even begun; whose arches wanted their key-stones; whose parts had no coherency; and whose pillars, in the very moment of being thrown open to public view, were already crumbling into ruins." (*Essays on the Poets,* "Alexander Pope," Ticknor & Fields, 1856, p. 193.)

[3] My French isn't nearly as bad as my Latin, which would have made Virginia Woolf cough discreetly behind her hand.

parison of George Sand's figures of speech to an old and exiled armchair, when he speaks of the "beauty and sweetness" of his mother's reading voice, and of how she

> supplied all the natural tenderness, all the lavish sweetness which they demanded to sentences which seemed to have been composed for her voice and which were all, so to speak, within the compass of her sensibility

—the thing worth noting is that Proust may be not only remembering George Sand's novels at bedtime, which in their quaint way supplied him with a stock of "narrative devices" that are "common to a great many novels," but also privately cherishing his mother's more recent literal renderings in French of Ruskin and (perhaps) other English masters of the longer-handled ladle. And it is just possible that Proust owes something of his feeling for his grandmother's linguistic furniture to Henry James's *Spoils of Poynton,* a novel about (to be crude) the sale of old furniture. Proust's grandmothery passage about the metaphors effaced by the *usure* of the modern tongue recalls James's lovely "She hated the effacement to which English usage reduced the widowed mother. . . ." from chapter 5. I don't know enough about Proust to say with any certainty that he had read James's *Spoils,* but it is his kind of book,[1] and Proust did after all write (in 1910), as quoted by Ronald Hayman:

> It is curious that in all the contrasted kinds of writing from George Eliot to Hardy, from Stevenson to Emerson, there is no literature

---

[1] As is Elizabeth Gaskell's *Wives and Daughters* (1864–66), a *Poynton* precursor in which some beloved old furniture of a dead mother is stored away by a tasteless stepmother: "Most girls would be glad to get rid of furniture only fit for the lumber-room," says Mrs. Kirkpatrick, on p. 189 of the Oxford Classics edition. I'm grateful to my wife for pointing out this reference. While I was reading *Wives and Daughters* (just to p. 189, where I

which exerts on me a power comparable to that of English and American literature.

On Proust's own authority, then, let's politely take leave of him and George Sand and of Flaubert, especially Flaubert: for if it is this fraught an undertaking to arrive at a full-bellied understanding of a plain English pork-chop of a word like *lumber-room,* as I am finding it to be, then it will be next to impossible to make sense of Flaubert's untranslatable *chutes* and *laideurs.* Let's return, instead, to the green and pleasant Samuel Johnson.

---

stopped, off to lumber-pastures new), I came across some passages about a certain Lord and Lady Cumnor and heard in their names the minuet-music of country gentry, and was reminded of Alexander Pope's game of *ombre* in the second version of *The Rape of the Lock.* It occurred to me that if one didn't know anything about the etymology of *lumber,* one might guess that it was from *l'ombre,* "shade" or "shadow"—and one would imagine that lumbery things were stored away in the shadows of l'umbra-rooms, over-seen by Pope's melancholy gnome, Umbriel, whose name is just *lumber* with the *l* displaced. The *Concise Oxford French Dictionary* has *mettre un homme à l'ombre* meaning (colloquially) to put a man in prison, and this is also one of *lumber*'s slang senses in English: *to be in lumber* can signify imprisonment (as can *to be in limber* and *to be in limbo*), per Partridge's *Dictionary of Slang.*

(v)

In his seventy-eighth *Rambler* essay, for Saturday, December 15, 1750, Johnson wrote:

> The most important events, when they become familiar, are no longer considered with wonder or solicitude, and that which at first filled up our whole attention, and left no place for any other thought, is soon thrust aside into some remote repository of the mind, and lies among other lumber of the memory, over-looked and neglected.

When I first read this sentence, in 1982, I had no notion of the long-bearded and -barded history of *lumber*. The phrase "lumber of the memory" appealed to me because it brought to mind dim palletized piles of pressure-treated two-by-fours, their end-grain sprayed bright nonwooden colors to distinguish grades and brands, laid out in a huge, fragrant mind-hangar—a place like the Home Depot, or Grossman's, or Chase Pitkin, where new sawdust, and not the dust of ages, covers the floor, and where unfinished ten-foot pieces of molding (quarter-rounds, coves, and coronado caps) are stored upright in allées of sequential pens; lengths that when you bring them up to the register, intending to Make Something New with them, spring in sympathy with your steps, like the rhythmic slow-motion warp of the sprinting vaulter's resilient prop: a forward-looking, American lumber of imminence, then, of unrolled plans and dormer punch-throughs and vest-pocket solariums, not a backward-looking European lumber of decrepitude and decay.[1] Remote repositories of the mind were just the sort of places you would need to store a heavy, dentable, sandable percept like lumber: the roundedness of the word implies the shearing scream of the tablesaw in some distant neighbor's yard on summer afternoons, which is always followed by a reassuringly melodic mallet-plink as the shorn end falls into the pile of angled scrap.

But if someone had quietly let me know back then that Johnson's chosen word had nothing directly to do with wood, that it was often used euphemistically to mean "rubbish," in metric placements where a single syllable like "trash" wouldn't work, I, though ashamed of the seriousness of my misunderstanding, would still have treasured the sentence. I connected it with Johnson's way of walking, his oddly love-inspiring "infirmity of the convulsive kind" (as Pope called it, when recommending some of Johnson's early verses to a friend)—an affliction "that attacks him sometimes, so as to

---

[1] "Up, my comrades! up and doing!" yodels John Greenleaf Whittier in "The Lumbermen"—an unintentionally funny poem, now that Monty Python's "I'm a Lumberjack and I'm OK" has transvestized forestry, and a poem that isn't in the *English Poetry Database,* because no American poems are—

> Up, my comrades! up and doing!
> Manhood's rugged play
> Still renewing, bravely hewing
> Through the world our way!

make Him a sad Spectacle." Boswell, attempting a diagnosis, quotes a description of St. Vitus's dance from a medical book: "It manifests itself by halting or unsteadiness of one of the legs, which the patient draws after him like an ideot." Thus Johnson lumbered into the drawing rooms of dancing masters like Chesterfield; and his gait easily merged with my reverence for the extensive mental millyards of knowledge that he was able to pack into his *Dictionary*, a book that as soon as it was published stood for the raw materials of prose, so definitive an inventory that even Pater, a century later, advised would-be Cyreniasts to be wary of any word that Johnson hadn't seen fit to define.

And I was also certain, when I first read it, that Johnson's sentence was the secret fuse-force that lay behind Coleridge's better-known description of the power of philosophy and of poetic genius: the sort of genius that "rescues the most admitted truths from the impotence caused by the very circumstance of their universal admission":

> Truths of all others the most awful and mysterious, yet being at the same time of universal interest, are too often considered as *so* true, that they lose all the life and efficiency of truth, and lie bed-ridden in the dormitory of the soul, side by side, with the most despised and exploded errors.

Johnson's lumbered "repository of the mind" reforms itself as Coleridge's slumbering "dormitory of the soul." Even Coleridge's use of "exploded errors" has a Johnsonian sound: Johnson elsewhere (*The Adventurer*, no. 126) censures the recluse who "thinks himself in possession of truth, when he is only fondling an error long since exploded." Coleridge wrote his version for the fifth issue of *The Friend*, a short-lived periodical (it ran from 1809 to 1810) that seems to have been modeled in part on Johnson's Ramblers, Idlers, and Adventurers; but he liked his passage so much that he worked it into his

Biographia Literaria (1817).[1] Right he was to fondle it a second time, too: he had renovated and Sardanopalized Johnson's truth, which had itself become so true that it lay bedridden in a multivolume collection of passé eighteenth-century moral essays by a critic who, in the eyes of the Lakers (as Jeffrey called Wordsworth et al.), stood for the falsely orotund diction of the Popists. Those hinted shapes that you can almost detect in the turbid shadows of Coleridge's sentence—the sprawling forms of despised and exploded opium-eaters sleeping off their murky glassfuls in a communal paralysis of indolence, bad dreams, and missed deadlines—force the inherited assertion to assume once again all the life and efficacy of truth.

Both quotations, I hope I am the first to note, can be traced back to a particular passage in Saint Augustine, whom Johnson read carefully and occasionally quoted from in essays and ghost-written sermons. In Chapter X of the *Confessions,* Augustine thinks about how *cogo* (to gather) and *cogito* are allied words, and how in remembering something, we must gather, or re-collect, truths that *sparsa prius et neglecta latitabant*—that before lay hidden away, scattered and ignored; or, in Coleridge and Johnson's variations, lay "despised and exploded" or "overlooked and neglected." "If," writes Augustine, in Pine-Coffin's Penguin translation,

> If, for a short space of time, I cease to give them my attention, they sink back and recede again into the more remote cells of my memory, so that I have to think them out again, like a fresh set of facts, if I am to know them. I have to shepherd them out again from their old lairs. . . .

(Augustine also refers here to the mind's contents as *thesauri,* "treasures," and compares his memory to a "huge temple"

---

[1] Chapter 4, "On Fancy and Imagination," in *Collected Works,* vol. 7, ed. James Engell and W. Jackson Bate, p. 82.

and a "spacious palace" and, with a little more neurological justification, to a place with *ineffabiles sinus*—ineffable sinuses, or secret recesses, folds, fastnesses, or deep pockets in the financial sense.) The first version of Johnson's *Rambler* essay, which has "the remoter repositories of the mind"[1] rather than the (better) singular "some remote repository," further points up the Augustinian source, which is plural.

There is another figure behind Johnson's and Coleridge's rooms full of neglected memory-lumber, as well. In Locke's "Of the Conduct of the Understanding," a work posthumously published in 1706 and probably intended as a coda to the much better-known but less interesting and human (and *lumber*less) *Essay Concerning Human Understanding,* Locke writes that "General Observations drawn from Particulars, are the Jewels of Knowledge, comprehending great Store in a little Room; but they are therefore to be made with the greater Care and Caution," since, Locke warns, we are always in peril of overdoing our jewel-storage, making

> the Head a Magazine of Materials, which can hardly be call'd Knowledge, or at least 'tis but like a Collection of Lumber not reduc'd to Use or Order; and he that makes every thing an Observation, has the same useless Plenty and much more falsehood mixed with it.

Some pages later, Locke (who was in the habit of using metaphors to point out the dangers of metaphor) says that he who has not a mind to represent to himself an author's sense "divested of the false lights and deceitful ornaments of speech," will make

> his understanding only the warehouse of other men's lumber; I mean false and unconcluding reasonings, rather than a repository

---

[1] See W. J. Bate's and Albrecht B. Strauss's edition of the *Rambler* essays, vol. II, p. 46.

of truth for his own use, which will prove substantial, and stand him in stead, when he has occasion for it.[1]

This is a form of the great scholarly worry—a worry which hydroptically book-thirsty poets like Donne, Johnson, Gray, Southey, and Coleridge all felt at times—the fear that too much learning will eventually turn even an original mind into a large, putty-colored regional storage facility of mislabeled and leaking chemical drums. Locke wasn't much of a poetry reader,[2] so it isn't likely that he got his *lumber* from Butler or

---

[1] In this second quotation I'm following a 1901 Maynard, Merrill, & Co. student edition of "Of the Conduct of the Understanding," with spelling and capitalization modernized, p. 121, bought for a dollar at an estate sale. Locke's "Of the Conduct," may I say in passing, in its discussion of the ways to train and subjugate the caprices of ideational succession, in order that no "foreign and unsought Ideas will offer themselves," and so that we will be able to keep these anarchic ideas "from taking off our Minds from its present pursuit, and hinder them from running away with our Thoughts quite from the Subject in hand," seems to have influenced several of Samuel Johnson's best *Rambler* essays, viz.: "Lest a power so restless should be either unprofitably, or hurtfully employed, and the superfluities of intellect run to waste, it is no vain speculation to consider how we may govern our thoughts, restrain them from irregular motions, or confine them from boundless dissipation." (*Rambler* no. 8.) Coleridge, an expert on muddle-headedness, attacks Locke in a letter to the Wedgewoods for his "complete Whirl-dance of Confusion" over mental terminology: "Sometimes again [in Locke's *Essay*] the Ideas are coincident as objects of the mind in thinking, sometimes they stand for the mind itself, and sometimes we are the thinkers & the mind is only the Thought-Box. In short, the Mind in Mr Locke's *Essay* has three senses—the Ware-house, the Wares, and the Ware-house-man. . . ." (Quoted in *A Locke Miscellany*, edited by Jean S. Yolton, 1990, pp. 274–5.) Laurence Sterne was of the contrary opinion that Locke's "glory [was] to free the world from the lumber of a thousand vulgar errors." (*Tristram Shandy*, vol. III, ch. 20.) See Patricia Graves's meticulous *Computer-Generated Concordance to Sterne's Tristram Shandy* (unpublished Ph.D. dissertation, Emory University, 1974, p. 807).

[2] Judging by his library and the slighting things he says in the *Essay* about the poetic imagination. Locke did, though, own Rabelais, Shakespeare, and Congreve's *The Mourning Bride*. (See Richard Ashcraft, "John Locke's Library: Portrait of an Intellectual," in *A Locke Miscellany*.)

Dryden. But he might have had Charles Cotton's translation of Montaigne in mind. I know I do now, as I retype Locke. One of the first places I looked for *lumber* was in Florio's 1603 translation of Montaigne's *Essays,* figuring that Florio would have given it to Shakespeare, and Shakespeare would have passed it on to everyone else (via *The Tempest,* say), since that was one of vocabulary's known spice-routes—but vexingly I didn't find it in Book 1, Chapter XXIV, "Of Pedantisme," where it should have been, and the *Harvard Concordance to Shakespeare* was able to cough up only the one unremunerative Lumbert Street address from *Henry IV, Part II.* So I set Florio's Montaigne aside, in one of my floor-piles, as a false lead—regretfully, since E. J. Trechmann, one of Montaigne's later translators, likens the nineteenth-century rediscovery of Florio's version to "the finding of a valuable piece of old furniture."[1] But then I discovered, working my way through some of the screens from the *Library of the Future* CD-ROM, that Charles Cotton (1630–1687) found a way to put *lumber* into his 1685 translation of the *Essays.* (It was Cotton's version, not Florio's, that Pope and Emerson read.) "Some one may say of me," Cotton has Montaigne say (in the late essay called "Of Physiognomy"), "that I have here only made a nosegay of culled flowers, and have brought nothing of my own but the thread that ties them."[2] Mon-

---

[1] *The Essays of Montaigne,* Oxford University Press, vol. 1, "Translator's Preface."

[2] And it *is* contemptible and wrong of Montaigne to have melted whole stolen crayons from Seneca into his paragraphs without announcing it, or for that matter for Georges Perec to work entire Frenched-over sentences from Joyce's *Ulysses* into his *Life: A User's Manual* without so much as a peep to his readers about it, or for Sterne to plagiarize paragraphs of Locke, or for Emerson to plagiarize a paragraph of Samuel Johnson's *Preface to Shakespeare*—it isn't cute, it isn't postmodern, it's cheating, and always has been—and once we learn that a prose writer is capable of such silent filchery, we dismiss him, rightly, as a liar and a con-man, and no matter how good he is, we no longer completely trust anything he gives us.

taigne has a thousand quote-crammed volumes ranged about him in his circular library as he writes, and he can borrow, if he wants to, "from a dozen such scrap-gatherers, people about whom I do not much trouble myself, wherewith to trick up this treatise of Physiognomy." But he will try to resist, since

> These lumber pies of common-places, wherewith so many furnish their studies, are of little use but to common subjects, and serve but to show us, and not to direct us. . . .

Lumber *pies*? What are these succulent-sounding baked goods that Cotton serves us, in his version of Montaigne's unusual phrase "pastissages de lieux communs"? Florio's translation kneejerks here with "rapsodies of common places," a cliché; modern versions by J. M. Cohen and Donald Frame offer the relatively vague "concoctions of commonplaces." Yet a *pastissage* is, according to Godefroy's *Dictionnaire de l'Ancienne Langue Française,* a "making, or baking of pies, or pastmeats," or figuratively, a mélange. Possibly Donald Frame would object that Cotton erred on the side of overspecificity. But Cotton seems to be aware of the range of metaphorical meaning that *pastissage* can have, since he translates the only other use of the word in the *Essays,* in "Of the Resemblance of Children to Their Fathers," less colorfully: "we call the piling up [*pastissage*] of the first laws that fall into our hands, justice."[1]

---

[1] A sentence that (as I determined only after much incredulous scrolling and searching) you will not find anywhere on the *Library of the Future*'s Third Series CD-ROM (you will in Roy E. Leake's *Concordance des Essais de Montaigne,* 1981)—since the *Library of the Future*'s version of the *Essays* leaves out more than four fifths of the original Cottonian translation. (Rather scandalously, given that World Library, Inc., repeats the claim that "All books are complete & unabridged" five times in its product catalog.) The CD-ROM includes, for example, only two of the first twenty-five essays, leaving out "Of Pedantry," "Of Liars," and "Of Fear," nowhere warning us, onscreen or off, that any material is cut. If this *Library of the*

Trechmann translates *pastissage* as "pasties" and M. A. Screech, most recently, substitutes "meat pies." But to my nose, Cotton's translation retains more of the steamy savoriness of the original, a lumber pie being, depending on the dictionary you consult, a "highly seasoned meat-pie, made either of veal or lamb" (*lumbard-pie* in Halliwell's *Dictionary of Archaic and Provincial Words, Obsolete Phrases, Proverbs, and Ancient Customs, from the Fourteenth Century,* 10th ed., 1881), or "A pie in which balls of minced meat or fish are baked with butter and eggs" (*Webster's Second;* definition omitted in *Webster's Third*), or even possibly an uncle or nephew of the *numble, umble,* or *humble* pie, a pie made from the *lombles* (cf. *loins* and *lumbar*-organs) or "certain inward parts" of the deer, according to Dr. Ernest Klein's *Comprehensive Etymological Dictionary of the English Language* (Elsevier, 1966–67), whose dedication pages made me cry furtively and without warning at the copying machine of the Berkeley Public Library. Volume I of Klein's dictionary is

---

Future really is a foretaste of the Library of the Future, I hope we won't, overawed by its exquisite searchability (and I am deeply indebted to it at present myself—although I would like to go on record as saying that I had *already found* the use of *lumber* in Boswell's *Life of Johnson* by reading an old Everyman Library edition on the T in Boston in 1987), compromise the university Library of the Present, which typically holds Hazlitt's full annotated nineteenth-century edition of Cotton's translation, as well as a convenient one-volume 1952 Great Books edition that prints every word. (The electronic text that *Library of the Future* uses looks to be a scanned version of Doubleday's handsome, footnote-free distillation of 1947, edited by Salvador Dali—an edition that in its physical paper form is accompanied by some interestingly autopsy-esque Dali illustrations not included on the disk—and I wonder, in passing, if Doubleday's permissions department is aware that their selection was scanned, and if Dali's act of essay-selection constitutes sweat-of-the-brow intellectual value that exists on top of a work in the public domain.)

DEDICATED TO THE SACRED MEMORY OF THE BEST PARENTS
MY DEAR *MOTHER*
WHO AFTER A LIFE OF SELF-SACRIFICE DIED IN SZATMAR IN 1940
AND MY DEAR *FATHER,*
THE WORLD-RENOWNED RABBI AND SCHOLAR
RABBI IGNAZ (ISAAC) KLEIN OF SZATMAR,
WHO DIED A MARTYR OF HIS FAITH IN AUSCHWITZ IN 1944;
AND TO THE SACRED MEMORY OF MY *WIFE*
AND OF MY ONLY *CHILD JOSEPH (HAYYIM ISRAEL)*
WHO ALSO FELL VICTIMS TO NAZISM IN AUSCHWITZ IN 1944

And Volume II is

DEDICATED TO THE BLESSED MEMORY OF
ARTHUR MINDEN, Q.C.
THE DEAREST FRIEND I EVER HAD,
THE NOBLEST MAN THAT EVER LIVED,
WHO DIED IN TORONTO IN 1966
MAY HIS SOUL BE BOUND IN THE BOND OF LIFE

Dr. Klein: a quiet and disciplined scholar who, after these awful deaths, was left with an extended etymological word-family to keep him company. I would like to thank him, if he is still with us, and even if he is not, for his help with the numbles and umbles and other inward parts that I hereby bake in this lumber pie—a pie that is, regardless of which fishes or meats may have participated in its recipe at various times, above all a mixed dish: Montaigne intended us to think of his "pastissage de lieux communs" as a shepherd's pie, a calzone, a frittata, a scrapple, a haggis, a pizza *ai quattro formaggi,* of commonplaces. Frame's "Concoction" sounds water-based and medicinal and unchewable—it is a non-nutritive pestle-product that Homais the apothecary would formulate in his capharnaüm. The *English Poetry Database* offers further elucidation: a lumber pie is a "compound paste" in a poem called "A Farewel to Wine, by a Quondam

Friend to the Bottle" (1693 is the date of the edition used by the database), by one Richard Ames. Several screens in, Ames samples one vintage and rejects it:

> I've tasted it—'tis spiritless and flat,
>   And has as many different tastes,
>   As can be found in Compound pastes,
> In Lumber Pye, or soporifrous Methridate.

The lumber pie also appears to be made, at least at some periods, without benefit of milk or butter or beef, and possibly *with* ox-heel—or so I nervously conclude (feeling in matters of culinary and bovine history more than a little out of my depth) from a 1717 poem by Edward ("Ned") Ward entitled "British Wonders: Or, A Poetical Description of the Several Prodigies and Most Remarkable Accidents That have happen'd in Britain since the Death of Queen Anne," another finding from the *Poetry Database*. Ward sings of the "horn-plague" that "like a fatal Rot or Murrain, / Turn'd all our Bulls and Cows to Carrion," leaving a queasy populace unwilling to touch beef or anything made with dairy products, such as "custard," for instance—an "open pie" (according to the *OED*) often containing meat in an egg and cream sauce:

> Custard, that noble cooling Food,
> So toothsome, wholsome, and so good,
> That Dainty so approv'd of old,
> Whose yellow surface shines like Gold . . .
> That crusty Fort, whose Walls of Wheat,
> Contain such tender lusheous Meat,
> And us'd so often to be storm'd
> By hungry Gownmen sharply arm'd,
> Was now, alas, despis'd as nought,
> And slighted wheresoe'er 'twas brought;
> Whilst Lumber-Pies came more in play,
> And bore, at Feasts, the Bell away.
> *So in wet Seasons, when our Mutton*

Is e'ery where cry'd down as rotten,
Cow-heel becomes a Dish of State,
And climbs the Tables of the Great.

The *OED* also informs us that "cow-heel" can mean "ox-heel." So a lumber pie was at one time a non-dairy ox-product. Or not: I may be misapplying the last four lines, which possibly do not refer specifically to the pie that precedes them.[1]

Another and (to be honest) incompatible explanation for the appearance in the *Essais* of the rare phrase "pastissage de lieux communs" is that Montaigne was quietly adapting, as was his way, and not quite understanding, a *pie*-figure from a text that was originally in English, or English mediated by

---

[1] I like to think that Samuel Johnson ate lumber pies, too—one of the best passages in Macaulay's article about Johnson in the *Encyclopaedia Britannica* goes: "Even to the end of his life, and even at the tables of the great, the sight of food affected him as it affects wild beasts and birds of prey. His taste in cookery, formed in subterranean ordinaries and *à la mode* beef shops, was far from delicate. Whenever he was so fortunate as to have near him a hare that had been kept too long, or a meat pie made with rancid butter, he gorged himself with such violence that his veins swelled and the moisture broke out on his forehead." But even Johnson might have had some difficulty with this gut-buster from the *True Gentlewoman's Delight* (1676), quoted in Robert Nares's *Glossary*, as supplemented by Halliwell and Wright (1867): "*A lumber pie.*—Take three or four sweet-breads of veal, parboil and mince them very small, then take the curd of a quart of milk, turned with three eggs, half a pound of almond-past, and a penny-loaf grated, mingle these together, then take a spoonful of sweet herbs minced very small, also six ounces of oringado, and mince it, then season all this with a quarter of sugar, and three nutmegs, then take five dates, and a quarter of a pint of cream, four yolks of eggs, three spoonfuls of rose-water, three or four marrow-bones, mingle all these together, except the marrow, then make it up in long boles, about the bigness of an egg, and in every bole put a good piece of marrow, put these into the pie; then put a quarter of a pound of butter, and half a sliced lemon, them make a caudle of white wine, sugar and verjuice, put it in when you take your pie out of the oven, you may use a grain of musk and ambergriece."

Latin. *Pie* is—as I happened to discover while looking for
lumber in Froude's *Short Studies on Great Subjects, Second
Series*, vol. II[1]—a printer's term. In "On Progress," Froude
writes:

> When a block of type from which a book has been printed is broken
> up into its constituent letters the letters so disintegrated are called
> "pie." The pie, a mere chaos, is afterwards sorted and distributed,
> preparatory to being built up into fresh combinations. A distin-
> guished American friend describes Democracy as "making pie."

(I take it the distinguished American friend was Emerson? Or
Oliver Wendell Holmes?) The *OED* doesn't include Froude's
passage, but the quotations there establish that, at least from
the mid-seventeenth century, *pie* could mean "A mass of type
mingled indiscriminately or in confusion, such as results from
the breaking down of a forme of type." Quoting from a
writer, too, is the breaking of his work down to constituent
pieces, with an eye to an alternative typeset reassembly. And
a few inches above the *OED* entry for the typographical *pie* is
the information that, in the fifteenth century and after, *Pyes*
were the English church's name for certain elaborate ordinals,
or books of commemorational scheduling; and the secular
pye book became, perhaps relatedly but probably later, "an
alphabetical index to rolls and records." So even in Montaigne's own time, *pies* or *pyes* were, unfiguratively, books,
and maybe were, as well, the hashed dark-matter of type—the
Drydo-Ovidian "rude and indigested mass"—from which

---

[1] No *lumber* in Froude that I found, but I came across an interestingly
indigestible equivalent: "To cram a lad's mind with infinite names of things
which he never handled, places he never saw or will see, statements of facts
which he cannot possibly understand, and must remain merely words to
him—this, in my opinion, is like loading his stomach with marbles." ("Education: An Address Delivered to the Students at St Andrew's, March 19,
1869," in *Short Studies on Great Subjects, Second Series*, p. 455.)

books were formed. Perhaps Montaigne encountered this more specialized use of *pie* somewhere and mistakenly concretized it as a pasty, causing the scrupulously flour-powdered Cotton to liven it up further as a *lumber pie*.

Under either conjectural prehistory of *pastissage,* we can speculate that Locke read Montaigne/Cotton's "lumber pies of commonplaces" and wrote of men who make their understandings into "warehouses of other men's lumber," and of false knowledge as "a Collection of Lumber not reduc'd to Use or Order," and then Samuel Johnson read Locke and wrote about those overlooked and neglected thoughts, lying among "other lumber of the memory." At least, that's one possible amateur genealogy. Then Ralph Waldo Emerson, reading Coleridge, Locke, Saint Augustine, and Johnson attentively,[1] sensed he was in the presence of something very

---

[1] Emerson mentions Saint Augustine as one of the writers one must read in his "Books." There is a helpful essay on Emerson's fascination with Johnson by Stephen Swords called "Emerson and the Ghost of Doctor Johnson," in *The Age of Johnson,* vol. 6, ed. Paul J. Korshin (New York: AMS Press, 1994). Swords does not mention one notable remaking of Johnson by Emerson. Johnson, in his "Life of Congreve," says of a passage in Congreve's *The Mourning Bride:* "He who reads those lines enjoys for a moment the powers of a poet: he feels what he remembers to have felt before, but he feels it with great increase of sensibility; he recognises a familiar image, but meets it again amplified and expanded, embellished with beauty, and enlarged with majesty." Emerson condensed this into his famous line (which I am temporarily unable to locate) about recognizing, in works of genius, our own rejected thoughts: "They return with an alienated majesty." *The Mourning Bride* (first produced in 1697) is the only one of Congreve's plays (according to David Mann's *Concordance to the Plays of William Congreve*) that contains *lumber.* Zara says (II, ii),

> what are Riches, Empire, Power,
> But larger Means to gratifie the Will?
> The Steps on which we tread, to rise and reach
> Our Wish; and that obtain'd down with the Scaffolding
> Of Sceptres, Crowns, and Thrones; they've serv'd their End,
> And are like Lumber, to be left and scorn'd.

special in the way of recyclable truisms here; and, some twelve years following the appearance of Coleridge's *Biographia Literaria,* in "The American Scholar" (1837), after giving an enthusiastic plug for the Romantic movement, and on his way to a denunciation of the "cold and pedantic" style of Pope, Johnson, and Gibbon, he worked his own preacherly numbers on the mind-lumber theme. "That, which had been negligently trodden under foot by those who were harnessing and provisioning themselves for long journeys into far countries, is suddenly found to be richer than all foreign parts," he declaimed to the slack-jawed Phi Beta Kappans; and then:

> let me see every trifle bristling with the polarity that ranges it instantly on an eternal law; and the shop, the plough, and the ledger referred to the like cause by which light undulates and poets sing;—and the world lies no longer a dull miscellaney and lumber-room, but has form and order; there is no trifle, there is no puzzle, but one design unites and animates the farthest pinnacle and the lowest trench.

Emerson was expressing, in fact, the nineteenth century's constantly repeated desire—the wish to find unexpected foreignness and beauty in the lumber at one's feet. Wordsworth had set things in motion in 1800 by announcing (in the second edition of the *Lyrical Ballads*) that he was imparting to incidents and situations from common life "a certain colouring of imagination, whereby ordinary things should be presented to the mind in an unusual aspect." But everyone tried out the idea. Hazlitt gave it an entomological turn:

> Let the naturalist, if he will, catch the glow-worm, carry it home with him in a box, and find it next morning nothing but a little grey worm; let the poet or the lover of poetry visit it at evening, when beneath the scented hawthorn and the crescent moon it has built itself a palace of emerald light. (*Lectures on the English Poets,* 1818.)

Shelley, in 1821, in his *Defence of Poetry* (published in 1840), gave it a haremy flavor: "Poetry lifts the veil from the hidden beauty of the world, and makes familiar objects be as if they were not familiar"; and later he says that it "strips the veil of familiarity from the world, and lays bare the naked and sleeping beauty."

Edward Bulwer-Lytton used it to pit prose and poetry against each other:

> Verse cannot contain the refining and subtle thoughts which a great prose writer embodies: the rhyme eternally cripples it; it properly deals with the common problems of human nature which are now hackneyed, and not with the nice and philosophising corollaries which may be drawn from them: thus: though it would seem at first a paradox, commonplace is more the element of poetry than of prose.[1]

Leigh Hunt, essayist and teacher of Keats, in his *The Seer; Or, Common-Places Refreshed* (1840), wants to break open

> the surfaces of habit and indifference, of objects that are supposed to contain nothing but so much brute matter, or common-place utility, and show what treasures they conceal. ("Pleasure.")

And in a very Leigh Huntian essay called "A Christmas Tree" in the Christmas 1850 number of *Household Words,* Dickens himself, entranced by the sight of the tree, invokes (as I clumsily did some pages ago, before I ran across this page of Dickens) the *Arabian Nights:*

> Oh, now all common things become uncommon and enchanted to me. All lamps are wonderful; all rings are talismans. Common flower-pots are full of treasure, with a little earth scattered on the

---

[1] *The Pilgrims of the Rhine,* 1834, quoted approvingly by the sixteen-year-old Ruskin in 1836 in his "Essay on Literature," in *Three Letters and an Essay on Literature by John Ruskin, 1836–1841: Found in His Tutor's Desk* (George Allen, 1893), p. 36.

top; trees are for Ali Baba to hide in; beef-steaks are to throw down into the Valley of Diamonds, that the precious stones may stick to them, and be carried by the eagles to their nests, whence the traders, with loud cries, will scare them.[1]

In 1856, Coventry Patmore said it again in the *Edinburgh Review:* "The poet is doing his noblest work in resuscitating moral truths from the inert condition of truisms and conferring upon them a perennial bloom and power. . . ." John Stuart Mill gave the theme a try himself in his *On Liberty* (1859):

> There is only too great a tendency in the best beliefs and practices to degenerate into the mechanical; and unless there were a succession of persons whose ever-recurring originality prevents the grounds of those beliefs and practices from becoming merely traditional, such dead matter would not resist the smallest shock from anything really alive, and there would be no reason why civilization should not die out, as in the Byzantine Empire." (*On Liberty,* Chapter III.)

---

[1] The essay is in the Penguin Classics edition, *Selected Short Fiction,* ed. Deborah A. Thomas, p. 131. In Dickens's "Seven Dials," included in the Penguin collection, there are "shops for the purchase of rags, bones, old iron, and kitchen-stuff" but no lumber-rooms. This may be as good a place as any to point out, if nobody has, that one of Leigh Hunt's essays from *The Indicator,* published in 1833, contains a sentence that was possibly the piece of old iron that Dickens hammered and alloyed into the entirety of *The Old Curiosity Shop.* In "Of the Sight of Shops," Hunt writes:

> The curiosity-shop is sometimes very amusing, with its mandarins, stuffed birds, odd old carved faces, and a variety of things as indescribable as bits of dreams.

Here is Dickens's version in the first chapter of *The Old Curiosity Shop:*

> There were suits of mail standing like ghosts in armour here and there, fantastic carvings brought from monkish cloisters, rusty weapons of various kinds, distorted figures in china and wood and iron and ivory: tapestry and strange furniture that might have been designed in dreams.

Matthew Arnold, who once absurdly criticized Wordsworth for being under-read,[1] weighs in, repetitive and humorless and uninspired as usual,[2] in 1863: "The grand power of poetry," he booms,

> is its interpretative power; by which I mean, not a power of drawing out in black and white an explanation of the mystery of the universe, but the power of so dealing with things as to awaken in us a wonderfully full, new, and intimate sense of them, and of our relations with them.

Bulwer-Lytton gave the notion of the renovated commonplace a second try, this time in rhyme, in 1869:

> Thou also, old picture of Paradise, well
> In the cobwebb'ed lumber-chamber of Hell
>   Hast thou rested, rotted, and rusted:
>   Beelzebub's masterpiece, painted
>   Long since, though the canvas be old,
> And the hues of it tarnisht and fainted,
>   Yet retoucht with our purple and gold,
> Thou shalt brighten, and glitter, and glow, for him,
> With the colours of Eden ere they wax'd dim.
>   Come forth, and be furbisht and dusted!
>   ("Orval.")

"Cobwebb'd lumber-chamber of Hell" is nicely torchlit; but better still is W. E. Henley's sad wave at the past, "that wharf of aery lumber," in his tribute, "My Meerschaum Pipe" (1875), which lifts the veil, or hanky, of custom from the sleeping beauty of that once commonplace appliance. This

---

[1] "But surely the one thing wanting to make Wordsworth an even greater poet than he is,—his thought richer, and his influence of wider application,—was that he should have read more books, among them, no doubt, those of that Goethe whom he disparaged without reading him." ("The Function of Criticism at the Present Time.")

[2] In his critical prose, that is. "Rugby Chapel" and the corded bales at the end of "The Scholar-Gypsy" are awfully good.

lyric (found in the *English Poetry Database*) is fortunately short enough to quote in full, and it is a good example, too, of the congeners *slumber, cumber,* and *lumber,* which poets and prose writers have found useful in close proximity:

> My Meerschaum Pipe is exquisitely dipped!
>   Shining, and silver-zoned, and amber-tipped,
>   In close chromatic passages that number
>   The tones of brown from cinnamon to umber,
>   Roll the rich harmonies of shank and crypt.
>
> Couchant, and of its purple cushions clipped,
>   Its dusky loveliness I wake from slumber.
>   Was ever maid than thou more softly lipped,
>   My Meerschaum Pipe?
>
> How many pangs herethro' have lightly tripped
>   Into the past, that wharf of aery lumber?
>   How many plans, bright-armed and all equipt,
>   Out of this glowing brain have skyward skipped?
>   Memories that hallow, O regrets that cumber
>   My Meerschaum Pipe!

W. E. Henley, we may learn from Drabble's *Oxford Companion to English Literature,* lost a foot early on to tubercular arthritis, and for this reason as well as his general piratical mien inspired the character of Long John Silver in *Treasure Island* (1883), which has in it just one *lumber,* a treasure handily unburied from the sandbanks of chapter 5 with the help of the *Library of the Future* CD-ROM:

> This appeal seemed to produce some effect, for two of the fellows began to look here and there among the lumber [the bushes of broom?], but half-heartedly, I thought, and with half an eye to their own danger all the time, while the rest stood irresolute on the road.

Interesting that Henley, a forgotten poet of the meerschaum pipe, is thesaurized by Stevenson as Silver, the unforgettable pirate of the maritime poop. "You have your hands on thousands, you fools," Blind Pew tells the men poking around the bushy lumber for the map. "You'd be as rich as kings if you could find it, and you know it's here, and you stand there malingering." And earlier: "Oh, shiver my soul," he laments, "if I had eyes!"

But only the poets and storytellers have eyes. Even Macaulay isn't quite up to par, according to Saintsbury's *History of Nineteenth Century Literature* (1896–1910): "A poet of the very highest class Macaulay was not; his way of thought was too positive, too clear, too destitute either of mystery or of dream, to command or to impart the true poetical mirage, to 'make the common as if it were not common.' "[1] James Russell Lowell similarly qualifies his praise for Dryden:

> But if he [Dryden] have not the potent alchemy that transmutes the lead of our commonplace associations into gold, as Shakespeare knows how to do so easily, yet his sense is always up to the sterling standard.

Christina Rossetti entitled an entire book *Commonplace, and Other Short Stories* (1870). One of the stories is an account of

---

[1] Saintsbury seems to be half-remembering the aforequoted passages of Shelley here, or perhaps paraphrasing Horace, who had said some helpful things in his *Art of Poetry* about how difficult it is to treat in one's own way what is common (line 128), and about the desirability of a poetry made of familiar things (line 240), and about the "beauty that may crown the commonplace" (line 243)—passages more helpful when pulled out of context, as they frequently were. (For instance, the "unutterably tedious" Alexander Gottlieb Baumgarten writes in his *Reflections on Poetry* that a "confused recognition, if it occurs, represents in the most poetic way a mingling of the familiar and the unfamiliar," and then he says, "Hence Horace, 'I should look for my poetic fictions in familiar things.' ") In one of the early translations into English of Horace's *Ars Poetica*, by Oldham (1683), a word leaps up:

> For there's no second Rate in Poetry
> A dull insipid Writer none can bear,
> In every place he is the publick jeer,
> And Lumber of the Shops and Stationer.

a lost masterpiece by Titian—a landscape with a female nude and some grapes—that is overpainted with a crude image of a flaming dragon by one of Titian's envious and less talented friends. The story ends:

> Reader, should you chance to discern over wayside inn or metropolitan hotel a dragon pendent, or should you find such an effigy amid the lumber of a broker's shop, whether it be red, green, or piebald, demand it importunately, pay for it liberally, and in the privacy of home scrub it. It *may* be that from behind the dragon will emerge a fair one, fairer than Andromeda, and that to you will appertain the honour of yet further exalting Titian's greatness in the eyes of a world.

The superficial exoticism of the dragon hides the long-limbed lumber-luster of the naked and fruitful commonplace.

"Make It New," Pound's manifestoid call, and "Make It Strange," the Formalists' onion-dome of a translation, is thus shorthand for a hundred years of poetical and critical orthodoxy. By 1914, Saki had stocked a six-page short story with the esthetic theory. In "The Lumber-Room" (collected in *Beasts and Super-Beasts*), young Nicholas announces that there is a frog in his breakfast. His elders scold him for thinking such a thing. As it happens, however, there *is* a frog in Nicholas's breakfast—his meal being a predecessor of Marianne Moore's horticultural definition of poetry, an imaginary breakfast with a real frog in it. (Nicholas has put the animal there himself.) As punishment, he is kept from visiting the beach with his vile cousins; and, watched over instead by his antipathetic aunt, he is forbidden to visit the gooseberry garden. So Nicholas decides to visit the lumber-room instead:

> The key turned stiffly in the lock, but it turned. The door opened, and Nicholas was in an unknown land, compared with which the gooseberry garden was a stale delight, a mere material pleasure.

In keeping with the general features of dark rooms of the Human Understanding, it is "large and dimly lit, one high window opening on to the forbidden garden being its only source of illumination." Like Saint Augustine's memory, it is a "storehouse of unimagined treasures." There is a piece of framed tapestry with a wolvish hunting scene, a roll of Indian hangings, some twisted candlesticks in the shape of snakes, a duck-shaped teapot, brass figures of peacocks and bulls, and, of course, a book: a "large square book" containing pictures of birds. ("And such birds!" A catalog of bird-wonders follows.) Just as Nicholas is "assigning a life-history" to the mandarin duck, his bad aunt calls accusingly from the gooseberry garden, and our hero is quietly pleased:

> It was probably the first time for twenty years that any one had smiled in that lumber-room.

Naturally the other children turn out to have a crummy time at the beach, while Nicholas, deprived of two layers of purported treats (beach and garden), meditates happily on possible plot-twists for the dusty hunting tapestry, having suddenly come into a fabulous inheritance in the nineteenth-century lumber-room of fiction. We are left with the expectation that Nicholas will grow up to write quick, cruel, funny stories about nasty grownups and sharp-toothed beasts, as his creator had.

Mervyn Peake changes the sex of his fifteen-year-old visitor to the fictional lumber-room in his *Titus Groan* of 1946, but Fuschia's hiding place is very similar to Nicholas's:

> The fact that this room was filled with lumber did not mean that she ignored it and used it only as a place of transit. Oh no, for it was here that many long afternoons had been spent as she crawled deep into the recesses and found for herself many a strange cavern among the incongruous relics of the past. (p. 60.)

Mervyn Peake, since he must as a writer go beyond Saki, posits for Fuschia two even more secret areas beyond the lumber-room—the acting room, and the secret attic. Fuschia describes the tripartite house of fiction to herself:

I know where I go. I go here. This is where I go. Up the stairs and into my lumber room. Through my lumber room and into my acting room. All across my acting room and up the ladder and on to my verandah. Through the door and into my secret attic. And here it is I am. I am here now. I have been here lots of times but that is in the past. That is over, but now I'm here it's in the present. This is the present. I'm looking on the roofs of the present and I'm leaning on the present window-sill and later on when I'm older I will lean on this window-sill again. Over and over again. (p. 62.)

So useful and welcome does the curiosity-shop model of literary activity become that by 1961, Muriel Spark could confidently assume, when she had a character in her book *The Prime of Miss Jean Brodie* write a treatise called "The Transfiguration of the Commonplace," that we would know pretty much what she was getting at. The commonplace was the entire arbitrarily window-framed world, the world of moral clichés, the world of cardboard-character types, the world of material junk, so familiar it was rejected and put in storage, and the transfigurer was the connoisseur-pawnbroker-auctioneer who saw where he or she might tie a dangly hand-written price on a little white string, assigning value and ownership where there had before been only oppressiveness and shopworn confusion.

Arthur Danto, a philosopher at Columbia, "admired and coveted" Muriel Spark's title, and, having evidently secured her permission (as he tells us in his Introduction), he used it as the title of his own book, *The Transfiguration of the Commonplace: A Philosophy of Art* (1981), a "takeover" (Danto's word) that, whatever the merits of his book, may not sit quite right with some observers, since Spark was obliged to give her gracious consent regardless of whatever private misgivings she might have felt in seeing a professional esthetician detach her quiet invention from the warmth and privacy of its living chapter and plaster it all over a study (mainly) of the smirking, loveless twentieth-century "transfigurations" of Duchamp and Warhol and their camp-followers—handlebar mustaches on the Mona Lisa, fake Brillo boxes, etc. Danto devotes a paragraph to *Hamlet,* passingly mentions Proust's long sentences and Hemingway's short ones, and alludes to "Johnsonian symmetries" and "Shakespearean fustian" (p. 197), but he says nothing about Wordsworth or Coleridge or Tennyson; his coverage of the textbook pop-art Modernists is not at all the sort of *Transfiguration* that Muriel Spark's Tennyson-reciting Sister Helena of the Transfiguration, or Miss Brodie herself, would have wanted anything to do with in their prime.

Muriel Spark's approximate contemporary Elizabeth Bishop is a modern poet-commonplacer for whom Sister Helena would more likely have had some affinity. The *Concordance to Elizabeth Bishop,* one of a whole series of Garland Concordances put together under the supervision of Todd K. Bender, directed me to the *lumber* in Bishop's late book of poetry, *Geography III.* Bishop, adopting the voice of Robinson Crusoe, has a passage about how Crusoe's few island possessions, which once "reeked of meaning" when they were all he had, are now no more than "uninteresting lumber."[1] This by an American in 1976. It is the most recent

---

[1] Some lines from G. K. Chesterton's *Orthodoxy* help explain Bishop's choice of Crusoe. In the chapter called "The Ethics of Elfland" he says that *Robinson Crusoe* "celebrates the poetry of limits," and then writes: "Crusoe is a man on a small rock with a few comforts just snatched from the sea: the best thing in the book is simply the list of things saved from the wreck. The greatest of poems is an inventory. Every kitchen tool becomes ideal because Crusoe might have dropped it in the sea." I must thank my mother for reminding me of this passage. " 'Saved from the wreck,' as Chesterton said, 'saved from the wreck,' " she said, helping her grandchildren build a lean-to out of sticks on a beach.

use of the older English sense of the word by an American writer that I have found—with the exception of the title of an essay in *Government Publications Review,* vol. 13, 1986, called "A Mystery Tour Through the Lumber Room: United States Census Publications, 1820–1930, A Descriptive Essay," by Michele Fagan,[1] and also excepting a poem (assuming he is American) by a person named Hugh Croft that was part of a wedding ceremony between Keith and Kirsten Evans-Orville whose "online recreation" was posted in a series of messages in September 1993 on the WELL. I found the poem by typing a Unix command, "!extract -f lumber misc," to extract lines from any messages holding "lumber" (or "golden slumbers" or "convention of plumbers") from the WELL's Miscellaneous Conference. The relevant stanza is:

> I love you because you
> Are helping me to make
> Of the lumber of my life
> Not a tavern
> But a temple,
> Out of the works
> Of my every day
> Not a reproach
> But a song.[2]

---

[1] Michele Fagan said by phone that the "Mystery" in her title was an editorial addition—she had intended it simply to be "A Tour Through the Lumber Room." The Beatles reference does confuse things a little. Her essay is a survey of the oddments that can be found in old census reports; I found it by searching the *Wilson Library Literature* CD-ROM.

[2] The WELL, Miscellaneous Conference, Topic 871, no. 8, September 22, 1993. The topic has since been retired and frozen and is no longer extractable unless you add an "-r" (for "retired") to the command string; i.e., "!extract -f 'lumber of my life' -r misc." If it is like most topics, it will eventually be deleted entirely, and my citation of it will be the only record of its existence. Electronic media have an underdeveloped sense of the value of their own history; all but a small fraction of what was actually posted on the WELL since 1985 has vanished.

Who Hugh Croft is I don't know. He isn't in the anthologies of wedding poetry or the library catalogs that I checked, and he isn't in *Books in Print,* and he isn't as good as Elizabeth Bishop. Even so, he is someone worth thanking—he has helped keep the old sense of the l.-word current in the U.S. through 1993.

I was looking forward to quoting Elizabeth Bishop's *lumber* in this warehouse-in-progress—I was inching my way toward it—when Sven Birkerts's funereal *Gutenberg Elegies,* about the decline and fall of the culture of print, arrived on December 14, 1994, sent by book-loving, book-reading Barbara Epstein of *The New York Review of Books,* and sent extravagantly by Federal Express even though Ms. Epstein knew then, because I had warned her, that my lumberfest had grown fifteen times too long for her noble tabloid. Sven Birkerts quotes Bishop's "Crusoe in England," including the lines

> I'm bored, too, drinking my real tea,
> surrounded by uninteresting lumber

but he neglects to write with wonderment about Bishop's atypical use of this word, *my* word. Did Birkerts stop to think about it when he was retyping the passage? Bishop, despite the fact that she is as American a poet as you could ask for, uses the word in the English way, defiantly, as if our Crown Zellerbachs and Georgia-Pacifics and International Papers had not successfully pruned out the old-growth meaning, even though Daniel Defoe's own novel doesn't use it at all.[1] (Defoe contents himself with "provisions," "divers pieces," "goods," "luggage," and "warehouse"—no *lumber* or *lumber-*

---

[1] What got Bishop interested in *lumber*? Had she been reading Lady Mary Wortley Montagu, who is her kind of writer in several ways, funny and observant and lesbian and mail-loving, and who has a passage in a letter of

room.)[1] Of course it isn't an error on Birkerts's part to use this innocent, very good poem by Bishop to do something big and floppy like run down "our cultural condition and its prospects," as Birkerts does (poems can and should be used for all sorts of apoetical purposes—it keeps us thinking about them), and Birkerts does follow his Bishop quotation up with a thought-provoking half-sentence: "The more complex

---

October 10, 1716 (partially quoted in the *OED*'s history of *lumber*) about the cabinets of curiosities in the Emperor's repository in Vienna? It sounds a lot like Bishop: "Two of the rooms were wholly filled with relics of all kinds, set in jewels, amongst which I was desired to observe a crucifix, that they assured me had spoken very wisely to the Emperor Leopold. I won't trouble you with the catalogue of the rest of the lumber; but I must not forget to mention a small piece of loadstone that held up an anchor of steel too heavy for me to lift." Horace Walpole, another letter-writer who would have appealed to Bishop, cattily dismisses Versailles (a symbol of civilization one could set in opposition to Crusoe's island) as a "lumber of littleness," which is an adaptation of a couplet in one of Pope's *Moral Essays*, about a use-lessly grand house:

> Lo, what huge heaps of littleness around!
> The whole, a labour'd Quarry above ground.

(I found the Walpole reference in an endnote to *Essays and Criticisms,* Thomas Gray, ed. Clark Sutherland Northup, 1911. Gray, on May 22, 1739, says of Versailles, "What a huge heap of littleness!") Or had Bishop been reading Anthony Powell's *Books Do Furnish a Room*, which came out in 1971, about the time she may have been writing her poem: "In the dozen years or so since I had last been at Thrubworth more lumber than ever had collected in these back parts of the house, much of it no doubt brought there after requisitioning. There was an overwhelming accumulation: furniture: pictures: rolled-up carpets: packing cases." Or had Bishop simply grown dissatisfied with "junk" and "stuff" in earlier drafts of her poem and looked in a thesaurus? It's always a possibility.

[1] Moll Flanders, though, says of a stolen trunk, or "Portmanteua," as Moll spells it, which she has safely gotten past the Custom-House officers: "I did not think the Lumber of it worth my concern." (Oxford ed., p. 266.) Owens and Furbank's *A KWIC Concordance to Daniel Defoe's Moll Flanders* (1985) took me there. Woolf's and Nabokov's customs-inspection similes are traceable to this scene in Defoe's proto-novel.

and sophisticated our systems of lateral access, the more we sacrifice in the way of depth." The half-sentence isn't true, though, in my experience: I have made "lateral access" my catechism for the past nine lumberlost months, and I have as a result read more, read deeper, read with more curiosity, joy, fanaticism, found more writers I look forward to reading more of, loved the Printed Page in the abstract more, saw more thrilling future in its past, than I have since early college. Lateral access uncovers new places to go deep. I have been reading my great-grandfather Nicholson's five-volume 1767 Tonson edition of Dryden,[1] and my grandfather Nicholson's copy of Meredith's poems, books I once doubted I would ever get to—and I owe these reactionary pleasures in great part to the ostensibly heartless, plastic *English Poetry Database,* whose thousand sideways shocks air-hockey us into an unusually vivid realization of the number of poems there are out there, waiting for us—good, funny poems sometimes, and not (as we might hope, because then we would feel better about not having looked them up) wasted efforts. A passing fret that literacy is under siege is good for reading; it lends grandeur to a commonplace pastime. *I am not merely reading Elizabeth Bishop,* one can say, *I am doing my part to preserve culture from the Straw Men.* And is there, I wonder, any point in Birkerts's lamenting how few there are who now read books with the trough-snortingly ludic absorption with which many allegedly used to read books, if the few who still do—readers like Birkerts himself—forget to bring to them the verbal attentiveness, the readiness to hear what Pater called

---

[1] Or I was reading it, anyway, until vol. III was stolen from the front seat of my car. The thief either was planning on pawning it, or possibly wanted to add to his book collection.

the "finer edge of words still in use" that will demonstrate by example why one given piece of lithography merits attention over all its laterally accessible alternatives? Bishop's poem is itself no more than "uninteresting lumber" unless you can hear the strangeness of her use of *lumber*. Or do I censure Sven Birkerts for being unfruitfully dour about electronic encroachments only because he managed to quote the *lumber*-passage from "Crusoe in England" in his book before I did in this essay? Am I so petty?[1] Or is it really just because Birkerts's meditation on reading doesn't find space to mention somewhere my own meditation on reading, called *U and I,* published in 1991? Am I indignant at Birkerts's sourness about our unbookish culture because *U and I* failed to cheer so thoughtful a man up about the future of the book? What unbecoming garbage!

---

[1] I don't resent the witty Anthony Lane, who, in *The New Yorker* of February 20–27, 1995, beat me to an American review of the *English Poetry Database*. Lane pursues the word *lard* for a moment, and mentions "the old Housman principle that good verse should make the hair stand up on the back of your neck" (did Housman really shave the *back* of his neck?), and he makes an excellent point: "Yet I found myself stirred, not engulfed, by the flow of mediocrity. 'English Poetry' offers a way out of the crucial, and frankly tedious, impasse that has stiffened within the academy in recent years—the standoff, in broad terms, between the élitist and the democratic."

Ah, and A. R. Ammons's *Garbage* (1993), a book-length poem of paired run-on lines, is the latest attempt at the ultramundane. It announces its age-old transfigurative hope right up front, on its dedication page, which reads:

> *to the bacteria, tumblebugs, scavengers,*
> *wordsmiths—the transfigurers, restorers*

Some of the poem, heavily metaled with lumps of arrhythmic Green-Party pulpitry, sounds surprisingly like Cardinal Newman's little brother, quoted many pages ago. For example:

> . . . the ditchwork of the deepest degradation
>
> reflects waters brighter than common ground:
> poetry to no purpose! all this garbage! all
>
> these words: we may replace our mountains with
> trash: leachments may be our creeks flowing
>
> from the distilling bottoms of corruption . . .

But some of the dross-dressing is, on its bewildering syntactical spree, good, and aptly self-critical:

                                              my
    poetry is strawbags full of fleas the dogs won't

    sleep on or rats rummage: I am the abstract inexact's
    chickenfeed: I am borderlines splintered down

    into hedgerows: I am the fernbrake ditches
    winter brown, the shaggy down springs' flows

    accrue: but think what it would be like to get
    every word in

And at one point the grandly spatted old Wordsworthian commonplace of renewal gets suddenly reshod, made new by a kicker at the end about poetry's post-transfigurational residue: the poem, Ammons writes,

                reaches down into the dead pit
    and cool oil of stale recognition and words and

    brings up hauls of stringy gook which it arrays
    with light and strings with shiny syllables and

    gets the mind back into vital relationship with
    communication channels:[1] but, of course, there

    is some untransformed material, namely the poem
    itself

Ammon's National-Book-Awarded *Garbage* is in fact the latest of many books of poetry and collections of essays or stories that, in low-mimetic contrast to Renaissance fardle-words like *jewels* or *flowers* or *garland,* point proudly to the unpromising material that will be remade in the trash-compaction of the book they entitle.

How might we find some of the others? One way is to begin with the second (1853) edition of the *Thesaurus of*

---

[1] The lurching ugliness of "communication channels" must be intentional, a wave of the toilet-brush to the abstract nouns that can suddenly start marching energetically in place in the middle of an otherwise fine passage in Wordsworth's *Prelude.*

English Words and Phrases, Classified and Arranged so as to Facilitate the Expression of Ideas and Assist in Literary Composition (by Peter Mark Roget, M.D., F.R.S., F.R.A.S., F.G.S, "Author of the 'Bridgewater Treatise on Animal and Vegetable Physiology,' etc."), which gives several *lumber* groups. Under INUTILITY it has

> Litter, rubbish, lumber, trash, orts, weeds.

And under UNIMPORTANCE it has

> Refuse, lumber, litter, orts, tares, weeds, sweepings, scourings, off-scourings; rubble, *débris*, slough, dross, *scoriae*,[1] dregs, scum, flue, dust, *see* Dirt.

If you search a library catalog with this handful of alternatives in mind, and add a few more as they occur to you, you can amass a relevant poets' and writers' *Garbage* checklist without too much trouble. There is an *Orts* by Ted Hughes (1977) and an *Orts* by George MacDonald (1882); an *Orts and Scantlings* by H. C. Dillow (1984), and *Scantlings: Poems, 1964–1969*, by Gael Turnbull. (An *ort* is a morsel of leftover food.) There

---

[1] Ruskin uses "scoria" in the preface to his *Crown of Wild Olive*, in one of his eulogistic antipollution paragraphs, which I must quote: "And, in a little pool, behind some houses further in the village, where another spring rises, the shattered stones of the well, and of the little fretted channel which was long ago built and traced for it by gentler hands, lie scattered, each from each, under a ragged bank of mortar, and scoria; and bricklayers' refuse, on one side, which the clean water nevertheless chastises to purity; but it cannot conquer the dead earth beyond; and there, circled and coiled under festering scum, the stagnant edge of the pool effaces itself into a slope of black slime, the accumulation of indolent years." (This too has a hint of the Gibbon-Poggio lament over the ruins of the Forum.) A sentence earlier, Ruskin mentions "street and house foulness; heaps of dust and slime, and broken shreds of old metal, and rags of putrid clothes." *Scoria, refuse, scum, slime, foulness, dust, old metal,* and *rags*: nearly an entire thesaurus list, *lumber* excepted, in a single paragraph—and all of them made beautiful, Edenized by one perfect phrase: "which the clean water nevertheless chastises to purity."

is *Tares,* by a poet named R. S. Thomas (1961), and *Tares: A Book of Verses* by Rosamond Marriott Watson (1898). Or you can try the charming-sounding *Chaff and Wheat: A Few Gentle Flailings* (1915), by Francis Patrick Donelly, or *Sweepings* (1926), by Lester Cohen, or *Slough Cup Hope Tantrum,* by Alan Davies (1975). Stephen Vincent Benet brought us *The Litter of the Rose Leaves* (1930), following up on Frank William Boreham's *Rubble and Roseleaves, and Things of That Kind* (1923). The poets of the Sludge Collective came out, in 1973, with *Sludge: Daughter of Ooze, Son of Stain.* Ohio University Press published Conrad Hilberry's *Rust: Poems* in 1974; Turkey Press produced Michael Hogan's *Rust: Poems* in 1977. *Out of the Dunghill: A Series of Fifty Odes* by Gordon Jackson came out in 1981. Allen Ginsberg published 150 copies of *Scrap Leaves: Hasty Scribbles* circa 1968; Marietta Minnigerode Andrews gave us *Scraps of Paper* in 1929; Edwin C. Hickman is the author of *Scraps of Poetry and Prose,* from 1854, preceded by *Scraps and Poems,* by Mrs. R. A. Searles, published by Swormstedt and Power of Cincinnati in 1851, and by *Scripscrapologia, or Collins' Doggerel Dish of All Sorts,* a collection by John Collins from 1804.[1] There is a book of prose pieces by Rod Mengham called *Beds & Scrapings,* and *Scrut,*[2] poems by George Roberts, published by Holy Cow! Press in 1983. Someone named Tuschen published *Junk*

---

[1] One of Collins's poems, "Tomorrow," was chosen by Palgrave for his *Olden Trashery* (as Christopher Ricks permutes the book's title on p. 450 of the Penguin edition)—the last two lines of the poem are: "As this old worn-out stuff, which is threadbare Today, / May become Everlasting Tomorrow." Palgrave explains that "Everlasting" is used "with side-allusion to a cloth so named, at the time when Collins wrote."

[2] "Scrut" is from *scruta,* an uncommon (though Horatian) Latin word meaning, "discarded goods, junk" (*Oxford Latin Dictionary*). A *scrutarius* is a junk-merchant. For *scruta,* Cooper's seventeenth-century *Thesaurus*

Mail: Poems in 1970; Richard Le Galliene published *The Junk-Man and Other Poems* in 1920; Jack Kerouac's "Junk" came out as a postcard poem in 1976. In *Old Junk* (1918, revised 1933), a little-known though moving collection of World War I essays intersprinkled with thoughts on toadstools and bedside reading, H. M. Tomlinson describes entering a French town after the German withdrawal and has a G. K. Chestertonian moment:

> The gardens beyond are to be seen through the thin and gaping walls of the streets, and there, overturned and defaced by shell-bursts and the crude subsoil thrown out from dug-outs, a few ragged shrubs survive. A rustic bower is lumbered with empty bottles, meat tins, a bird-cage, and ugly litter and fragments. . . . It is perplexing to find how little remains of the common things of the household; a broken doll, a child's boot, a trampled bonnet. Once in such a town I found a corn-chandler's ledger. . . .
>
> I don't know that I ever read a book with more interest than that corn-chandler's ledger; though at one time, when it was merely a commonplace record of the common life which circulated there, testifying to its industry and the response of earth, it would have been no matter to me.

Tomlinson even gives a wartime inflection to *lumber* in his preface: "My friend added his own gas-mask and apparatus to the grim lumber on the hat-rack. The floor was wet, and was cumbered with heavy boots, guns, and dirty haversacks."

Back to cheerfuller *Garbage*-heaps, though. Charles Ira Bushnell published *Crumbs for Antiquarians,* a book of

---

Linguae Romanae has "Olde garments, horse shoes, and such other baggage solde for necessitie." Close scrutiny, then, on the etymological evidence, is a kind of ragpicking. And until recently, if you looked up *lumber* in the English side of Traupman's *New College Latin & English Dictionary* you were given *scruta* as the translation—as you still are with Cassell's, and with Langenscheidt's tiny *Universal Latin Dictionary,* bound in a yellow plastic cover that resists spills—but in the brand-new edition of Traupman (1995), *materia* ("timber") is the equivalent offered.

revolutionary war studies, in 1864–66; and the Reverend Elnathan Corrigton Gavitt came up with the fine title *Crumbs from My Saddle Bags* for a book of pioneer reminiscences published in 1884. About then T. De Witt Talmage tried the simpler *Crumbs Swept Up*. Dylan Thomas published "The Crumbs of One Man's Year" in *The Listener* in 1947. Nathaniel Parker Willis offered *The Rag-Bag, a Collection of Ephemera* (1855); Seamus Heaney and Ted Hughes produced an anthology called *The Rattle Bag* in 1982. There is *Waste Basket, Husks of Wheat, Dump Truck, Debris, Sewage, Bin Ends, Stubble Burning, Stubble Poems, Dirty Washing, The Waste Land, Out of the Bog, Bog Poems*, and *Disgust*, which are books of poetry by Charles Bukowski, Diane Wakoski, Keith Abbott, Madge Morris, Valerie Hannah Weisberg, Victoria Rothschild, Roland Gant, Willie, Sylvia Kantaris, T. S. Eliot, Harold Strong Gulliver, Seamus Heaney, and Algernon Charles Swinburne, respectively. Layton Irving is the author of *Droppings from Heaven* (1979); Thomas MacKellar in 1844 wrote a book of occasional poetry called *Droppings from the Heart*; and the poet Duncan McNaughton titled one of his books *Shit on My Shoes* (1979). There is even a *Poop, and Other Poems* (1972) by Gerald Locklin. Douglas Houston produced *With the Offal Eaters: Poems* in 1986, and Ordinary Madness Press published Doug Hornig's *Feeding at the Offal Trough: Poems* in 1983.

Ammons, performing a subject search in an online catalog for "Garbage Disposal," was (so he tells us in *Garbage*, p. 49) pleased to retrieve nothing, since it gave him a "clear space and pure / freedom to dump whatever." Ammons's online catalog (presumably it is Cornell's) has more clear spaces than mine: on the day I devoted to this offal search (December 1, 1994), I found several books by typing FIND SUBJECT GARBAGE DISPOSAL: one was a *Combustible Refuse Collection Survey* performed in Cleveland, circa 1940, by the WPA. But I found no books of poetry or collected prose entitled *Sullage,* or *Dregs,* or *Rinsings,* or *Squeezings,* or *Medical Waste,* or *Filth-Inhabiting Flies,* or *Draff,* or *Vetch*—and I hereby reserve the right (nonexclusive, of course) to use any or all of these, alone or in combination, for future books. Most surprisingly, there is no book of poetry or gathering of fugitive review-essays called simply *Lumber. Lumber and Other Essays:* one can imagine some minor turn-of-the-centurion like Augustine Birrell or Edmund Gosse or W. E. Henley[1] settling on it as a title, but as it happens, none of them quite saw their way to it. There is, however, an ahead-of-its-time book by one Selina Gaye called *The World's Lumber Room* (1885) that A. R. Ammons would probably like. Its epigraph is a slightly emended quotation from Goldsmith's *Vicar of Wakefield:*

> I regarded myself as one of those vile things that Nature designed should be thrown by into her *lumber room,* there to perish in obscurity.

Selina Gaye (also the author of *The Maiden of the Iceberg: A Tale in Verse,* published in 1867 and not included in the *English Poetry Database,* though it is available on microfilm) has left out an adjective: Goldsmith's sentence actually reads (I flipped through the *Vicar* three times before I found it), ". . . there to perish in *unpitied* obscurity." *The World's Lumber Room* is an interdisciplinary study of "dust" and its sources and users—it occupies itself with decomposition, the

---

[1] In a preface, Henley called his collection, *Views and Reviews* (1890), "less a book than a mosaic of scraps and shreds recovered from the shot rubbish of some fourteen years of journalism." While he was editor of the *National Observer,* Henley published a series of colorful essays on legal history by Francis Watt that were collected in 1895 as *The Law's Lumber Room.*

recycling of Victorian household refuse, the social hierarchy of Parisian ragpickers (or *chiffonniers*), kitchen middeners, ants, flies, coral reefs, volcanoes, beetles, the medicinal jelly made from ivory dust, brewers' refuse ("draff") pressed into cakes and fed to horses, and old rugs:

> A carpet which covered the floor of one of the rooms in the mint of San Francisco for five years was, when taken up, cut in small pieces, and burnt in pans, with the result that its ashes yielded gold and silver to the value of 2,500 dollars.

The following passage in particular, from Gaye's preface, is oddly inspiring:

> The World's Lumber Room, comprising the three great departments of Earth, Air, and Water, is in fact co-extensive with the World itself, and, so far from being the sort of place which the worthy Vicar's son seems to have pictured to himself, is rather a workshop or laboratory, where nothing is left to "perish," in his sense of the word, but the old becomes new, and the vile and refuse, instead of being "thrown by" in their vileness, are taken in hand and turned to good account.

Perhaps I am not so very misguided, then, in deliberately making a lumber-room of my head with the present study, so long as that room is, as Gaye contends, coextensive with the world itself. No decomposing quotation is so vile that it can't be taken in hand and turned to good account. Still, if I'm going to quote from the long and illustrious line of lumber-into-treasure commonplaceholders, if I'm going to cite Horace and Wordsworth and Emerson and W. E. Henley and Saki and A. R. Ammons, there is no excuse for my having left out of this series the most adept and amazing commonplace-transfigurer there ever was, or will be. "He unfortunately worked up the rubbish as well as the gems," Leslie Stephen writes, in an essay called "Pope as a Moralist," but in another passage Stephen grants, as we all must, that Alexander Pope has "a probably unequalled power of coining aphorisms out of common-place." Of Pope's *Essay on Criticism* the harsh Reverend Elwin says that all the classical doctrines of criticism in it "might have been picked up from his French manuals in a single morning," and he concurs with De Quincey's dismissal of it as "mere versification, like a metrical multiplication table, of common-places the most mouldy with which criticism has baited its rat-traps." And yet what an extraordinary multiplication table it is, and what lucky sewer rats we readers are! Tiny known quantities of sense, operated upon in accordance with known metrical law, yield in Pope's arithmetic hands infinitely long and unrepeating decimals of truth:

> True Wit is Nature to Advantage drest
> What oft was Thought, but ne'er so well Exprest.

Not much has been more oft thought over the centuries than the notion that the writer writes what oft was thought but ne'er so well exprest; nobody, though, has exprest it with such politely imploded conviction as Pope exhibits here.[1] At twenty-five, Pope possessed (this is Leslie Stephen again) "the rare art of composing proverbs in verse, which have become

---

[1] Christopher Smart attempted to turn these two lines (from the *Essay on Criticism* again) into Latin:

> Vis veri ingenii, natura est cultior, id quod
> Senserunt multi, sed jam scite exprimit unus.

A. E. Housman claimed that Smart didn't write any good poetry until after he became insane, somewhere around 1756. His Latin version of Pope's poem was published in 1752. One wonders whether a growing sense of the utter futility of trying to Latinize an egg as ideally ovoid as Pope's couplet was what caused the sad "estrangement" of Smart's mind, and led to his confinement in St. Luke's Hospital, where he versified Horace and first wrote poetry that the exacting Housman could admire. Smart translated "loads of learned lumber" as *nugarum docta farrago*—"a learned trail-mix of trivia," more or less. Smart carefully preserved a faintly praising note that Pope wrote him in 1743 and even had it painted in his portrait. See Arthur Sherbo, *Christopher Smart, Scholar of the University* (1967), p. 33.

part of the intellectual furniture of all decently educated men." Even De Quincey, in spite of the ornate scorn he reserves for the *Essay,* seems to have come into a few Queen Anne tea-tables from Pope's estate. In the *Confessions of an English Opium-Eater,* he denounces certain works of political economy as being "the very dregs and rinsings of the human intellect." Compare Pope:

> Still run on Poets in a raging Vein,
> Ev'n to the Dregs and Squeezings of the Brain.

Not that Pope's "dregs and squeezings" isn't itself a second pressing: a footnote in the Twickenham edition calls our attention to a line in Oldham's *Satyrs upon the Jesuits* that goes, "With all the *dregs,* and *squeesings* of his rage." Mark Pattison writes that Pope was

> very industrious, and had read a vast number of books, yet he was very ignorant,—ignorant, that is, of everything but the one thing which he laboured with all his might to acquire, the art of happy expression. He read books to find ready-made images, and to feel for the best collocations of words. His memory was a magazine of epithets and synonymes, and pretty turns of language. Whenever he found anything to his purpose, he booked it for use, and some time or other, often more than once, it made its appearance in his verse.[1]

We pardon Pope, most of the time, because he rehabilitates nearly every second-hand phrase that comes through his shop. He unscrews a line he likes, sorts and cleans its pieces, stores them, finds matches, does some seemingly casual beveling, drills a narrow caesural ventilation-hole, squirts the Krazy Glue of genius into several chinks, gives the prototypical whole a sudden uniting twist, and hands the world a tiny two-

---

[1] "Pope and His Editors," in Mark Pattison, *Essays,* vol. II, 1889.

cylinder perpetual-motion machine—a heroic couplet. Even when we know his sources phrase by phrase, we must still remain in awe (following a week in a darkened room devoted to adjusting to the horrifying extent and specificity of the thefts) of his divine clockmaker's gift. Dryden (in his "Preface to the Fables") explains that "the genius of our countrymen in general [is] rather to improve an invention, than to invent themselves; as is evident not only in our poetry, but in many of our manufactures." And Samuel Wesley (a poet too minor to receive an entry of his own in Drabble's *Oxford Companion,* though Swift gives him the honor of being the fourth fatality in *The Battle of the Books*),[1] in a passage from his *Epistle to a Friend Concerning Poetry* (1700) defends Dryden's own frequent raids on the already articulated:

> If from the modern or the antient Store
> He borrows ought, he always pays 'em more:
> So much improv'd, each Thought, so fine appears,
> Waller or Ovid scarce durst own 'em theirs.
> The Learned Goth has scowr'd all Europe's Plains,
> France, Spain, and fruitful Italy he drains,
> From every Realm and every Language gains:
> His Gains a Conquest are, and not a Theft;
> He wishes still new Worlds of Wit were left . . .

This is a sort of versification of Dryden's own praise of Boileau, in the essay "On the Origin and Progress of Satire":

> What he [Boileau] borrows from the ancients he repays with usury of his own, in coin as good and almost as universally valuable.

Samuel Butler, a few decades earlier, came up with one of the tripier casings for this old trope:

---

[1] Aristotle shoots Descartes with an arrow in the right eye; Homer's horse tramples D'Avenant; then Homer gets John Denham with a long spear, and Samuel Wesley is slain by a kick of Homer's horse's heel.

Our moderne Authors write Playes as they feed hogs in West-
phalia, where but one eate's peas, or akornes, and all the rest feed
upon his and one anothers excrement.[1]

I happened on Wesley's *Epistle to a Friend Concerning
Poetry* in the *English Poetry Database* simply because it mentions the "lumber-thoughts" of a poetical first draft. (Some
you should keep, and some "the sponge should strike.") But I
liked the poem and paused over it, for it looked to be something Pope had read carefully:

> Draw the Main Strokes at first, 'twill shew your Skill,
> Life-Touches you may add whene'er you will.
> Ev'n Chance will sometimes all our Art excel,
> The angry Foam we ne'er can hit so well.
> A sudden Thought, all beautiful and bright
> Shoots in and stunns us with amazing Light;
> Secure the happy Moment e'er 'tis past,
> Not Time more swift, or Lightning flies so fast.

Any self-respecting source-seeker who reads Wesley's *Epistle*
just after a fresh run-through of Pope's *Essay on Criticism*

---

[1] Samuel Butler, *Prose Observations,* ed. Hugh de Quehen (Oxford:
Clarendon Press, 1979), p. 131. Pope, it turns out, lunched on this very
image in his *Epilogue to the Satires, Dialogue II* (1738):

> Let Courtly Wits to Wits afford supply,
> As Hog to Hog in Huts of *Westphaly;*
> In one, thro' Nature's bounty or his Lord's,
> Has what the frugal, dirty soil affords,
> From him the next receives it, thick or thin,
> As pure a Mess almost as it came in.

How Pope came to read Butler's distinctive passage, when it wasn't published
until after Pope's death, is a matter of conjecture. One wants Swift to have
had something to do with it, but Robert Thyer, the first editor of Butler's
posthumous manuscripts (*Genuine Remains*, 1759), suspects (vol. II, p. 497)
the agency of Bishop Atterbury, who earlier had helped Charles Boyle in his
attack on Bentley's *Phalaris*. See also John Butt's note to l. 172 of the Twickenham edition of the *Epilogue to the Satires, Dialogue II,* p. 323.

will notice that some of its phrases and ideas were reset a decade later in Pope's precocious assemblage. Indeed, Pope's use of Wesley extends beyond phrasing, to the metaphorical structure of whole sections. Here is Wesley:[1]

> Style is the Dress of Thought; a modest Dress,
> Neat, but not gaudy, will true Critics please:
> Not Fleckno's Drugget, nor a worse Extream
> All daub'd with Point and Gold at every Seam:
> Who only Antique Words affects, appears
> Like old King Harry's Court, all Face and Ears;
> Nor in a Load of Wig thy Visage shrowd,
> Like Hairy Meteors glimm'ring through a Cloud:
> Happy are those who here the Medium know,
> We hate alike a Sloven and a Beau.
> I would not follow Fashion to the height
> Close at the Heels, nor yet be out of Sight:
> Words alter, like our Garments, every day,
> Now thrive and bloom, now wither and decay.
> Let those of greater Genius new invent,
> Be you with those in Common Use content.

And here is Pope, as he tracks Wesley's passage:

> Expression is the Dress of Thought, and still
> Appears more decent as more suitable;
> A vile Conceit in pompous Words exprest,
> Is like a Clown in regal Purple drest;
> For diff'rent Styles with diff'rent Subjects sort,
> As several Garbs with Country, Town, and Court.
> Some by Old Words to Fame have made Pretence;
> Ancients in Phrase, meer Moderns in their Sense!
> Such labour'd Nothings, in so strange a Style,

---

[1] And I am aware that I am overquoting—I know that there is an ideal rhythm of quotation and text, a museum-goer's pace that you must offer the reader that isolates each labeled display-case of small print from the next— but I nonetheless haven't been able to keep from close-packing the page: this piece of ham-scholarship is, I think, the one chance I will get to cite freely, without shame, without constraint: I'll never let myself fall so utterly in lumber again.

> Amaze th'unlearn'd, and make the Learned Smile.
> Unlucky, as Fungoso in the Play,
> These Sparks with aukward Vanity display
> What the Fine Gentleman wore Yesterday!
> And but so mimick ancient Wits at best,
> As Apes our Grandsires in their Doublets drest.
> In Words, as Fashions, the same Rule will hold;
> Alike Fantastick, if too New, or Old;
> Be not the first by whom the New are try'd,
> Nor yet the last to lay the Old aside.

(The startling figure of the meteor-wig is taken from Boileau; Pope replaces it with the reference to Fungoso, a character in Ben Jonson's *Every Man out of his Humour*.)

So Samuel Wesley's encomium to Dryden's artful borrowing-skills seems to have given Pope the go-ahead to pick Wesley's own pocket. The ingenue-poet (who later knew Wesley and his family) tries to put us off the scent by footnoting his "True Wit" couplet with a vaguely apropos tidbit from Quintilian,[1] and Elwin's commentary adduces a parallel prose passage from Boileau, but the truth is that

> True Wit is Nature to advantage drest,
> What oft was Thought, but ne'er so well Exprest

is closer to Reverend Samuel Wesley's good sense than anything else:

> Good Sense[2] is spoild in Words unapt exprest,
> And Beauty pleases more when 'tis well drest.

---

[1] *Naturam intueamur, hanc sequamur: id facillimè accipiunt animi quod agnoscunt*, Pope piously quotes, which is adapted from Quintilian's *Institutio Oratoria*, Book VIII, ch. 3, paragraph 71: "We must look to nature, and follow her . . . the mind easily admits what it recognizes as true. . . ." I'm following the translation by John Selby Watson.

[2] Pope replaces Wesley's "Good Sense" with the first two words of the Prologue to Dryden's *Mr. Limberham* (from the passage that six lines later mentions "machining lumber"):

But there are all degrees of imitation and embezzlement in poetry. Wesley, too, I note, now splashing backward a decade or two in the *English Poetry Database,* had come up with his "sense well drest" couplet by tinkering with the following triplet from Roscommon's *Essay on Translated Verse* (1684):

> Abstruse and Mystick thoughts you must express,
> With painful Care but seeming easiness,
> For truth shines brightest through the plainest dress.[1]

> True wit has seen its best days long ago;
> It ne'er looked up, since we were dipt in show.

[1] The eagerest and most appealingly innocent version of this thought comes earlier still, in "At a Vacation Exercise," by the nineteen-year-old John Milton. Since it doesn't contain "drest" or "exprest," you can't reach it through mechanical retrievals; but it is in handy collections like *The Penguin Book of Renaissance Verse,* where I first encountered it. Milton addresses Philosophy:

> I have some naked thoughts that rove about
> And loudly knock to have their passage out;
> And wearie of their place do only stay
> Till thou hast deck't them in thy best array.

(It was written in 1623 and published in *Poems,* 1673.) And James Russell Lowell, writing a hundred and fifty-odd years after Pope, successfully nudged the apparently immovable Popianism forward several feet, in prose:

> in literature, it should be remembered, a thing always becomes his at last who says it best, and thus makes it his own. ("Dryden.")

And

> The thought or feeling a thousand times repeated becomes his at last who utters it best. ("Keats.")

And better still, in poetry:

> Though old the thought and oft expressed,
> 'Tis his at last who says it best.
>   ("For an Autograph.")

Bartlett's gives Lowell's couplet, and refers us in a footnote not to Pope but to Emerson's "Next to the originator of a good sentence is the first quoter of it." Emerson's problem, though, was that when he quoted he didn't always remember to use quotation marks.

As a matter of fact, Samuel Wesley justifies his adaptive reuse of Roscommon right in his poem:

> If English Verse you'd in Perfection see,
> Roscommon read, and Noble Normanby:[1]
> We borrow all from their exhaustless Store,
> Or little say they have not said before.

And in lines that must have made Pope's devious heart beat faster—lines that described in detail the Cave of the Muses, "a wondrous Storehouse," with Crystal Fountains, and Labyrinths, and "rich Mosaick Work divinely fram'd"— Samuel Wesley urges the beginner to fill his head with other people's poetry:

> Whate'er within this sacred Hall you find,
> Whate'er will lodge in your capacious Mind
> Let Judgment sort, and skilful Method bind;
> And as from these you draw your antient Store
> Daily supply the Magazine with more.

Pope, a congenital sorter and binder, wrote very good stuff by following Wesley's advice, which required him to do exactly what he wanted to do anyway—to fill his capacious mind with the scoria of reading. But our hero must have had some second thoughts: in 1717, when he still hadn't reached thirty and was collecting his *Works* (including the *Essay on Criticism*)—perhaps nipped at by an agenbite or two (for nobody knew better than himself what a "mosaic"—Elwin's word—of sources his poetry was)—he defended his method in an introduction:

---

[1] Normanby is John Sheffield, Earl of Mulgrave, Duke of Buckingham and Normanby (1648–1721), a patron of Dryden, Wesley, and Pope, and author of *An Essay Upon Poetry*, 1682. He, too, uses the phrase "true wit" in a couplet, following Dryden ("True Wit is everlasting, like the Sun"), and regarding the Soul of Poetry, he happily asks:

> what caverns of the Brain
> Can such a vast and mighty thing contain?

Therefore they who say our thoughts are not our own because they resemble the Ancients, may as well say our faces are not our own, because they are like our Fathers: And indeed it is very unreasonable, that people should expect us to be Scholars, and yet be angry to find us so.

Reverend Elwin, glaring up at this sentence from a footnote, snaps:

The sophistry is transparent. A man may be a scholar without being a plagiarist or an imitator.

True, and worth saying—but surprisingly sharp. The real point is that Pope took his license to steal from nearby, commonplace, unexciting Samuel Wesley. He did not take it from the ancients, or from the preface to Boileau's *L'Art Poétique;* not even from Dryden or Roscommon, who were too grand and prominent for systematic plunder. (Writers, D'Avenant explains, "commonly make such use of treasure found in Bookes, as of other treasure belonging to the Dead, and hidden under ground; for they dispose of both with great secrecy, defacing the shape, or images of the one, as much as of the other; through feare of having the Originall of their stealth, or aboundance discover'd.") Pope's method was to begin with a minor model—either an inadequate earlier translation (or two, or three), or an original but middling poem (*The Cave of Poverty*)—and then, squirming in its nutrients, to leave his own unspeakably iridescent verse-frass in its husk. Wesley's *Epistle* was thus ideal for his purposes: it was cast in the very form (metapoetical verse essay) in which Pope wanted to display himself, and the Reverend obviously had some talent, but, poor man, not enough of it, and he wrote too fast and erred on the side of self-deprecation[1]—and lacking the neces-

---

[1] Wesley's brother-in-law and editorial partner, John Dunton, tells us that Wesley "usually writ too fast to write well. Two hundred couplets a day are too many by two-thirds, to be well furnished with all the beauties and graces

sary complement of true wit, malice, arrogance, and metric tact, all of which Pope knew himself to have in abundance, Wesley, father of thirteen children, had left behind an *Epistle* that Pope could conveniently despise, and in despising could treat as the fly treats rotting fruit. "Next, o'er his Books his eyes began to roll," Pope wrote in the revised *Dunciad* (these four lines replacing the "learned lumber" couplet that he had used in the first version), "In pleasing memory of all he stole"; and though he is not describing himself here, there is an element of tonic self-disgust:

> How here he sipp'd, how there he plunder'd snug
> And suck'd all o'er, like an industrious Bug.

All writers are to some degree industrious Bugs—and Pope's transfiguration of the "oft thought" commonplace is an early miracle, unsurpassed by any distich of the nineteenth century. Nonetheless, there were two serious wrongs Pope did Reverend Sam (1662–1735) as he improved upon him. The first was not to mention him in the poem, or if not in the poem itself, then at least in a note. Wesley, a principled trades-man, imported wheelbarrowsful of Roscommon's and Dry-den's and Sheffield's plenty into *his* poem, but he had the good grace to say so in verse as he went. Pope, on the other hand, only briefly mentions Roscommon at the end of the

---

of that art." (John Nichols, *Literary Anecdotes of the Eighteenth Century,* ed. Colin Clair, p. 404. Nichols says that Wesley's poetry is "far from being excellent.") In the *Epistle* Wesley is resolutely humble, claiming that he is himself no poet, and is "Content to Rime," like Tom Durfey. Durfey (1653–1723) was a tireless dramatist, poet, and songster whom Dryden and (later, predictably) Pope made fun of. Defoe called him "Pun-Master-General Durfey." But Durfey had his good days, too, as Wesley did: he wrote "I'll Sail Upon the Dog Star," which Purcell set to music; Auden included it in his *Oxford Book of Light Verse.*

Essay on Criticism (briefly and equivocally, as being "not more learn'd than good"), alludes once to Normanby, and omits Wesley altogether. That on its own wouldn't be so terrible. But Pope then included Wesley's name in the first edition of *The Dunciad* in a ridiculing list of the dull books in Theobald's library. "Wesley, Watts, and Blome" (or rather "W——ly, W——s, and Bl——") quickly became "Withers, Quarles, and Blome" in a subsequent printing, when one of Wesley's sons, Samuel the Younger, a friend of Pope's, protested:[1] Pope hung a gooey footnote from the verse claiming that the slights to Wesley and Watts had appeared in "surreptitious" editions (in fact the surreptitious editions were entirely Pope's doing), and that both men were "eminent for good life." Wesley, Pope adds, barely repressing a snigger, "writ the Life of Christ in verse." This is factually correct, and you can read the whole thing as it was published in 1693, including an account of Jesus at Capernaum, in the *English Poetry Database*.[2] But there was an earlier book of poems, too. When he was twenty-three, Wesley published *Maggots: or, Poems on Several Subjects, Never before Handled* (1685),

---

[1] See the note to line 126 in the Twickenham *Dunciad*, Book 1, pp. 78–79, which cites Norman Ault as the source of this information.

[2] *The Life of Our Blessed Lord & Saviour Jesus Christ. An Heroic Poem Dedicated to Her Most Sacred Majesty, In Ten Books. Attempted by Samuel Wesley*. It was accompanied by laudatory poems by unknowns like Taylor, Pittis, Luke Milbourne, Peter Motteux (the translator of Rabelais and Cervantes) and Nahum Tate, then poet laureate—

> The vast Idea seem'd a subject fit
> To exercise an able Poet's Wit;
> But to Express, to Finish and Adorn,
> Remain'd for you, who for this Work was Born.

A poet named Cutts was stoutly Keatsian in his praise of Wesley's attempt:

> You, (with Columbus,) not alone descrie,
> But conquer (Cortez-like), new Worlds in Poetry.

a lively clutch of grotesqueries and obscenities. It contains a monologue by a Methuselaian maggot who travels from brain to brain, and takes credit for inspiring various historical figures, including Virgil and Cleopatra; a 245-line "Ode to a Tobacco Pipe" that draws some startling comparisons between the tobacco pipe and the "glyster pipe," or enema; and a "Dialogue Between a Chamber-pot and a Frying Pan," in which the Chamber-pot begins

> Stand off! nor with rude Smut disgrace
> The Glories of my *brighter* face!

Another of Wesley's poems is "On a CHEESE: A Pastoral," and there is a rousing one called "A Pindaricque, On the Grunting of a Hog." ("Harmonious *Hog* draw near!" "Harmonious *Hog!* warble some *Anthem* out!") Pope conceals from his readers this cheerfully indecent and commonplace-transfiguring side of Wesley (which helped him in writing the maggoty Rabelaisianisms in *The Dunciad*), and he is silent about the *Epistle* itself, which was the host corpse for his *Essay.* This is the sort of duplicity and unfairness to the memory of an important predecessor that makes many of Pope's commentators eventually hate him. Coleridge plagiarized and paraphrased, and he even used decoy Latin footnotes, as Pope had, to distract readers from less impressive contemporary precedents, but he was such a patent dysfunctional, lifting the gate on a sluiceway of stagnant metaphysics for anyone who would stand for it,[1] that we forgive him his thefts of Schelling; Pope on the other hand was clean and sober, a calculating wee-hour snarfer, and it doesn't seem fair that he should also be a great poet.

---

[1] There is a nice footnote to William Harness's memoir of Coleridge in the fourth volume (1875) of Stoddard's Bric-a-Brac Series: "Wordsworth and Rogers called on him [Coleridge] one forenoon in Pall Mall. He talked unin-

In 1709, when he was five years old, John ("Jacky") Wesley, not yet famous as the founder of Methodism, was saved from a fire in the rectory at Epworth that burned all of his father Samuel Wesley's books, including a valuable Hebrew collection, which Samuel had been using to compile a Latin commentary on the Book of Job.[1] Samuel Wesley described the narrow escape in a letter to Sheffield:

> When I was without, I heard one of my poor lambs, left still above the stairs, about six years old, cry out dismally, "Help me!" I ran in again to go up-stairs, but the staircase was now all afire. I tried to force up through a second time, holding my breeches over my head, but the steam of fire beat me down. I thought I had done my duty; went out of the house to that part of my family I had saved, in the garden, with the killing cry of my child in my ears. I made them all kneel down, and we prayed God to receive his soul.

A servant attempted another rescue:

> The man was fallen down from the window, and all the bed and hangings in the room where he was blazing. They helped up the man the second time, and poor Jacky leaped into his arms and was saved. I could not believe it till I had kissed him two or three times. My wife then said to me, "Are your books safe?" I told her it was not much now she and all the rest were preserved, for we lost not one soul, though I escaped with the skin of my teeth. A little

---

terruptedly for two hours, during which time Wordsworth listened with profound attention. On leaving, Rogers said to Wordsworth, 'Well! I could not make head or tail of Coleridge's oration: did you understand it?' 'Not a syllable,' replied Wordsworth." Stoddard's book (an ad for which was mentioned above, in an earlier footnote) is embossed on the cover with the motto "Infinite riches in a little room," as well as an image of a lumber-room filled with statues, halberds, missals, and urns. I bought it at the rare-book room of the Holmes Book Store in Oakland, California (since closed), for $12.50.

[1] The commentary was eventually finished and published posthumously, with a dedication to Queen Caroline. John Wesley knelt before the Queen and presented his father's book in October of 1735. "It is very prettily bound," said the Queen politely. She set it aside without opening it.

> lumber was saved below stairs, but not one rag or leaf above. We
> found some of the silver in a lump, which I shall send up to Mr.
> Hoare to sell for me.

Jacky Wesley took seriously his naked delivery from the
flames. It "fixed itself in his mind as a work of divine provi-
dence," says the *Dictionary of National Biography*. "The day
after the fire," Southey writes (in Note V to Volume 1 of his
life of John Wesley), "as Mr. [Samuel] Wesley was walking in
the garden, and surveying the ruins of the house, he picked up
part of a leaf of his Polyglot Bible, on which (says his son
John) just these words were legible: *Vade, vende omnia quae
habes, et attolle crucem, et sequere me.*—Go, sell all that thou
hast, and take up thy cross, and follow me." John Wesley
obeyed: he took up the cross and traveled incessantly, preaching (by some accounts) forty thousand sermons and covering
two hundred and fifty thousand miles before he died. The
substantial sums he made from the sale of instructive works
to the semiliterate, he gave away. One of these was *Wesley's
Complete English Dictionary*. In the preface to the second
edition of the dictionary, dated October 20, 1763, John Wesley writes:

> In this Edition I have added some hundreds of words, which were
> omitted in the former: chiefly from Mr. Johnson's dictionary,
> which I carefully looked over for that purpose. And I will now
> venture to affirm, that, small as it is, this dictionary is quite suffi-
> cient, for enabling any one to understand the best Writings now
> extant, in the English tongue.

But Wesley's dictionary is not sufficient. It has no entry for
Lombard or *lombard-house*, and it skips from LU'DICROUS to
A LUMINARY—even though Mr. Johnson had not shrunk from
a definition of *lumber*, as we have seen, and even though John
Wesley's father had used *a little ~ from below stairs* to refer to
everything besides little Jacky Wesley himself that was saved

from the portentous fire. That the word isn't there may be evidence, though, if evidence is needed, of its spoken currency among the rural poor, since John Wesley's is essentially a hard-word dictionary for the unschooled-but-willing-to-learn.

My discovery, in Samuel Wesley's letter, of a casual l.-phrase[1] was, I think, the happiest para-scholarly moment I experienced while working on this entire piece of laxicography. It will be years before Samuel Wesley's letters are searchable electronically, if they ever are, which means that I can safely cast myself as a philological John Henry, holding my own against the tireless steam-drill in the railroad song: the steam-powered *English Poetry Full-Text Database* located Wesley's use of "lumber-thoughts" (and the *EPFTD is* steam-turbine-powered, assuming the usual sources of electric power), but I alone—steamed-milk-and-espresso-powered manual rhabdomancer—have found the humbler, below-stairs epistolary use (a use that demonstrates unpremeditated currency, no fossil of poetic diction) with my own untooled hands, by paging through a small-press book that lacks an index. I don't seem to tire of Muriel Spark's transfiguration: Wesley's letter-lumber becomes a lump of silver for me, since I have chosen to search for it, and I will bundle it in this para-

---

[1] The letter is quoted in Franklin Wilder's *Father of the Wesleys,* pp. 79–82, a biography of Samuel Wesley "proudly dedicated" to Mr. Wilder's late son, Robert Seab Wilder. ("Born January 2, 1948—Died September 10, 1966.") I found the letter on the evening of November 23, 1994, in the library of the Graduate Theological Union in Berkeley, California, where I'd never been before, accompanied by my own beautiful son, who had just had his first birthday, and who was in a deep sleep, with his head flopped sideways in the stroller, unaware of the silent aisles of book-lumber towering above him. It must have been painful for Mr. Wilder to type Wesley's account of the miraculous survival of a son.

graph and send it up to a latter-day "Mr. Hoare" to sell.[1] At the same time, I will do what I can to rescue Wesley's poetry, which I want to like, because Wesley is, despite episodes of marital stubbornness and fatherly pig-headedness (he ruined one daughter's life by forbidding her to marry the man she wanted), a considerably more appealing person than Pope. Indeed Reverend Wesley could have been a real-life model for the good-hearted, stoical Vicar of Wakefield. Like Reverend Wesley, Goldsmith's hero (Dr. Primrose) lives in the country with his large family, where he undergoes a series of Job-like trials and is forever in debt; and like Wesley, the Vicar just barely saves his children from a fire:

> That moment I heard the cry of the babes within, who were just awaked by the fire, and nothing could have stopped me. "Where, where, are my children?" cried I, rushing through the flames and bursting the door of the chamber in which they were confined. "Where are my little ones?"—"Here, dear pappa, here we are," cried they together, while the flames were just catching the bed where they lay. I caught them both in my arms and snatched them through the fire as fast as possible, while just as I was got out, the roof sunk in. "Now," cried I, holding up my children, "now let the flames burn on, and all my possessions perish. Here they are, I have saved my treasure. Here, my dearest, here are our treasures, and we shall yet be happy." We kissed our little darlings a thousand times, they clasped us round the neck, and seemed to share our transports, while their mother laughed and wept by turns.

It's at least possible that Goldsmith was recalling some account of the 1709 fire at Wesley's Epworth Rectory (either Wesley's actual letter to Sheffield or something written or preached by one of his famous Methodist sons) when he was writing this scene in his 1766 novel.

---

[1] The Mr. Hoare in Wesley's letter, the silver-broker, not the coincidental Hoare who wrote about "loads of learned lumber" in the special collections of the university library.

Despite Pope's evident reliance on Wesley's unsung *Epistle* while he was working on the *Essay on Criticism*, Wesley's "lumber-thoughts" are not responsible for the *lumber* in (and let me quote it whole again for convenient reference) Pope's great couplet:

> The Bookful Blockhead, ignorantly read
> With Loads of Learned Lumber in his Head.

I now believe, however, that I know where Pope's phrase came from. The *EPFTD*-florist has delivered it to me. While I may preserve some pedantic pride by citing the pre-Popian lumber-finds that I made solo, unaided by concordances, indexes, the *OED,* the *Library of the Future,* or Chadwyck-Healey (the only significant find, come to think of it, is the *lumber*-pair in Locke's "Of the Conduct of the Understanding"),[1] it is Chadwyck-Healey that triumphed

---

[1] Except for a use by John Ozell in 1708, to be footnoted shortly. Without artificial retrieval-tools, I also found this ante-Papal line from the Prologue to Book IV of the Urquhart-Motteux translation of Rabelais (1694): "Since

in the end.[1]

For several months I misunderstood what it was trying to tell me. In November of 1994 I was confident that I had the chronology of the derivation of Pope's couplet sketched out. There was a "learned Lombard" prominently mentioned (Book I, canto i) in D'Avenant's huge poem *Gondibert* (1651), set in Lombardy.[2] This use prepped the ear for "learned lumber" without inventing it. And then there was a fairly complicated Lombardy-lumber pun, probably the handiwork of the debt-harassed Sir John Denham (1615–1669), in one of the anonymous satires on *Gondibert* that were bundled with the second edition of D'Avenant's poem (1653) and attributed to "severall of the Authors Friends":

> Of all Ill Poets by their Lumber known,
> Who nere Fame's favor wore, yet sought them long,

---

tools without their hafts are useless lumber." And in Book IV, chapter 59, Rabelais's Gastrolators offer their god some "lumber pies with hot sauce," a translation of "pastéz à la saulce chaulde." But I saw no instance of the word in Book III, chapters 3–5, in which Panurge and Pantagruel debate the advantages of debt. In translating *pastéz* (Book II, chapter 5 and elsewhere) Sir Thomas Urquhart (1611–1660) seems generally to have employed "pasties"; Peter Motteux, his successor (and Wesley's acquaintance), introduced the *lumber* into the pie. *Pastissage,* Montaigne's curious word, does not appear anywhere in Rabelais, according to Dixon and Dawson's *Concordance des Oeuvres de François Rabelais* (1992).

[1] De hammer dat John Henry swung,
  It weighed over nine pound;
  He broke a rib in his lef'-han' side,
  An' his intrels fell on de groun',
  Lawd, Lawd, an' his intrels fell on de groun'.
            ("John Henry," in Auden, *The Oxford Book of Light Verse*)

[2] But here the learned Lombard whom I trace
  My forward Pen by slower Method stays . . .

Pope's first published poem, a translation of Chaucer's "Merchant's Tale" that was published in 1709, begins in Lombardy, too:

There liv'd in Lombardy, as Authors write
In Days of old, a wise and worthy Knight . . .

Sir Daphne [D'Avenant] gives precedency to none,
And breeds most business for abstersive Song.

From untaught Childhood, to mistaking Man,
An ill-performing Agent to the Stage;
With Albovin in Lumber he began,
With Gondibert in Lumber ends his rage.

"Albovin" refers to D'Avenant's first play, *The Tragedy of Albovine*. To be "in lumber" can mean to be in debt, but (as we have seen) it can also mean to be imprisoned, or simply (see Partridge's *Dictionary of Slang*) to be in big trouble—senses that Denham wants here, since D'Avenant "began" with a bad case of syphilis about the time *Albovine* came out (the illness was, according to Drabble's *Companion,* "a subject referred to in his own works and in the jests of others"), and he was held captive in the Tower from 1650 to 1652, while working on *Gondibert*.[1]

Then there was Dryden's

> Damn me, whate'er those book-learned blockheads say

from his translation, the "Third Satire of Persius," line 152 (1693). It impelled Pope toward the "bookful blockhead" in the first half of his couplet. ("Bookful" itself is a rare word; Pope's choice of it over Dryden's "book-learned" is characteristic of his fine-tunefulness.) And finally there was this anonymous translation of some lines from the beginning of the Fourth Satire of Boileau, dated 1687:

> The haughty Pedant, swoln with Frothy Name
> Of Learned Man, big with his Classick Fame;
> A thousand Books read o're and o're again,

---

[1] Denham's parody, contained in Disk 1 of the *English Poetry Database*, is reprinted in an appendix to David Gladish's edition of *Gondibert*, 1971, where there are also some lines about D'Avenant's "sad mis-haps, / Of drinking, riming, and of claps."

> Does word for word most perfectly retain,
> Heap'd in the Lumber-Office of his Brain;
> Yet this cram'd Skull, this undigested Mass,
> Does very often prove an arrant Ass;
> Believes all Knowledge is to Books confin'd,
> That reading only can inform the Mind. . . .

The "lumber-office" here—a colorful pawnbrokering of what is merely a "teste entassez" (a heaped head) in the original[1]—was perhaps the first time the lumber-room metaphor was applied inside the skull.

These poetical uses—"learned Lombard," "Ill Poets by their Lumber known," "book-learned blockheads," and "the Lumber-Office of his Brain"—in addition to others by Dryden, Butler, Rochester, Oldham, and Swift, supplemented by Locke's figure of the contents of the mind-magazine as "a Collection of Lumber not reduc'd to Use or Order"—were the various tributary strands, I theorized, that Pope boondoggled into the great keychain of his couplet.

But then in December of 1994, more knowledgeable by this time about Pope's habits, I went through the hundred-odd instances of lumber from 1660 to 1800 one more time, onscreen. I stopped again at the four *lumber*-uses in Samuel Garth's *Dispensary,* more than in any other single poem. Here

---

[1] Un Pêdant enyvré de sa vaine science,
Tout herissé de Grec, tout bouffi d'arrogance,
Et qui, de mille Auteurs retenus mot pour mot,
Dans sa teste entassez, n'a souvent fait qu'un Sot,
Croit qu'un livre fait tout . . .

Entasser des écus is a common phrase for hoarding money, according to the *Concise Oxford French Dictionary*—maybe the anonymous Englisher is trying to preserve the financial clink in "entassez" with "lumber-office." The translation is from the *Poems on Affairs of State* (1697), vol. 1, p. 210, entitled "The Fourth Satyr of Boileau to W.K."—it was left out of the modern edition of the *Poems on Affairs of State,* but it is on the *EPFTD.*

was a poet who really liked the word.[1] One *lumber* comes in a description of Chaos's underground home:

> To these dark Realms much learned Lumber creeps.

Up till then I had dismissed this particular "learned ∼" as a straightforward borrowing by Garth from Pope—just as Samuel Boyce's "With loads of lumber treasur'd in his head" (1757), and Paul Whitehead's "Loads of dull lumber, all inspir'd by Pay" (1733), and Thomas Paget's "Much hoarded Learning but like Lumber lies" (1735), and George Ogle et al.'s "Small Store of learned Lumber fills my Head" (1741) were all borrowings—since on the bibliographical screen of the database, Garth's work (a popular and much discussed mock-heroic satire on uncharitable apothecaries) was dated 1714, three years after the *Essay on Criticism*. But Chadwyck-Healey is in the business of text-conversion, not literary history: the year they so scrupulously associate with each electrified book is the year of the edition from which they keyed their text, which is not necessarily the year that the text was first published. Presented with a poem published sometime in the seventeenth century, but transcribed from an edition published in 1908, you know, of course, not to trust 1908 as your rough date of original appearance, but in the case of poems that went through multiple editions in close succession, the nearly correct year can sometimes throw you off. Here (through simple ignorance on my part: Samuel Garth was one of the best-known poets of the period) I had been thrown off badly. *The Dispensary* first came out in

---

[1] Garth's heavy use of *lumber* was infectious: Geoffrey Tillotson, in his introduction to the Twickenham edition of Pope's *The Rape of the Lock* (1940, rev. ed, 1954, p. 113), writes: "Among the medical lumber of [Garth's] poem are satiric references to the 'beau monde' (the phrase of the time) which provide Pope with hints and materials."

1699, and was "universally and liberally applauded," according to Samuel Johnson, in his "Life of Garth." Chadwyck-Healey had worked from the seventh edition, advertised on the title page as having "several Descriptions and Episodes never before printed." What I had to find out, then, and what the database couldn't tell me, was whether Garth's "learned lumber" had appeared in one of the editions prior to the 1711 publication of Pope's *Essay on Criticism,* or in one of the editions subsequent to it.

There would, however, be no difficulty in establishing that Pope could have read Garth's "learned lumber" if Garth's use of the phrase did precede Pope's. It was not possible, in other words, that the two poets discovered it independently, for Pope and Garth were friends and collaborators. Garth read Pope's early *Pastorals* (1709) in manuscript, and "Summer," the second pastoral, was dedicated "To Dr. Garth" in editions after 1717. Later still, Pope (anxious to show the world that he didn't feud with everyone) added this note:

> Dr. *Samuel Garth,* Author of the *Dispensary,* was one of the first friends of the author, whose acquaintance with him began at fourteen or fifteen. Their friendship continu'd from the year 1703, to 1718, which was that of his death.

Both poets' biographers (John F. Sena and Maynard Mack) are cautious about accepting the 1703 date as marking the inception of the friendship. Fifteen seems a trifle early, and Pope was childishly vain about his literary precocity, confusing and falsifying the epistolary record whenever he could, and even in middle age decking his reissued poems with boy-wonder dates and testimonials in the most pathetic way. ("Written in the Year 1704," "Written at sixteen years of age," etc.) John Sena thinks Garth may have met Pope at Will's Coffee House—1706 or 1707 might be a better date than 1703. Whatever the circumstances, they knew each other several years before Pope published the *Essay on Criticism,* and remained friends after it was published. (Garth was probably fortunate in dying before Pope had a chance to become infuriated at some imagined slight and draw-and-quarto him in verse, as he was wont to do with old friends and allies.)

Moreover Pope owned at least two different editions of *The Dispensary*—that of 1703, in which he wrote his name and a note that the book was a "Donum Autoris," and that of 1706, with annotations that Frank H. Ellis (who edited the poem in *Poems on Affairs of State,* Volume 6) called "disappointing." In his "Life of Garth," Samuel Johnson wrote that "It was remarked by Pope that *The Dispensary* had been corrected in every edition, and that every change was an improvement." This fact Johnson got (according to G. Birkbeck Hill's footnote) from Jonathan Richardson's *Richardsoniana:*

> Mr. Pope told me himself that "there was hardly an alteration of the innumerable ones through every edition that was not for the better."

All right, then—was "learned lumber" one of those innumerable alterations for the better that came about before 1711, or after 1711? Unaware of Ellis's excellent modern scholarly collation of all the *Dispensary* editions, I went (on December 14, 1994) to the Bancroft Library at Berkeley, and examined their fragile 1699 edition. It uses *lumber,* but not *learned lumber:*

> With sordid Age his Features are defac'd;
> His Lands unpeopl'd, and his Countries waste.
> Here Lumber, undeserving Light, is kept,
> A *P—p*'s[1] Bill to this dark Region's swept:

---

[1] P—p's = Sir John Philipps, who, according to Ellis's note, introduced a bill in 1699 for the suppression of "all sorts of *Debauchery.* . . . Adultery

> Where Mushroom Libels silently retire;
> And, soon as born, with Decency expire.

"Lumber, undeserving Light" is not at all bad—its scansion is identical with Pope's "Blockhead, ignorantly read" and it has the *L*-iteration-alliteration that is important to Pope's couplet. But apparently it wasn't good enough for Garth, since by 1706 (as I determined at the Special Collection of the Green Library at Stanford, which fortunately owns a Sixth Edition *Dispensary*), Garth had updated it to:

> A grifly Wight, and hideous to the Eye;
> An aukward Lump of fhapelefs Anarchy.

---

was propos'd to be punished with Death." The bill died in committee. Defoe, in "An Encomium Upon a Parliament" (1699) wrote:

> 'Twas voted once, that for the Sin
>   Of Whoring Men should die all;
> But then 'twas wisely thought again,
> The House would quickly grow so thin,
>   They durst not stand the Tryal.

(See *Poems on Affairs of State,* vol. 6, pp. 56, 121.) There is a "W——" attacked in Canto 5 of the 1699 edition of *The Dispensary,* who is none other than Samuel Wesley:

> Had W—— never aim'd in Verse to please,
> We had not rank'd him with our *Ogilbys.*

To this unprovoked and stupid libel (John Ogilby, who died in 1676, was evidently a clunky translator of Homer and Virgil and the object of much ridicule-*reçu*), Wesley responded a year later in his *Epistle* in a restrained passage about the pasteboard poetical machinery of the sort Garth used in *The Dispensary:*

> And G—h, tho barren is his Theme and mean,
> By this has reach'd at least the fam'd Lutrine.

Wesley alludes here to charges by Blackmore, Defoe, and others that Garth took his idea for *The Dispensary* from Boileau's *Le Lutrin* (the story of a disputed reading-desk)—charges that Pope would later encounter in connection with his *Rape of the Lock.* The couplet is also, by virtue of the mispronunciation of *lutrin* forced by the rhyme-word *mean,* a pun on *latrine,* apt because of the internecine urinal-throwing in Garth's poem.

With fordid Age his Features are defac'd;
His Lands unpeopl'd, and his Countries wafte.
To these dark Realms much learned Lumber creeps,
There copious M——[1] fafe in Silence fleeps
Where Mufhroom Libels in Oblivion lye,
And, foon as born, like other Monfters die.

Therefore 1706 is the crucial publication date in the history of *learned lumber;* the point at which all dull, voluminous commentary receives its most succinct dismissal. The Yale Medical Library, as it happens, owns an interleaved Fifth Edition Dispensary (1703), in which (as Frank Ellis writes in his *Affairs of State* collation) "extensive manuscript revisions have been made, in a hand not Garth's, both on the blank leaves and in the text itself." This marked-up 1703 edition, which Ellis calls *1703A,* is probably, as he says, "a fair copy of the text that actually went to the printer" of the 1706 edition; one of the manuscript revisions is "To these dark Realms much learned Lumber creeps." We deduce, then, that "learned lumber" was a molecule successfully synthesized by Garth in his mock-epic alembic at some point between 1703 and 1706—five years, at the very least, before it appeared in Pope's published patch-box of an *Essay.* Of the two men, sad to say, Garth was the one who fused all the Lombardic antecedents into "learned lumber"; Pope merely made a more

---

[1] M—— looks to be Luke Milbourne (1649–1720), who attacked Dryden's Virgil in 1698, and attempted what Sir Walter Scott later called "a rickety translation of his own." I made this tentative identification by looking through the two-syllable trochaic surnames under M in the index to Ellis's *Affairs of State* volume; there is a note about Milbourne on p. 164, in explication of a passage in Daniel Defoe's exuberant *The Pacificator* (1700), one of many poems by Defoe that aren't included in the *English Poetry Database.* (Defoe devotes a whole page to the opposition between Wit and Sense in poetry; e.g., "*Wit* is a King without a Parliament, / And *Sense* a Democratick Government.")

pointed use of Garth's condensation.[1] "Pope's admirer,"
writes Peter Quennell, in his biography of Pope,

> if he troubles to study [*The Dispensary*], is often haunted by a
> vague suspicion that he has met a line or couplet elsewhere, in a
> very different, much more spacious context; and it soon occurs to
> him that, although Pope may not have borrowed from Garth . . .
> his old friend's poem may have lingered in the background of his
> mind, and that, while he was imagining and writing, he was also
> unconsciously remembering.

On the evidence, "may not have borrowed" is much too charitable, as is "unconsciously remembering": throughout his
life, Pope's mimicry and mosaicry has every sign of being
entirely conscious—brilliant and beautiful, but at the same
time contemptible.

Why, though, an untutored twentieth-century reader might
ask, wouldn't Garth put up some sort of minor fuss about
Pope's many petty thefts? Because he was good-natured? Bol-

---

[1] John Ozell's important 1708 verse translation of Boileau's *Le Lutrin*
(not a part of Chadwyck-Healey's gathering) includes, in Canto III, a very
close imitation of Garth's 1706 passage:

> There undisturb'd volum'nous H———sleeps,
> Him under Twenty faithful Locks he keeps;
> Secure from Chandlers, and devouring Fire,
> The learned Lumber there remains intire.

(I don't know who "H———" is.) *L'amas* ("heap," "hoard," "load") is the
curt original in Boileau that Ozell expands into the Garthian "learned Lumber." Nicholas Rowe, in his introduction to Ozell's translation, writes:
"Those who will take the Trouble to compare 'em now they are both in one
Language, will be best able to judge, how near the Translator of the *Lutrin*
comes to the Beauties which all the World has so justly admired in Dr.
Garth." Indeed. Since Ozell (whom Pope disliked enough to write a short,
nasty epigram against the English *Lutrin*, published in 1727) had already
stolen Garth's "Learned Lumber" by 1708, Pope may have felt that it had
become public property. (The first covert quoter is a thief; the second is
merely well read.) The difficulty (for Pope) is that we tolerate a higher
degree of importation in a translation like Ozell's than in a professedly original poem like Pope's *Essay*.

ingbroke said Garth was "the best-natured ingenious wild man I ever knew," and Pope in "The Epistle to Arbuthnot" calls him "well-natur'd Garth," and he is quoted in Spence's *Anecdotes* as saying that Garth was "one of the best natured men in the world." In an age of wig-wearers, Garth wore one of unusual magnitude and copiousness (his portrait was painted in it)— and it could be that Pope, whose praise always came at the end of a long series of calculations, thought so highly of Garth's character because Garth didn't get angry and shriek, as Belinda did in *The Rape of the Lock* (a poem about plagiarism), upon seeing his flowing curls so expertly forfexed. Reverend Wesley's phrase about overdressed style-wigs "Like Hairy Meteors glimm'ring through a Cloud" may supply a hint as to what Pope is doing: he's snipping Garth's locks in *The Rape of the Lock,* but because he is writing a better poem than *The Dispensary,* Pope's appropriations will immortalize and meteorize the wiggy victim (Garth), who would otherwise be forgotten:

> But trust the Muse—she saw it upward rise,
> Tho' mark'd by none but quick Poetic Eyes: . . .
> A sudden Star, it shot thro' liquid Air,
> And drew behind a radiant *Trail of Hair.*
> (*Rape of the Lock,* Canto V)

I may have come up with this theory (Pope as hairdresser) because not far from where I live is a hair-styling salon called simply Alexander Pope. I haven't had a haircut there yet.

Maybe all this talk of Pope's theft is unfair to him. Yet even Maynard Mack, who is sympathetic to his lifelong poet, brings himself to say that "there remains a reserve in him that in some circumstances can edge over into evasiveness, deceit, or chicanery."[1] Professor Mack tentatively attributes the chicanery to Pope's being a Catholic in a Catholic-hating age, an

---

[1] *Alexander Pope: A Life,* p. 103.

only child, and a hunchback, which doesn't seem fair to all the good-hearted siblingless Catholic hunchbacks who have ever lived. Pope was bad because it helped him to write to be bad—he snuck things from other writers without thanking them, and then, having wronged them that way, he took offense at them publicly, too. One after another, he unjustly attacked the figures in or at the periphery of his circle, from John Dennis to Lewis Theobald to Lady Mary Wortley Montagu, not because he cared to right wrongs and expose incompetencies, but because the glove-flinging, spittle-spraying indignation that accompanied an autochthonous squabble was his best muse. He hated being hated, but he found he liked being angry, and he loved versifying his revenge.

In the early case of "learned lumber," though, there is another way the derivation might have worked. Say a seventeen-year-old, vastly talented but still byline-shy Pope, encouraged by his reception at Will's, offered to comment on some of the less successful passages in Garth's gift to him, *The Dispensary*. Say that Pope, in the course of going over the poem, came up with some fine alternative lines and outright interpolations and showed them to Garth, who, very impressed (and confusing self-interest with generosity toward lyric youth), *stuck them in his poem.* Under this supposition, the reason why Pope said that each edition of *The Dispensary* was an improvement over the last was that Pope had himself supplied some of the improvements. Here is the whole "learned lumber" passage from the *Essay on Criticism*, italics included this time for variety. Notice that it goes on to mention Samuel Garth by name:

> The Bookful Blockhead, ignorantly read,
> With *Loads* of *Learned Lumber* in his Head,
> With his own Tongue still edifies his Ears,
> And always *List'ning to Himself* appears.
> All Books he reads, and all he reads assails,
> From *Dryden's Fables* down to *Durfey's Tales*.

> With *him,* most Authors steal their Works, or buy;
> *Garth* did not write his own *Dispensary.*

Near the end of his life, Pope added a self-congratulating footnote to this last line:

> A common slander at that time in prejudice of that deserving author. Our poet [i.e., Pope] did him this justice, when that slander most prevail'd; and it is now (perhaps the sooner for this very verse) dead and forgotten.

Perhaps the "justice" Pope is doing Garth with that line is rather a trickier kind of betrayal. Pope is pretending to be holding a false charge up to ridicule—the charge that Garth stole or bought his creation—while actually saying what he in fact literally says: that Garth did not write his own *Dispensary.* He is spreading gossip without spreading it—hiding his true confession behind a pretend-sneer at a blockhead critic. One can speculate that Pope got paid, either in amazed respect or in actual cash, for his contributions to Garth's poem, just as, later on, Pope paid (underpaid) the poets who quietly helped him translate *The Odyssey.* I haven't seen the marked-up Yale copy, *1703A,* in which those 414 added and 82 revised lines are included "in a hand not Garth's"—but even if the modifications aren't in Pope's handwriting, and they probably aren't, it is entirely possible that Pope was responsible for some of the added couplets, including the Tennysonian moment that G. Birkbeck Hill and Peter Quennell choose to quote:

> To Die, is landing on some silent Shoar,
> Where Billows never break, nor Tempests roar.[1]

---

[1] "Tennysonian" is stretching it—I'm thinking of:

> And Enoch Arden, a rough sailor's lad
> Made orphan by a winter shipwreck, play'd
> Among the waste and lumber of the shore . . .

The sparkling line in *The Dispensary* about the healing Pine that will "Lament your Fate in tears of Turpentine" is a post-1703 addition, too. Both of these passages sound to me like Pope at his precocious best—and if Pope was capable of introducing these improvements into Garth's cantos, he could also have thought up "To these dark Realms much learned Lumber creeps / There copious M[ilbourne] safe in Silence sleeps" and given it to Garth as well.[1]

What we can earnestly strive to believe, then (although it may well not be true), is that Pope, who is after all the greater poet, slipped Garth the "learned lumber" under the tabula rasa around 1705, and then found he liked it so much that he wished he hadn't, and used it in his own poem in 1711, reclaiming it from Ozell's *Lutrin*. Garth didn't protest these and other later borrowings, because Pope was a friend and Garth was good-natured, and because if he did, he would then have had to admit that some number of lines in

---

See the Tennyson concordance by "Arthur E. Baker, F.R.Hist.S., F.L.A., Secretary and Librarian, Taunton. Author of 'A Brief Account of the Public Library Movement in Taunton,' etc.," which gives only that one *lumber,* as against six uses of *luminous* that immediately follow. Richard Blackmore (an enemy of Garth and eventually of Pope), in his *Creation* (1712), offers a beautiful intermediating image. Without the winds, he writes, a ship would

> lye a lazy and a useless Load,
> The Forest's wasted Spoils, the Lumber of the Flood.

[1] "Creeps" also sounds Popish; unfortunately, though, Pope's famous prosodic precept about monosyllables—"And ten low Words oft creep in one dull Line"—happens to be, as the Twickenhamites note, straight from Dryden's "Essay of Dramatic Poesy": "he creeps along with ten little words in every line." The presence of Milbourne in the new passage (if it is he) does perhaps attest to Pope's authorship, though: Pope went on to condemn Milbourne several times, e.g., in *The Essay on Criticism* (l. 463), and in *The Dunciad* (Book II and Appendix). Milbourne came to be thought of by Pope as Dryden's Theobald.

the revised and amplified poem were not from his own pen.
I don't know whether to subscribe to this sequence of events
or not. Either the young Pope stole his *learned lumber* outright from Garth (and Ozell), which would diminish him forever in my eyes, since I thought of him, when I began my
lumberjahr, as being at the center of the metaphor of study
that I had chosen to study, or the young Pope first loaned it
to Garth and then repossessed it, which adds to the picture of
his tiresome sneakiness, but leaves his original talents unim-
peached. At the moment, I can't help reading the following
additions in the 1706 *Dispensary* as being the stealthy work
of a teenage Pope, a warmup for his *Rape of the Lock,* rather
than the work of a secure and successful forty-five-year-old
Garth:

> But still the offspring of your Brain shall prove
> The Grocer's care, and brave the Rage of Jove.
> When Bonfires blaze, your vagrant Works shall rise
> In Rockets, till they reach the wondring Skyes.

The lines sound so *young,* so ambitious (though ironic), and
in their "you" address, so like the last four lines of the *Rape*—

> When those fair Suns shall sett, as sett they must,
> And all those Tresses shall be laid in Dust;
> *This Lock,* the Muse shall consecrate to Fame,
> And mid'st the Stars inscribe *Belinda's* Name!

Pope learned what he had in him to say by helping Garth
say things he didn't know he wanted to say, but was happy
to be thought to have said. Surely Garth had help: the fact
that there are four *lumber*s in *The Dispensary*'s final version
is, I now see, an argument not for Garth's uncontrollable
enthusiasm for *lumber* as a word, but rather for the existence of multiple contributors to his poem (one of whom
was Pope): helped by one or more hands, Garth lost track of

what he had and was no longer able to suppress unwanted repetitions.[1]

And there I'm going to have to stop. The long-overdue *English Poetry* disks, housed in their plastic jewel-boxes, must be returned to Chadwyck-Healey. One book after another I have sliced in half and jammed down on the juicing hub—at times my roistered brain-shaft has groaned like a tiny electric god in pain with the effort of noshing and filtering all this verbal pulp. No doubt there are other important early *lumber*-formations waiting to be found—I never got around to checking Jeremy Taylor's *Holy Dying* (1651), and I was only cursory in my scan of *The Compleat Angler* (1653)—but I'm stopping anyway. I have poked through verbal burial mounds, I have overemphasized minor borrowings, I have placed myself deep in the debt of every accessible work of reference, and I have overquoted and overquibbled—of course I have: that is what always happens when you pay a visit to the longbeards' dusty chamber. *Lumber-room* loans the short-sold world back to the reader, while storing all of poetry and prose within as a shrouded pledge. It contains the notion of containment; it keeps in mind how little we can successfully

---

[1] Apropos of word-frequency: of those writers whose careers preceded or overlapped Pope's, Edward ("Ned") Ward, the one who mentioned "lumber pies" some sections back, is the one who, according to the *English Poetry Database,* employs *lumber* the most frequently—eight times. He is followed by Pope himself: six unique *lumbers* and one *lumberhouse* (which must be searched for separately), after you subtract the duplicate lines from *Dunciad I* and *Dunciad II.* Dryden is next with five *lumbers,* if you add in the one from *Mr. Limberham* that the concordance gives, but which isn't in the *EPFTD* because it's from a play. Butler, Garth, Oldham, and Swift (though Swift isn't on the disks) are next with four apiece; Denham has three; while underachievers like John Byrom, Aaron Hill, William Meston, and Samuel Wesley have career totals of only two *lumbers.* A relatively lumber-rich poetical loam, then, seems to be a good predictor of literary merit. Based on the statistics, it may be time for a revaluation of Ned Ward.

keep in mind. I will miss looking upon every author as the potential employer of a single perversely chosen unit of vocabulary. All the pages I have flipped and copied and underlined will turn gray again and pull back into the shadows, and have no bearing on one another. Lumber becomes treasure only temporarily, through study, and then it lapses into lumber again. Books open, and then they close.

(1995)

ABOUT THE AUTHOR

NICHOLSON BAKER was born in 1957 and attended the Eastman School of Music and Haverford College. He is the author of four novels—*The Mezzanine* (1988), *Room Temperature* (1990), *Vox* (1992), and *The Fermata* (1994)—and one work of nonfiction, *U and I* (1991). His essays have appeared in *The New Yorker, The Atlantic Monthly, The New York Review of Books, Esquire,* and *The Best American Essays 1994.* He is married with two children.